THE
COLLECTED
POEMS
OF
AMY
CLAMPITT

THE
COLLECTED
POEMS
OF
AMY
CLAMPITT

NEW YORK

ALFRED A. KNOPF

1997

THIS IS A BORZOI BOOK
PUBLISHED BY ALFRED A. KNOPF, INC.

Copyright © 1997 by the Estate of Amy Clampitt
Introduction copyright © 1997 by Mary Jo Salter

http://www.randomhouse.com/

This collection of poetry is a compilation of previously published
Alfred A. Knopf, Inc., titles:

The Kingfisher, copyright © 1979, 1980, 1981, 1982, 1983 by Amy Clampitt;
What the Light Was Like, copyright © 1985 by Amy Clampitt;
Archaic Figure, copyright © 1982, 1984, 1985, 1986, 1987 by Amy Clampitt;
Westward, copyright © 1990 by Amy Clampitt; and *A Silence Opens,*
copyright © 1993 by Amy Clampitt.

Owing to limitations of space, all acknowledgments for permission to
reprint previously published material may be found on page 473.

Library of Congress Cataloging-in-Publication Data
Clampitt, Amy.
   [Poems]
   Collected poems / Amy Clampitt.
    p.   cm.
   ISBN 0-375-40008-7
   I. Title.
   PS3553.L23A17 1997   97-5163
   811'.54—dc21   CIP

Manufactured in the United States of America
First Edition

CONTENTS

CONTENTS

III   HEARTLAND

IV   TRIPTYCH

V   WATERSHEDS

VI   HYDROCARBON

WHAT THE LIGHT WAS LIKE (*1985*)

I   THE SHORE

II   THE HINTERLAND

III   VOYAGES: A HOMAGE TO JOHN KEATS

IV   THE METROPOLIS

CONTENTS

ARCHAIC FIGURE   (1987)

IV   ATTACHMENTS, LINKS, DEPENDENCIES

WESTWARD   *(1990)*

I   CROSSINGS

CONTENTS

II   HABITATS

III   A SORT OF FOOTHOLD

IV   THE PRAIRIE

A SILENCE OPENS   (1994)

I

CONTENTS

FOREWORD

H ER earliest memory was of blue violets. At the age of seventy, in an essay called "Providence," Amy Clampitt retrieved with remarkable clarity her sensations on the day of a younger brother's birth:

> *It is the twenty-sixth of April, 1923, I am not yet three years old. . . . My father's sister Edith . . . is leading me past barns and through feedlots to the outermost grove. What holds these details in place is the sight, out under those trees, of a bed of violets whose hue I cannot reach except by way of a later metaphor: the contained intensity of a body of water. It is as though I became in that instant aware of edges, shores, boundaries, limitations. The shell had cracked: an exodus, an expulsion, was under way.*

What holds these details in place: it's a quintessential Clampitt touch, implying that even our memories have their physical home, and could lose it.

The firstborn of Roy and Pauline Clampitt's five children never lost the sense of her early childhood as a paradise from which she was expelled. Its area was some three hundred acres, land belonging to her paternal grandfather and partly farmed by her parents, in the hamlet of New Providence, Iowa (pop. 200). There she developed an ease in the natural world that was a delight in itself, and also linked with the pleasures of naming and remembering. She knew, for instance, that her passion for bird-watching began at the age of five, when the same Aunt Edith showed her a rose-breasted grosbeak.

The expulsion somehow foreseen in the violets came when she was ten. Her parents took out a mortgage, one that proved a great hardship, on a farm less than three miles away. Unlike the comforting home her grandparents had shaded with fruit trees and silver poplar and red cedar—and brightened, too, with beds of transplanted wild-flowers whose colorful names she mastered—the bleak new house on Pioneer Farm was on a windswept, nearly treeless crest overlooking a graveyard of the prairie's first settlers. Amy Clampitt never forgot that she was the descendant of pioneers. The widespread modern experi-ence of being uprooted, willingly or not, would be a signature theme in her poems, from the purely autobiographical "Black Buttercups" (where she is pictured as a girl "weeping at the thought of exile") to the panoramic "Sed de Correr," where the poet Cesar Vallejo is shown "running away from what made one."

She wouldn't know she was a poet for many years—and wouldn't publish a book, amazingly, until she was sixty-three. But she had known as a child that she was different from the others, some of whom teased her on the bus ride to the New Providence Consoli-dated School, which she attended for all twelve grades. Conformity and complacency were what she came to feel was being inculcated. She had an early conviction of not wanting to grow up to do what women apparently did—get married, have children, be imprisoned by household chores—and she always identified less with her mother than with her father, an independent-spirited man of literary interests who had turned down a job as school principal to become a farmer.

Her parents sent her to Sunday school with everybody else. New Providence had been settled by Quakers from North Carolina who, after the Great Revival, had fallen into a "benighted" hybrid, as she thought, of church and meetinghouse—hymns but no baptism, ser-mons but no communion—and she received a good biblical educa-tion. Impatient with authority all her life, as a child she shrugged off organized religion as "already obsolete." Throughout periods of reli-gious experience in adulthood that ranged from doubt to intense Episcopalianism to disillusionment, and then to some sort of private peace with her enduring inconsistencies, she retained a love of the bells and candles and gestures, the multilayered music and language of church. Praise of God's works always pleased her deeply. Gerard Manley Hopkins was the first poet she loved, and she often said she'd never have become a poet without him.

Social discomfort, hymns ringing in the ear, a Quaker's respect for silence, a farmgirl's penchant for naming the things of the natural world: together an ideal formula for creating a poet. Add, too, that childhood view of a graveyard, where (as a number of Clampitt poems will tell you) the wind polishes names away.

When I knew Amy Clampitt—from 1979 until her death in 1994—she was often interpreting the lessons of her childhood, however indirectly, through her poetry. Oddly, then, my sense of who she was is clearest in the first and last fifteen years of her life, while she's only an acquaintance in the decades in between.

In fact she was thirty-four years my senior, and we would probably never have become such close friends if I hadn't assumed she was roughly my age. I was working as the sole reader of unsolicited manuscripts at *The Atlantic Monthly,* and my torpor at the end of each day was such that only a really luminous poem could have burned through the fog. Fittingly, two of the sensuous, playful, musically complicated poems in the envelope I emptied one afternoon were called "Fog" and "Gradual Clearing." I recognized the author's name from a quirkily vivid poem, "The Sun Underfoot Among the Sundews," recently published in *The New Yorker* (her first in the magazine—so wouldn't she be rather young?), and I decided, after passing on the new poems to the *Atlantic*'s poetry editor, Peter Davison (who took one), that I would write this Amy Clampitt of New York a fan letter. In it I mentioned that I was twenty-four, wrote poems, and would like to trade a few with her sometime; but enclosed none.

Her immediate reply—on June 5, 1979, a day that expanded the boundaries of my life—was so exuberantly grateful that you could practically see her jumping up and down. (Later Amy would write me that she'd begun to get an inkling of who she was when traveling in Europe in the forties, or more precisely "the minute I crossed the border into Italy at Ventimiglia—I was free to show excitement, as I'd never quite been anywhere else.") Despite all *my* gratitude, in the years to come, for her help with my poems and for what I learned from being sent most of hers in progress, I was surprised by her first letter's declaration that "to have evoked such friendliness from a younger poet amounts to nothing less than a milestone." We were "of different generations," she wrote, though she never did stop refusing to tell me her age, or even her birthday, which she made a point of not celebrating. (She was born on June 15, 1920: sometime in the nineties, after she got into reference books, I secretly looked her up.)

Hoping I wouldn't feel "swamped," she enclosed in her first letter a booklet of her poems, *Multitudes, Multitudes,* which a friend had printed for his short-lived private press in 1974, and she demurred, "You'll find lots of excesses, throes of self-expression, and all the weight of the grand tradition. *Milton,* yet!" But apparently she had subtler tastes too: she was writing from the "delectably silent and foggy lobstering village" of Corea, Maine. She signed the typed letter in an angular, nearly illegible hand that the amateur graphologist in me felt sure belonged to a birdlike frame.

Which it did, as I discovered when she opened her door to me and my husband-to-be in New York not long after. Tall, seemingly weighing nothing at all in her ballet slippers, she had a lightness of foot and manner that put one in mind, immediately, of a child. Her dark brown hair, graying only a little then, was put up behind with a hippie's leather barrette, though she had also trained two wide chin-length locks to fall over her rather comically large ears. She was less able (though she tried, with long, elegant fingers that were always flying upward) to hide a beautiful gap-toothed smile. She listened intently, but when she spoke she became a rapid, revved-up, high-pitched machine that rarely paused except for an attack of the giggles.

Amy had been living for a decade with Harold Korn, a Columbia Law School professor, whom she'd met at a gathering for Democratic Party supporters. She'd been a doorbell-ringer for Eugene McCarthy. The unconventionality of her life with Hal, added on to her girlishness, was reason to feel—as I always did, rather jealously—that she was actually younger than I. Amy and Hal had a fraying psychedelic poster of Bob Dylan's profile tacked to the living-room wall (though it got paler and less psychedelic every year), and piles of papers and books and LPs installed permanently, it seemed, on the floor and on the dining-room table. Things got done because one wanted to do them; whenever Amy or Hal bought a present on impulse, they'd say, "You haven't had a birthday in a while." She was, I would learn, a step-saving cook, an infrequent dishwasher, and—most liberating of all—merely a visitor in her own home. The Upper East Side apartment wrapped with large windows, where she woke up every day and kept her manual typewriter, was not hers; it was Hal's. She had a little place of her own in the West Village which she rarely occupied, offering it now and then to friends, but whose mere existence occupied an enormous, freeing space in her imagination.

Over a cup of tea one day, on a visit to that autonomous but otherwise nondescript Village apartment, I began to understand how ungirlish and grave, how attuned to the tragedy of life, my new friend could be. Prompted by her fond references to a nephew, I asked if she had ever wanted children. "Oh no," she said, "when we dropped the bomb on Hiroshima I knew that this wasn't a world I wanted to bring children into." Even then I guessed that her reasons had been more complex, but there was no gainsaying her sincerity. Nor did I dare smile when she added, as deadly serious as if she'd seen combat, that she'd "had to take tranquilizers all through the Vietnam War." Amy took politics—and everything else—personally. I later learned that she had left the Episcopal church (after years of commitment so fervent she had considered becoming a nun) because she felt its leaders had not been sufficiently outspoken against the war.

Such personalizing of the world was a burden and a virtue that enabled her to write her most brilliant, because most far-fetched, poems—like "The Dahlia Gardens," in which she gets inside the burning body of the young Quaker, Norman Morrison, who doused himself with gasoline as an anti-Vietnam protest. Or like "Beethoven, Opus 111," in which her father's ill-advised attempt to rid his farm of poison ivy by setting a patch ablaze is compared to the struggles of the revolutionary Romantic composer. Or "The Prairie," in which the coincidence of her grandfather's birthyear with Chekhov's opens the drama of the Clampitt family's migrations and aspirations and nervous ailments, of the dispossession of Native American lands, the exile of Joseph Brodsky, and the "landless, exquisite" nomadism of Henry James.

Even very local politics—the protracted legal efforts of her Greenwich Village landlord to evict his nonresident tenant, so that the building could go co-op—helped shape "The Prairie," her longest and perhaps most ambitious poem. As she wrote me in January of 1989,

> *Given the obvious shortage of apartments anybody can afford, not to* mention *the homeless, I can't write about it in the fairly ironic tone I once affected. A couple of weeks ago, I woke one morning before daylight, so angry that I began phrasing a piece about it in the manner of the Talk of the Town; but by the time I sat down . . . I'd gotten out my manuscript of "The Prairie" and made Manhattan the springboard.*

The poem, which she had sent me earlier in fifteen-line stanzas, was sliced into tercets and reshuffled ingeniously, almost beyond recognition: it now began in a Manhattan elevator shaft, and its original first line, imagining the birth of Chekhov, was inserted deep into page three.

Amy's Greenwich Village struggle also colored years' worth of nature poems with obliquely political content—charmingly observed but moral-laden sketches of weeds too stubborn to be eradicated. Though she would preserve for book publication only two of her "Vacant Lot" series, they were thematic cousins of poems she did keep like "Kudzu Dormant" and "Fireweed" and "Nothing Stays Put" and "The Spruce Has No Taproot" and "Real Estate." I thought of her childhood uprooting, and also of her Village landlord, when in a late interview she declared her role as a poet to be "maintaining a subversive attitude, the opposite of going along with anybody's program whatever. It amounts to wariness about being co-opted."

A political protest had given her the courage to call herself a poet for the first time. In 1971, participating in what was called the Daily Death Toll, she had demonstrated outside the White House against the bombing of North Vietnam. Identifying signs were provided for the protesters—Teacher, Student, Farmer, Poet—and she picked up the sign marked Poet.

But what was she doing *before* that—before owning up to her vocation at fifty-one? It took me a while to piece together Amy's gestation as a writer. She had written a few poems while at Grinnell College in Iowa, but by the time she escaped the Midwest for New York City she was fairly sure she would become a novelist. Dropping out in the first year of a graduate fellowship at Columbia University—she was no scholar, she insisted with some justice, though her curiosity was keener and broader than anybody's I've ever met—she took a job as a secretary at Oxford University Press. Secretary? Remembering her filing, or piling, system at home, I can only conclude she was valued at work for her literary sharpness. She wrote advertising copy and won a company-sponsored essay contest, whose prize was a trip to England. It, and a follow-up journey around Europe a few years later, when she quit the Oxford job, changed her life; it confirmed in her, as she said later, "the *livingness* of the past."

You feel her enduring Anglophilia in joyful poems that surfaced years later, like "Exmoor" or "On the Disadvantages of Central Heating," and her sense of England's historical "livingness" in her poems in which the Wordsworths and Keats and George Eliot and Virginia Woolf speak and write. It was in England, too, that she embarked on a serious romance, which was resumed unhappily in New York. I never asked her about it, but clearly the affair upended her. The title poem of her first book, *The Kingfisher,* would record a breakup that had mired her in "uninhabitable sorrow."

The return to New York brought a new job that was ideal for a Central Park bird-watcher—reference librarian for the Audubon Society—and a renewed commitment to distill her copious journals into fiction. She wrote three novels in the fifties, none of them to see publication, though she took herself seriously enough to find an agent. (The manuscripts, which I haven't read, were recently discovered in an overlooked cupboard more than two years after her death.) The novelist Edmund White knew nothing of Amy's attempts at fiction when for *The Nation* in 1983 he wrote his extraordinarily canny review of *The Kingfisher.* He praised her for "a strange fusion of an ambition to narrate and a talent for suppressing the tale. . . . No story has been told, but the high heat of alchemy has been generated." A close friend from the forties on, Phoebe Hoss, read the novels as they were written. She remembers them as intricately plotted and ornately descriptive, and as illustrating a difficulty Amy had in real life: so morally charged herself, she couldn't always accept the shades of gray in people. Yet the portrayal of character independent from plot—character in itself—could be one of Amy's fortes.

The portraitist emerges not only in her biographical poems on great figures but in little-remarked poems like "A Hedge of Rubber Trees," which deftly sketches a few funny-sad encounters with a Greenwich Village eccentric. Amy's letters to her many friends and family were Dickensian in their vitality, brimming with humorous accounts of people she'd met once and might never meet again, yet for whom she often felt some instant shock (always surprised: that was her mode) of admiration or empathy. Not only people. Asking after my cat, she wrote,

> *I don't know if I ever told you about the time, the only time, Hal and I ever had what could be called a pet—namely a housefly that lingered on in cold weather, and whose tactful behavior (such as* not *alighting on the edge of a coffee cup, but merely somewhere near by) finally endeared itself to us, and who acquired the name of Leporello, for no reason except that when I asked Hal what his*

> *name was, that was what came out. Eventually, of course, some-*
> *thing happened to him—we were never sure what—and we had*
> *by then endowed him with so many traits that there was some-*
> *thing more than a mock desolation.*

Surely her failure to publish fiction reinforced her diffidence about going public with the poems she turned to in the sixties. But upon moving in with Hal, and buoyed by his encouragement, she took up the banner of Poet and published her chapbook and began to send poems to magazines. In 1977 (by now she was an editor at E. P. Dutton) she took a poetry workshop whose graduation ceremony, so to speak, was a group-reading in a bar. A breakthrough: she relished having an audience. And then, in 1978, she won her most coveted audience yet, the poetry editor of *The New Yorker.*

Howard Moss embraced the richness of language in Amy's poems—as he saw them, they were an antidote to the prevailing literary minimalism—and the career boost afforded by his loyal championship can hardly be exaggerated. But despite her frequent appearances in *The New Yorker* from 1979 onward, and her accelerated leaps of development, book editors weren't biting. The manuscript she thought of as her first book—having outgrown and dismissed the pamphlet *Multitudes, Multitudes*—changed title and contents and organization many times. The book's more Maine-focused incarnation as *The Outer Bar,* which I proposed unsuccessfully to The Atlantic Monthly Press in 1980, contained a handful of poems never seen again. She tried versions out on several more publishers before my husband, Brad Leithauser, suggested she send *The Kingfisher* to his new editor at Knopf, Ann Close, in 1982. Alice Quinn, the originator of the Knopf Poetry Series (and the successor to Howard Moss at *The New Yorker* upon his death in 1987), called up with the news that she was accepting the book and would edit it.

A few hours later, Ann Close, who would eventually edit Amy's three last books, made a follow-up call to congratulate her. "She's not here," Hal answered breezily, "she's outside. In fact, I think she's outside *skipping.* You know, she's only three years old."

The sixty-three-year-old girl skipping the streets of New York was about to receive one of the warmest receptions for a first book of poems by any American in this century. Helen Vendler in *The New York Review of Books* predicted that a hundred years from now, the book would

take on the documentary value of what, in the twentieth century,
made up the stuff of culture. And later yet, when (if man still
exists) its cultural terminology is obsolescent, its social patterns
extinct, it will, I think, still be read for its triumph over the resis-
tance of language, the reason why poetry lasts.

How could one respond to such praise? The "poetry factory," as Amy liked to call the gears racketing in her head, was producing so furiously that for all the powerful gratification she felt, nothing could slow her. She had to make up for lost time, she said. She was flustered, incredulous, happy, nervous, sometimes unaccountably blue; but she was thinking very clearly.

By the fall of 1983, the same year of *The Kingfisher*'s debut, she had already composed a working manuscript of her 1985 book, *What the Light Was Like,* many of whose poems she'd excluded from the first volume as not fitting into its scheme. Her sense of a book as a shaped thing was acute. By 1984, a year before *What the Light Was Like* appeared, and under the influence of an introductory Classical Greek course at Hunter College that had led to revelatory travels in Greece, she had already begun "The Mirror of the Gorgon" series for her third, myth-saturated book, *Archaic Figure,* published in 1987. But she held the poems back, suspecting that others on similar subjects—the fear and suppression of strong women was often their theme—would follow. Enclosed in a single letter of 1984 I find nine minor poems that were never collected at all. That same year, she sent me a three-part poem called "A Manhattan Elegy," which despite a chapbook appearance as "Manhattan" was kept out of three Knopf collections until her fifth and final one, *A Silence Opens,* a decade later.

Reading that final volume, you can't help seeing many of the poems as valedictory not only to life but to language. In "The Cove," the opening poem of her first book, she had begun with fog and a gale that made people indoors feel all the cozier; in "Syrinx," the poem that inaugurates *A Silence Opens,* the first lines bring the sound of foghorns and wind chimes and of wind itself "in a terrible fret, without so much / as a finger to articulate / what ails it." The book ends with "A Silence," which features the typographical device of extra spaces between unpunctuated phrases—a visual hint both at God's silence and at poetry's limitations. Yet the path into ineffability wasn't so direct after all. Amy's poems had from the beginning consciously addressed the boundaries words cannot cross (see "Easter Morning" or "The August Darks") while employing language with such dizzying variety and ease and wit that she sometimes fooled us into believing that there are no boundaries. (Look again at those lines in "Syrinx," with the bullseye pun on "fret.")

Nobody can read Amy Clampitt without a dictionary. Her vocabulary may well be the widest of any modern American poet, making use as it does of various sub-lexicons (botany is a favorite) and foreign languages (French appears often) and, perhaps most important, the nearly limitless aural corollaries, as it were, to the often arcane words that came naturally to her. In "Gooseberry Fool," for instance, the taste of the gooseberry takes getting used to, like "trepang, / tripe à la mode de Caen, / or having turned thirteen"—an insistent repetition of consonants and vowels as tangy as the fruit. Omni-sensuality was at the heart of Amy's linguistic fluency and economy: when she came up with the internal rhyme of "a suede of meadow," you saw and heard and touched it at once.

Yet a deliberate rejection of grammatical economy was often one of her hallmark devices, too, a tendency to clustered and circular phrases rather than linear argument. It was her baroque syntax and vocabulary, her near-meters that weren't meter, her line breaks that worked against expected grammatical or metric pauses, that brought Amy her most zealous admirers and her most dismissive detractors. Eventually they brought her into the wholly unforeseen role of Exhibit A whenever the direction of American poetry was discussed. One critic who liked where she seemed to be taking it, Willard Spiegelman, put the paradox of Amy's style most memorably: he said she had "a Keatsian lusciousness" and "a Quaker austerity."

Another way to characterize her method might be to compare it to the ocean in "Beach Glass," a collector for whom "nothing / is beneath consideration." Or to the flatbed truck that transports defunct cars in "Salvage," where she finds "esthetic / satisfaction in these / ceremonial removals // from the category of / received ideas." Or to the bower birds and magpies and other scavenging creatures that her poems saluted for making beautiful things out of seeming randomness. Accretion and winnowing in an unending loop were what Amy saw at work in life: a principle, too, by which she composed her sentences and her books.

For the killdeer in "Camouflage," a mosaic of stones set cleverly into gravel is a "treasury"—which is an old-fashioned word for a poetry collection, too. Given her prolific output, the reprinting of only the five volumes of her lifetime in this treasury, *The Collected Poems of Amy Clampitt,* may well be questioned. But the poetry factory itself provides an answer. Poems are still turning up among Amy's papers—often, scarcely readable scrawls on the backs of post-card-sized legal announcements she recycled from Hal's mail—and in typed versions sent to friends; it isn't at all clear yet which drafts are final. A selection of heretofore unpublished poems will eventually be called for. But first this gathering—one that ratifies Amy Clampitt's own choices in the order she scrupulously placed them. These poems tell us what she most wanted to say; they are what she wanted her reputation to stand on.

As her poems went public, so did her person. Into her eleven years of life as a famous older poet she packed more activity than most people half her age would have attempted. She continued to rent a summer cottage (and create many of her most radiant poems) in Corea, Maine, a sort of no-home away from no-home; she treasured her Down East friends, the view of 'Tit Manan lighthouse and the walk to the outer bar, but she took a pointed pleasure in not really belonging to Corea any more than she did to Manhattan or had to Iowa. Hal would drive them up in a car named Ralph. She who loved to arrive in new places, and so often wrote about masses of people on the move, had no wish to learn to drive. After one mishap on Amtrak (I forget what), she also shunned American trains for years, and was so determined not to fly that she regularly got to Europe by boat. Such convictions would make it impossible, you'd think, for her to accept invitations to give poetry readings all over the country; but she leapt upon even the most far-flung and ill-paid offers and made a virtue of eccentricity, writing poems about America as seen from a Greyhound bus.

Quitting her freelance editing work, she dared with increasing pleasure and confidence to try herself as a visiting professor—at William and Mary, Amherst, Smith, and elsewhere—and her generosity to students made her a sort of favorite aunt. Rewarded by a once-distrusted literary establishment with one honor after another, she used her influence to further the careers of the many younger writers she saw promise in. She edited a selection of Donne. She began writing essays and reviews and published a prose collection, *Predecessors, Et Cetera,* though she doubted—and underestimated—

her talents as a critic. She wrote and rewrote and rewrote a play, *Mad with Joy,* about Dorothy Wordsworth (in whose nervous energy, frustrated literary talent, and lonely life in the cottage at Grasmere one detects the early Amy Clampitt on the prairie). In one of the great thrills of her life, the play was given a staged reading in Cambridge, Massachusetts, in 1993.

By then, to my shame, I had become a less reliable correspondent, and so the final, surprising chapter of her life—set in the Berkshire Mountains—had begun almost without my knowing. A poet Amy had befriended in Italy in 1991, Karen Chase, was from Lenox, Massachusetts, and introduced her to it. One attraction was its literary heritage, as I remember from a visit with her to The Mount, home of one of her most beloved writers, Edith Wharton. One day in the summer of 1992, Amy and Hal had just left Lenox, where they'd been visiting Karen, when the local paper, *The Berkshire Eagle,* landed on the lawn with the news that Amy had won a MacArthur Fellowship. When Karen phoned her—she had been on her way to Maine—Amy was annoyed; such teasing wasn't funny. But at length convinced this was no prank, she decided that very day to buy a summer place in Lenox. The small but well-proportioned gray clapboard house with a spacious backyard was her first purchase of any magnitude. She and Karen went on expeditions they called "junking," and soon the house was full of imaginatively chosen furniture. The "poet of displacement," as she once termed herself, had a foothold.

Then, while teaching at Smith in the spring of 1993, Amy learned that she had ovarian cancer. I was living in Paris that year and was shocked, on a brief trip back to New York in October, to see how thin and frail her surgery had left her. We were reading at an overlong poetry festival, and her valor was remarkable as she mounted the stage, chic in a new dress and a turban that masked her hair loss from chemotherapy. The following spring, when she learned she would probably not recover, she and Hal moved to Lenox for whatever time she had left. She called me in Paris not to tell me the worst but to say in as bubbly a voice as ever that they were getting married in a few days.

And so, on June 10, 1994, days before her seventy-fourth birthday (which I still pretended not to know about), she married her companion of twenty-five years, Harold Korn, in the living room of their first home. Karen Chase, her husband, and Amy's housekeeper and friend, Vivian Banton, were the only guests. A photo shows the bride too weak to stand but not to smile—under a wide-brimmed, rakish straw hat that was to hang on the wall facing her bed for the three months that remained.

Her decline, as I saw when I returned to Massachusetts in August, was rapid and dignified. Though basically unable to eat, she refused intravenous feeding. Having asked that her bed be moved into her study, so she could watch the birds at their backyard feeder, she spent hours simply staring out the window. "What I like about this view," she said in one burst of energy, "is that there's so much going on." All I saw, miserably, was a gray squirrel scampering up a birch tree.

Sometimes a visitor would read aloud the poems she asked for. I got through Wordsworth's "Ode: Intimations of Immortality" all right, but choked on one of his Lucy poems ("But she is in her grave, and, oh, / The difference to me!"), and frustrated Amy sorely by not finding the complete Hopkins on her bookshelf. When she had breath, she dictated her plans for her funeral, to be held in the yard she looked out on. She wanted her ashes to be buried under the birch tree—an unconscious harking back, I like to imagine, to the bed of blue violets under the trees of her first memory, violets deeply tinted by her own undiminished capacity for awe. (In "The Woodlot" she had called them "a blue cellarhole / of pure astonishment.") As it turned out, it would be her brother Larry, born on the day of that memory, who dug the spade first into the ground. No poems of her own were to be read aloud, though we might listen to the Beethoven sonata that had inspired her elegy for her father. She asked only for a passage from Isaiah, the Twenty-Third Psalm, Hopkins, Wordsworth, Emily Dickinson, and certain favorite poems to be read by the friends who wrote them.

The Quaker in her was still very much alive: if anybody wanted to say something about her, she thought he should just stand up and say it.

Mary Jo Salter
1997

THE
KINGFISHER

(1983)

FOR HAL

As kingfishers catch fire, dragonflies draw flame . . .
GERARD MANLEY HOPKINS

One   Fire and Water

THE COVE

Inside the snug house, blue willow-ware
plates go round the dado, cross-stitch
domesticates the guest room, whole nutmegs
inhabit the spice rack, and when there's fog
or a gale we get a fire going, listen
to Mozart, read Marianne Moore, or
sit looking out at the eiders, trig
in their white-over-black as they tip
and tuck themselves into the swell, almost
as though diving under the eiderdown
in a *gemütlich* hotel room at Innsbruck.

At dusk we watch a porcupine, hoary
quadruped, emerge from under the spruce trees,
needle-tined paddle tail held out straight
behind, as though the ground were negotiable
only by climbing, to examine the premises,
and then withdraw from the (we presume)
alarming realm of the horizontal into
the up-and-down underbrush of normality.

From the sundeck, overhung by a gale-
hugged mountain ash, limbs blotched
and tufted with lichen, where in good
weather, every time we look up there's
a new kind of warbler flirting, all ombré
and fine stitchery, through the foliage,
one midday, looking down at the grass
we noticed a turtle—domed repoussé
leather with an underlip of crimson—
as it hove eastward, a covered
wagon intent on the wrong direction.

Where at low tide the rocks, like the
back of an old sheepdog or spaniel, are
rugg'd with wet seaweed, the cove
embays a pavement of ocean, at times
wrinkling like tinfoil, at others
all isinglass flakes, or sun-pounded
gritty glitter of mica; or hanging
intact, a curtain wall just frescoed
indigo, so immense a hue, a blue

of such majesty it can't be looked at,
at whose apex there pulses, even
in daylight, a lighthouse, light-
pierced like a needle's eye.

FOG

A vagueness comes over everything,
as though proving color and contour
alike dispensable: the lighthouse
extinct, the islands' spruce-tips
drunk up like milk in the
universal emulsion; houses
reverting into the lost
and forgotten; granite
subsumed, a rumor
in a mumble of ocean.
                    Tactile
definition, however, has not been
totally banished: hanging
tassel by tassel, panicled
foxtail and needlegrass,
dropseed, furred hawkweed,
and last season's rose-hips
are vested in silenced
chimes of the finest,
clearest sea-crystal.
                    Opacity
opens up rooms, a showcase
for the hueless moonflower
corolla, as Georgia
O'Keeffe might have seen it,
of foghorns; the nodding
campanula of bell buoys;
the ticking, linear
filigree of bird voices.

GRADUAL CLEARING

Late in the day the fog
wrung itself out like a sponge
in glades of rain,
sieving the half-invisible
cove with speartips;
then, in a lifting
of wisps and scarves, of smoke-rings
from about the islands, disclosing
what had been wavering
fishnet plissé as a smoothness
of peau-de-soie or just-ironed
percale, with a tatting
of foam out where the rocks are,
the sheened no-color of it,
the bandings of platinum
and magnesium suffusing,
minute by minute, with clandestine
rose and violet, with opaline
nuance of milkweed, a texture
not to be spoken of above a whisper,
began, all along the horizon,
gradually to unseal
like the lip of a cave
or of a cavernous,
single, pearl-
engendering seashell.

THE OUTER BAR

When through some lacuna, chink, or interstice
in the unlicensed free-for-all that goes
on without a halt out there all day, all night,
all through the winter,

one morning at low tide you walk dry-shod across
a shadow isthmus to the outer bar,
you find yourself, once over, sinking at every step
into a luscious mess—

a vegetation of unbarbered, virgin, foot-thick
velvet, the air you breathe an aromatic
thicket, odors in confusion starting up
at every step like partridges

or schools of fishes, an element you swim through
as to an unplanned, headily illicit
interview. The light out there, gashed
by the surf's scimitar,

is blinding, a rebuke—Go back! Go back!—
behind the silhouetted shipwreck (Whose?
When did it happen? Back in the village
nobody can tell you),

the bell buoy hunkering knee-deep in foam,
a blood-red-painted harbinger. How strange
a rim, back where you came from,
of familiar portents

reviewed from this *isola bella,* paradise
inside a prison rockpile—the unravished
protégé of guardians so lawless, refuge
moated up in such a shambles!

Your mind keeps turning back to look at them—
chain-gang archangels that in their prismatic
frenzy fall, gall and gash the daylight
out there, all through the winter.

SEA MOUSE

The orphanage of possibility
has had to be expanded to
admit the sea mouse. No one
had asked for such a thing,
or prophesied its advent,

sheltering under ruching
edges of sea lettuce—
a wet thing but pettable
as, seen in the distance,
the tops of copses,

sun-honeyed, needle-pelted
pine trees, bearded barley,
or anything newborn not bald
but furred. No rodent this
scabrous, this unlooked-for

foundling, no catnip plaything
for a cat to worry, not even
an echinoderm, the creature
seems to be a worm. Silk-spiny,
baby-mummy-swaddled, it's

at home where every corridor
is mop-and-bucket scrubbed
and aired from wall to wall
twice daily by the inde-
fatigable tidal head nurse.

BEACH GLASS

While you walk the water's edge,
turning over concepts
I can't envision, the honking buoy
serves notice that at any time
the wind may change,
the reef-bell clatters
its treble monotone, deaf as Cassandra
to any note but warning. The ocean,
cumbered by no business more urgent
than keeping open old accounts
that never balanced,
goes on shuffling its millenniums
of quartz, granite, and basalt.
                                      It behaves
toward the permutations of novelty—
driftwood and shipwreck, last night's
beer cans, spilt oil, the coughed-up
residue of plastic—with random
impartiality, playing catch or tag
or touch-last like a terrier,
turning the same thing over and over,
over and over. For the ocean, nothing
is beneath consideration.
                                  The houses
of so many mussels and periwinkles
have been abandoned here, it's hopeless
to know which to salvage. Instead
I keep a lookout for beach glass—
amber of Budweiser, chrysoprase
of Almadén and Gallo, lapis
by way of (no getting around it,
I'm afraid) Phillips'
Milk of Magnesia, with now and then a rare
translucent turquoise or blurred amethyst
of no known origin.
                                  The process
goes on forever: they came from sand,
they go back to gravel,
along with the treasuries
of Murano, the buttressed
astonishments of Chartres,
which even now are readying

for being turned over and over as gravely
and gradually as an intellect
engaged in the hazardous
redefinition of structures
no one has yet looked at.

MARINE SURFACE,
LOW OVERCAST

Out of churned aureoles
this buttermilk, this
herringbone of albatross,
floss of mercury,
déshabille of spun
aluminum, furred with a velouté
of looking-glass,

a stuff so single
it might almost be lifted,
folded over, crawled underneath
or slid between, as nakedness-
caressing sheets, or donned
and worn, the train-borne
trapping of an unrepeatable
occasion,

this wind-silver
rumpling as of oatfields,
a suede of meadow,
a nub, a nap, a mane of lustre
lithe as the slide
of muscle in its
sheath of skin,

laminae of living tissue,
mysteries of flex,
affinities of texture,
subtleties of touch, of pressure
and release, the suppleness
of long and intimate
association,

new synchronies of fingertip,
of breath, of sequence,
entities that still can rouse,
can stir or solder,
whip to a froth, or force
to march in strictly
hierarchical formation

down galleries of sheen, of flux,
cathedral domes that seem to hover
overturned and shaken like a basin
to the noise of voices,
from a rustle to the jostle
of such rush-hour
conglomerations

no loom, no spinneret, no forge, no factor,
no process whatsoever, patent
applied or not applied for,
no five-year formula, no fabric
for which pure imagining,
except thus prompted,
can invent the equal.

THE SUN UNDERFOOT
AMONG THE SUNDEWS

An ingenuity too astonishing
to be quite fortuitous is
this bog full of sundews, sphagnum-
lined and shaped like a teacup.
                              A step
down and you're into it; a
wilderness swallows you up:
ankle-, then knee-, then midriff-
to-shoulder-deep in wetfooted
understory, an overhead
spruce-tamarack horizon hinting
you'll never get out of here.
                              But the sun
among the sundews, down there,
is so bright, an underfoot
webwork of carnivorous rubies,
a star-swarm thick as the gnats
they're set to catch, delectable
double-faced cockleburs, each
hair-tip a sticky mirror
afire with sunlight, a million
of them and again a million,
each mirror a trap set to
unhand unbelieving,
                              that either
a First Cause said once, "Let there
be sundews," and there were, or they've
made their way here unaided
other than by that backhand, round-
about refusal to assume responsibility
known as Natural Selection.
                              But the sun
underfoot is so dazzling
down there among the sundews,
there is so much light
in the cup that, looking,
you start to fall upward.

BOTANICAL NOMENCLATURE

Down East people, not being botanists,
call it "that pink-and-blue flower
you find along the shore." Wildflower
guides, their minds elsewhere, mumble
"sea lungwort or oysterleaf" as a label
for these recumbent roundels, foliage
blued to a driftwood patina
growing outward, sometimes to the
size of a cathedral window,
stemrib grisaille edge-tasseled
with opening goblets, with bugles
in miniature, mauve through cerulean,
toggled into a seawall scree,
these tuffets of skyweed
neighbored by a climbing tideline,
by the holdfasts, the gargantuan lariats
of kelp, a landfall of seaweed:

Mertensia, the learned Latin
handle, proving the uses of taxonomy,
shifts everything abruptly inland,
childhoodward, to what we called then
(though not properly) bluebells:
spring-bottomland glades standing upright,
their lake-evoking sky color
a trapdoor, a window letting in distances
all the way to the ocean—
reaching out, *nolens volens,*
as one day everything breathing
will reach out, with just such
bells on its fingers, to touch
without yet quite having seen
the unlikelihood, the ramifying
happenstance, the mirroring
marryings of all likeness.

ON THE DISADVANTAGES
OF CENTRAL HEATING

cold nights on the farm, a sock-shod
stove-warmed flatiron slid under
the covers, mornings a damascene-
sealed bizarrerie of fernwork
                decades ago now

waking in northwest London, tea
brought up steaming, a Peak Frean
biscuit alongside to be nibbled
as blue gas leaps up singing
                decades ago now

damp sheets in Dorset, fog-hung
habitat of bronchitis, of long
hot soaks in the bathtub, of nothing
quite drying out till next summer:
                delicious to think of

hassocks pulled in close, toasting-
forks held to coal-glow, strong-minded
small boys and big eager sheepdogs
muscling in on bookish profundities
                now quite forgotten

the farmhouse long sold, old friends
dead or lost track of, what's salvaged
is this vivid diminuendo, unfogged
by mere affect, the perishing residue
                of pure sensation

MERIDIAN

First daylight on the bittersweet-hung
sleeping porch at high summer : dew
all over the lawn, sowing diamond-
point-highlighted shadows :
the hired man's shadow revolving
along the walk, a flash of milkpails
passing : no threat in sight, no hint
anywhere in the universe, of that

apathy at the meridian, the noon
of absolute boredom : flies
crooning black lullabies in the kitchen,
milk-soured crocks, cream separator
still unwashed : what is there to life
but chores and more chores, dishwater,
fatigue, unwanted children : nothing
to stir the longueur of afternoon

except possibly thunderheads :
climbing, livid, turreted alabaster
lit up from within by splendor and terror
—forked lightning's
                              split-second disaster.

A RESUMPTION,
OR POSSIBLY A REMISSION

For my sister Beth

Waking to all that white, as week by week
the inland ravines of a two-river city
filled up with it, was like the resumption
of a state of grace, as in dreams of being carried.
Nothing disturbed it: not the owl that came
rowing out at noon, soundless as fur,
nor the great horned ones' profundo
yelp from some outpost among oaks'
dun, nattering cling-leaves. In that
white habitat, the precarious architect
of ledges and cornices, of bridges
suspended with the ease of hammocks, even
those halloos came through as friendly.

Though on days of thaw a ponderous
icicle-fall, a more and more massively
glistening overhang, gave birth to daggers,
and though we'd hear our alcoholic landlord
(he came once beseeching the loan of
a bottle opener) being yelled at
by the spouse-in-charge, who would then
address herself to a parlor organ,
pumping out consolation with a vengeance,
from January nearly to the willowy
landfall of April, when new excitements
and misgivings began to intervene, to live
moated and immured inside the castle-keep
of all that white was to discover
even the Ur-nightmare of being
dropped, of waking up abandoned,
gone miraculously into remission.

I find I can no longer summon the layout
of that apartment. But the scene outside it
either reinvents, or subsumes uninterrupted,
a state that can't be gone back to: from
one window a pair of cardinals, she olive-
muted and red of beak, as though (you said)

she'd put on lipstick, he the scarlet-
suited royal mite of a Goya portrait,
meteors' scathing anomaly slowed down
and mollified to a quasi-domestic,
seed-eating familiar; next door
a silent house, walks uncleared week
after week, snowdrifts accumulating,
their tented pavilions overhung
by an old, crone-dark catalpa
metamorphosing, snowfall by snowfall,
into a hammock, the burden of all
that white, the deepening sag of it,
upheld as by a nursing mother.

A PROCESSION AT CANDLEMAS

I

Moving on or going back to where you came from,
bad news is what you mainly travel with:
a breakup or a breakdown, someone running off

or walking out, called up or called home:
death in the family. Nudged from their stanchions
outside the terminal, anonymous of purpose

as a flock of birds, the bison of the highway
funnel westward onto Route 80, mirroring
an entity that cannot look into itself and know

what makes it what it is. Sooner or later
every trek becomes a funeral procession.
The mother curtained in Intensive Care—

a scene the mind leaves blank, fleeing instead
toward scenes of transhumance, the belled sheep
moving up the Pyrenees, red-tasseled pack llamas

footing velvet-green precipices, the Kurdish
women, jingling with bangles, gorgeous
on their rug-piled mounts—already lying dead,

bereavement altering the moving lights
to a processional, a feast of Candlemas.
Change as child-bearing, birth as a kind

of shucking off: out of what began
as a Mosaic insult—such a loathing
of the common origin, even a virgin,

having given birth, needs purifying—
to carry fire as though it were a flower,
the terror and the loveliness entrusted

into naked hands, supposing God might have,
might actually need a mother: people have
at times found this a way of being happy.

A Candlemas of moving lights along Route 80;
lighted candles in a corridor from Arlington
over the Potomac, for every carried flame

the name of a dead soldier: an element
fragile as ego, frightening as parturition,
necessary and intractable as dreaming.

The lapped, wheelborne integument, layer
within layer, at the core a dream of
something precious, ripped: Where are we?

The sleepers groan, stir, rewrap themselves
about the self's imponderable substance,
or clamber down, numb-footed, half in a drowse

of freezing dark, through a Stonehenge
of fuel pumps, the bison hulks slantwise
beside them, drinking. What is real except

what's fabricated? The jellies glitter
cream-capped in the cafeteria showcase;
gumball globes, Life Savers cinctured

in parcel gilt, plop from their housings
perfect, like miracles. Comb, nail clipper,
lip rouge, mirrors and emollients embody,

niched into the washroom wall case,
the pristine seductiveness of money.
Absently, without inhabitants, this

nowhere oasis wears the place name
of Indian Meadows. The westward-trekking
transhumance, once only, of a people who,

in losing everything they had, lost even
the names they went by, stumbling past
like caribou, perhaps camped here. Who

can assign a trade-in value to that sorrow?
The monk in sheepskin over tucked-up saffron
intoning to a drum becomes the metronome

of one more straggle up Pennsylvania Avenue
in falling snow, a whirl of tenderly
remorseless corpuscles, street gangs

amok among magnolias' pregnant wands,
a stillness at the heart of so much whirling:
beyond the torn integument of childbirth,

sometimes, wrapped like a papoose into a grief
not merely of the ego, you rediscover almost
the rest-in-peace of the placental coracle.

I I

Of what the dead were, living, one knows
so little as barely to recognize
the fabric of the backward-ramifying

antecedents, half-noted presences
in darkened rooms: the old, the feared,
the hallowed. Never the same river

drowns the unalterable doorsill. An effigy
in olive wood or pear wood, dank
with the sweat of age, walled in the dark

at Brauron, Argos, Samos: even the unwed
Athene, who had no mother, born—it's declared—
of some man's brain like every other pure idea,

had her own wizened cult object, kept
out of sight like the incontinent whimperer
in the backstairs bedroom, where no child

ever goes—to whom, year after year,
the fair linen of the sacred peplos
was brought in ceremonial procession—

flutes and stringed instruments, wildflower-
hung cattle, nubile Athenian girls, young men
praised for the beauty of their bodies. Who

23

can unpeel the layers of that seasonal
returning to the dark where memory fails,
as birds re-enter the ancestral flyway?

Daylight, snow falling, knotting of gears:
Chicago. Soot, the rotting backsides
of tenements, grimed trollshapes of ice

underneath the bridges, the tunnel heaving
like a birth canal. Disgorged, the infant
howling in the restroom; steam-table cereal,

pale coffee; wall-eyed TV receivers, armchairs
of molded plastic: the squalor of the day
resumed, the orphaned litter taken up again

unloved, the spawn of botched intentions,
grief a mere hardening of the gut,
a set piece of what can't be avoided:

parents by the tens of thousands living
unthanked, unpaid but in the sour coin
of resentment. Midmorning gray as zinc

along Route 80, corn-stubble quilting
the underside of snowdrifts, the cadaverous
belvedere of windmills, the sullen stare

of feedlot cattle; black creeks puncturing
white terrain, the frozen bottomland
a mush of willow tops; dragnetted in ice,

the Mississippi. Westward toward the dark,
the undertow of scenes come back to, fright
riddling the structures of interior history:

Where is it? Where, in the shucked-off
bundle, the hampered obscurity that has been
for centuries the mumbling lot of women,

did the thread of fire, too frail
ever to discover what it meant, to risk
even the taking of a shape, relinquish

the seed of possibility, unguessed-at
as a dream of something precious? Memory,
that exquisite blunderer, stumbling

like a migrant bird that finds the flyway
it hardly knew it knew except by instinct,
down the long-unentered nave of childhood,

late on a midwinter afternoon, alone
among the snow-hung hollows of the windbreak
on the far side of the orchard, encounters

sheltering among the evergreens, a small
stilled bird, its cap of clear yellow
slit by a thread of scarlet—the untouched

nucleus of fire, the lost connection
hallowing the wizened effigy, the mother
curtained in Intensive Care: a Candlemas

of moving lights along Route 80, at nightfall,
in falling snow, the stillness and the sorrow
of things moving back to where they came from.

THE DAKOTA

Grief for a generation—all
the lonely people
gone, the riffraff
out there now mainly pigeons—
steps from its limousine
and lights a taper
inside the brownstone catacomb
of the Dakota. Pick up
the wedding rice, take out
the face left over from
the funeral nobody came to,
bring flowers, leave them woven
with the lugubrious ironwork
of the Dakota. Grief
is original, but it
repeats itself: there's nothing
more original that it can do.

TIMES SQUARE WATER MUSIC

By way of a leak
in the brickwork
beside a stairway
in the Times Square
subway, midway
between the IR
and the BM T, weeks
of sneaking seepage
had smuggled in,
that morning,
a centimeter
of standing water.

To ward off the herd
we tend to turn into,
turned loose on
the tiered terrain
of the Times Square
subway, somebody
had tried, with
a half-hearted
barricade or tether
of twine,
to cordon off
the stairway—

as though anyone
could tie up seepage
into a package—
down which the
water, a dripping
escapee, was surrep-
titiously proceeding
with the intent,
albeit inadvertent,
in time, at an
inferior level,
to make a lake.

Having gone round
the pond thus far
accumulated, bound
for the third, infra-
infernal hollow
of the underground,
where the N, RR,
and QB cars are
wont to travel,
in mid-descent I
stopped, abruptly way-
laid by a sound.

Alongside the iron-
runged nethermost
stairway, under
the banister,
a hurrying skein
of moisture had begun,
on its way down,
to unravel
into the trickle
of a musical
minuscule
waterfall.

Think of spleen-
wort, of moss
and maiden-
hair fernwork,
think of water
pipits, of ouzels
and wagtails
dipping into
the course of it
as the music
of it oozes
from the walls!

Think of it
undermining
the computer's
cheep, the time
clock's hiccup,
the tectonic
inchings of it
toward some
general crackup!
Think of it, think of
water running, running,
running till it
        falls!

Two   Airborne, Earthbound

THE EDGE OF THE HURRICANE

Wheeling, the careening
winds arrive with lariats
and tambourines of rain.
Torn-to-pieces, mud-dark
flounces of Caribbean

cumulus keep passing,
keep passing.   By afternoon
rinsed transparencies begin
to open overhead, Mediterranean
windowpanes of clearness

crossed by young gusts'
vaporous fripperies, liquid
footprints flying, lacewing
leaf-shade brightening
and fading. Sibling

gales stand up on point
in twirling fouettés
of debris. The day ends
bright, cloud-wardrobe
packed away. Nightfall

hangs up a single moon
bleached white as laundry,
serving notice yet again how
levity can also trample,
drench, wring and mangle.

AMARANTH AND MOLY

The night we bailed out Jolene from Riker's Island
tumbleweeds in such multitudes were blowing through the dark
it might almost have been Wyoming. Built like a willow
or a John Held flapper, from the shoulders up
she was pure Nefertiti, and out of that divine
brown throat came honey and cockleburs.
She had nine children and no identifiable husband.
She wore a headcloth like a tiara above a sack dress
improvised from a beach towel. She'd turned larceny
against the bureaucracy into an art form.
When they raised the subway fare and simultaneously
cut back on Human Resources, Jolene
began jumping turnstiles as a matter of principle.
The police caught up with her at approximately
the fifteenth infraction, and the next thing
anybody knew, she'd been carted off
to the Women's House of D.
                                 Now that it's
been shifted to the other side of the East River,
bailing anybody out becomes an all-night expedition—
a backhanded kind of joyride, comparable
to crossing the Styx or the Little Big Horn
in a secondhand Volkswagen. You enter a region
of landfill, hamburger loess, a necropolis
of coffee grounds, of desiccated *Amaranthus albus*
(rudely known as pigweed) on the run.
No roots. When a tumbleweed takes off, barbed wire
won't stop it, much less a holstered guard
or signs reading No Unauthorized Vehicles
Beyond This Point. A shuttlebus arrives
after a while to cart you to the reception area,
where people paid to do it teach you how to wait,
with no message, while one shift goes off
and the next comes on, and every half hour or so
you feed another batch of change into a pay phone,
jiggling all the levers of influence you can think of
to no effect whatever.
                        At a little after
three a.m., finally, Jolene came out—
the same beautiful outrageous gingersnap
with a whole new catalog of indictments.
On the shuttlebus, while a pimp was softly

lecturing his sullen girl on what to do next time,
Jolene described how at the precinct
they'd begun by giving her a
Psychiatric Assessment for which the City
then proceeded to bill her.
By the time the van arrived to take her
to the House of D., the officer
who'd brought her in in the first place
was saying, "Jolene, I love you." And she'd
told him, she told us, exactly what he could do.
All around us in the dark of Riker's Island
the tumbleweeds scurrying were no pigweed,
I was thinking, but the amaranth of antiquity.
And Jolene was not only amaranth and moly, she was poetry
leaping the turnstiles of another century.

SALVAGE

Daily the cortege of crumpled
defunct cars
goes by by the lasagna-
layered flatbed
truckload: hardtop

reverting to tar smudge,
wax shine antiqued to crusted
winepress smear,
windshield battered to
intact ice-tint, a rarity

fresh from the Pleistocene.
I like it; privately
I find esthetic
satisfaction in these
ceremonial removals

from the category of
received ideas
to regions where pigeons'
svelte smoke-velvet
limousines, taxiing

in whirligigs, reclaim
a parking lot,
and the bag-laden
hermit woman, disencumbered
of a greater incubus,

the crush of unexamined
attitudes, stoutly
follows her routine,
mining the mountainsides
of our daily refuse

for artifacts: subversive
re-establishing
with each arcane
trash-basket dig
the pleasures of the ruined.

BALMS

Hemmed in by the prim
deodorizing stare
of the rare-book room,
I stumbled over,
lodged under glass, a
revenant *Essay on Color*
by Mary Gartside, a woman
I'd never heard of, open
to a hand-rendered
watercolor illustration
wet-bright as the day
its unadulterated red-
and-yellow was laid on
(publication date 1818).

Garden nasturtium hues,
the text alongside
explained, had been
her guide. Sudden as
on hands and knees
I felt the smell of them
suffuse the catacomb
so much of us lives in—
horned, pungent, velvet-
eared succulence, a perfume
without hokum, the intimate
of trudging earthworms
and everyone's last end's
unnumbered, milling tenants.

Most olfactory experience
either rubs your nose
in it or tries to flatter
with a funeral home's
approximation of such balms
as a theology of wax alone
can promise, and the bees
deliver. Mary Gartside
died, I couldn't even
learn the year. Our one
encounter occurred by chance
where pure hue set loose
unearthly gusts of odor
from earthbound nasturtiums.

LINDENBLOOM

Before midsummer density
opaques with shade the checker-
tables underneath, in daylight
unleafing lindens burn
green-gold a day or two,
no more, with intimations
of an essence I saw once,
in what had been the pleasure-
garden of the popes
at Avignon, dishevel

into half (or possibly three-
quarters of) a million
hanging, intricately
tactile, blond bell-pulls
of bloom, the in-mid-air
resort of honeybees'
hirsute cotillion
teasing by the milligram
out of those necklaced
nectaries, aromas

so intensely subtle,
strollers passing under
looked up confused,
as though they'd just
heard voices, or
inhaled the ghost
of derelict splendor
and/or of seraphs shaken
into pollen dust
no transubstantiating
pope or antipope could sift
or quite precisely ponder.

THE CORMORANT IN ITS ELEMENT

That bony potbellied arrow, wing-pumping along
implacably, with a ramrod's rigid adherence,
airborne, to the horizontal, discloses talents
one would never have guessed at. Plummeting

waterward, big black feet splayed for a landing
gear, slim head turning and turning, vermilion-
strapped, this way and that, with a lightning glance
over the shoulder, the cormorant astounding-

ly, in one sleek involuted arabesque, a vertical
turn on a dime, goes into that inimitable
vanishing-and-emerging-from-under-the-briny-

deep act which, unlike the works of Homo Houdini,
is performed for reasons having nothing at all
to do with ego, guilt, ambition, or even money.

CAMOUFLAGE

For Jo and Roy Shaw

It seemed at first like a piece of luck,
the discovery, there in the driveway,
of an odd sort of four-leaf clover—
no bankful of three-penny greenery
but a worried, hovering, wing-dragging
        killdeer's treasury—

a mosaic of four lopsided olives
or marbles you had to hunt
to find again every time, set into
the gravel as if by accident.
We'd have turned that bird's
        entire environment

upside down to have preserved them.
But what was there, after all,
we could have told her about foxes,
coons, cats, or the vandal
with its eye out for whatever anyone
        considers special?

In her bones, in her genes, in
the secret code of her behavior,
she already knew more than all our
bumbling daydreams, our palaver
about safeguards, could muster
        the wit to decipher:

how her whereabouts could vanish
into the gravel, how that brilliant
double-looped necklace could amputate
into invisibility the chevroned
cinnamon of her plumage. Cleverer
        than any mere learned,

merely devious equivocation,
that broken-wing pageant—
who taught her that? We have
no answer except accident,
the trillion-times-over-again
        repeated predicament

sifted with so spendthrift
a disregard for casualties
we can hardly bear to think of
a system so heartless, so shiftless
as being in charge here. It's
    too much like us—

except, after having looked so close
and so long at that casual handful
of dice, squiggle-spotted by luck
that made them half invisible,
watching too often the waltzing swoop
    of the bird's arrival

had meant a disruption of more usual
habits. For all our reading in the papers
about blunderers and risk-takers with
the shrug of nothing-much-matters-
how-those-things-turn-out, we'd unlearned
    to be good losers.

Sorrow, so far as we know, is not
part of a shorebird's equipment.
Nor is memory, of either survival
or losing, after the event.
Having squandered our attention, we
    were less prudent.

For a day, we couldn't quite afford
that morning's black discovery.
Grief is like money: there is only
so much of it we can give away.
And that much grief, for a day,
    bankrupted our economy.

THE KINGFISHER

In a year the nightingales were said to be so loud
they drowned out slumber, and peafowl strolled screaming
beside the ruined nunnery, through the long evening
of a dazzled pub crawl, the halcyon color, portholed
by those eye-spots' stunning tapestry, unsettled
the pastoral nightfall with amazements opening.

Months later, intermission in a pub on Fifty-fifth Street
found one of them still breathless, the other quizzical,
acting the philistine, puncturing Stravinsky—"Tell
me, what *was* that racket in the orchestra about?"—
hauling down the Firebird, harum-scarum, like a kite,
a burnished, breathing wreck that didn't hurt at all.

Among the Bronx Zoo's exiled jungle fowl, they heard
through headphones of a separating panic, the bellbird
reiterate its single *chong,* a scream nobody answered.
When he mourned, "The poetry is gone," she quailed,
seeing how his hands shook, sobered into feeling old.
By midnight, yet another fifth would have been killed.

A Sunday morning, the November of their cataclysm
(Dylan Thomas brought in *in extremis* to St. Vincent's,
that same week, a symptomatic datum) found them
wandering a downtown churchyard. Among its headstones,
while from unruined choirs the noise of Christendom
poured over Wall Street, a benison in vestments,

a late thrush paused, in transit from some grizzled
spruce bog to the humid equatorial fireside: berry-
eyed, bark-brown above, with dark hints of trauma
in the stigmata of its underparts—or so, too bruised
just then to have invented anything so fancy,
later, re-embroidering a retrospect, she had supposed.

In gray England, years of muted recrimination (then
dead silence) later, she could not have said how many
spoiled takeoffs, how many entanglements gone sodden,
how many gaudy evenings made frantic by just one
insomniac nightingale, how many liaisons gone down
screaming in a stroll beside the ruined nunnery;

a kingfisher's burnished plunge, the color
of felicity afire, came glancing like an arrow
through landscapes of untended memory: ardor
illuminating with its terrifying currency
now no mere glimpse, no porthole vista
but, down on down, the uninhabitable sorrow.

THE SMALLER ORCHID

Love is a climate
small things find safe
to grow in—not
(though I once supposed so)
the demanding cattleya
du côté de chez Swann,
glamor among the faubourgs,
hothouse overpowerings, blisses
and cruelties at teatime, but this
next-to-unidentifiable wildling,
hardly more than a
sprout, I've found
flourishing in the hollows
of a granite seashore—
a cheerful tousle, little,
white, down-to-earth orchid
declaring its authenticity,
if you hug the ground
close enough, in a powerful
outdoorsy-domestic
whiff of vanilla.

A HAIRLINE FRACTURE

Whatever went wrong, that week, was more than weather:
a shoddy streak in the fabric of the air of London
that disintegrated into pollen
and came charging down by the bushelful,
an abrasive the color of gold dust, eroding
the tearducts and littering the sidewalks
in the neighborhood of Sloane Square,

where the Underground's upper reaches have the character,
almost, of a Roman ruin—from one
crannied arcade a dustmop of yellow blossom
hung with the stubborn insolence of the unintended,
shaking still other mischief from its hair
onto the platform, the pneumatic haste of missed
trains, the closing barrier—

wherever we went, between fits of sneezing we quarreled:
under the pallid entablatures of Belgravia,
the busy brown façades that were all angles
going in and out like a bellows, even the small house
on Ebury Street where Mozart, at the age of eight,
wrote his first symphony, our difference
was not to be composed.

Unmollified by the freckled plush of mushrooming
monkeyflowers in the windowboxes of Chelsea, undone
by the miraculous rift in the look of things
when you've just arrived—the remote up close,
the knowing that in another, unentered existence
everything shimmering at the surface is this minute
merely, unremarkably familiar—

it was as though we watched the hairline fracture
of the quotidian widen to a geomorphic fissure,
its canyon edge bridged by the rainbows of a terror
that nothing would ever again be right
between us, that wherever we went, nowhere
in the universe would the bone again be knit
or the rift be closed.

EXMOOR

Lost aboard the roll of Kodac-
olor that was to have super-
seded all need to remember
Somerset were: a large flock

of winter-bedcover-thick-
pelted sheep up on the moor;
a stile, a church spire,
and an excess, at Porlock,

of tenderly barbarous antique
thatch in tandem with flower-
beds, relentlessly pictur-
esque, along every sidewalk;

a millwheel; and a millbrook
running down brown as beer.
Exempt from the disaster,
however, as either too quick

or too subtle to put on rec-
ord, were these: the flutter
of, beside that brown water,
with a butterfly-like flick

of fan-wings, a bright black-
and-yellow wagtail; at Dulver-
ton on the moor, the flavor
of the hot toasted teacake

drowning in melted butter
we had along with a bus-tour-
load of old people; the driver

's way of smothering every *r*
in the wool of a West Countr-
y diphthong, and as a Somer-

set man, the warmth he had for
the high, wild, heather-
dank wold he drove us over.

DANCERS EXERCISING

Frame within frame, the evolving conversation
is dancelike, as though two could play
at improvising snowflakes'
six-feather-vaned evanescence,
no two ever alike. All process
and no arrival: the happier we are,
the less there is for memory to take hold of,
or—memory being so largely a predilection
for the exceptional—come to a halt
in front of. But finding, one evening
on a street not quite familiar,
inside a gated
November-sodden garden, a building
of uncertain provenance,
peering into whose vestibule we were
arrested—a frame within a frame,
a lozenge of impeccable clarity—
by the reflection, no, not
of our two selves, but of
dancers exercising in a mirror,
at the center
of that clarity, what we saw
was not stillness
but movement: the perfection
of memory consisting, it would seem,
in the never-to-be-completed.
We saw them mirroring themselves,
never guessing the vestibule
that defined them, frame within frame,
contained two other mirrors.

SLOW MOTION

Her liquid look as dark
as antique honey,
the auburn of her hide
improbably domestic,
the color of a collie or a
Jersey calf, she occupied
(unantlered, a knob-jointed
monument to mild inquiry)

the total sun of that July
mid-morning. Astonishment
sometimes (as it moved
then) moves slowly
to fill up the heart's abruptly
enormous hollow
with stilled cold
as from a well.

Daring her, I stole
a step. One ear
shifted its ponderous
velour to winnow
what my own bare
tympanum merely spilled
and scattered like
a gust of lost pollen.

The meshes of a life
at close attention
went dense; the heaved
limbs upended slowly,
the white scut half-
lifted in a lopsided
wigwag, as though
even the wildest of
surmises need be
in no great hurry.

SUNDAY MUSIC

The Baroque sewing machine of Georg Friedrich
going back, going back to stitch back together
scraps of a scheme that's outmoded, all
those lopsidedly overblown expectations
now severely in need of revision, re
the nature of things, or more precisely
(back a stitch, back a stitch) the
nature of going forward.

No longer footpath-perpendicular, a monody
tootled on antelope bone, no longer
wheelbarrow heave-ho, the nature of going
forward is not perspective, not stairways,
not, as for the muse of Josquin or Gesualdo,
sostenuto, a leaning together
in memory of, things held onto
fusing and converging,

nor is it any longer an orbit, tonality's
fox-and-goose footprints going round
and round in the snow, the centripetal
force of the dominant. The nature of next
is not what we seem to be hearing
or imagine we feel; is not dance,
is not melody, not elegy,
is not even chemistry,

not Mozart leaching out seraphs
from a sieve of misfortune. The nature
of next is not fugue or rondo, not footpath
or wheelbarrow track, not steamships'
bass vibrations, but less and less
knowing what to expect, it's
the rate of historical
change going faster

and faster: it's noise, it's droids' stone-
deaf intergalactic twitter, it's get ready
to disconnect!—no matter how filled
our heads are with backed-up old
tunes, with polyphony, with basso
profundo fioritura, with this Concerto
Grosso's delectable (back a stitch,
back a stitch) Allegro.

BEETHOVEN, OPUS 111

For Norman Carey

*There are epochs . . . when mankind, not content
with the present, longing for time's deeper layers, like
the plowman, thirsts for the virgin soil of time.*
OSIP MANDELSTAM

—Or, conversely, hungers
for the levitations of the concert hall:
the hands like rafts of *putti*
out of a region where the dolorous stars
are fixed in glassy cerements of Art;
the *ancien régime*'s diaphanous plash
athwart the mounting throb of hobnails—
shod squadrons of vibration
mining the air, its struck ores hardening
into a plowshare, a downward wandering
disrupting every formal symmetry:
from the supine harp-case, the strung-foot
tendons under the mahogany, the bulldozer
in the bass unearths a Piranesian
catacomb: Beethoven ventilating,
with a sound he cannot hear, the cave-in
of recurring rage.
            In the tornado country
of mid-America, my father
might have been his twin—a farmer
hacking at sourdock, at the strangle-
roots of thistles and wild morning glories,
setting out rashly, one October,
to rid the fencerows of poison ivy:
livid seed-globs turreted
in trinities of glitter, ripe
with the malefic glee no farmer doubts
lives deep down things. My father
was naïve enough—by nature
revolutionary, though he'd have
disowned the label—to suppose he might
in some way, minor but radical, disrupt
the givens of existence: set
his neighbors' thinking straight, undo
the stranglehold of reasons nations
send their boys off to war. That fall,

after the oily fireworks had cooled down
to trellises of hairy wicks,
he dug them up, rootstocks and all,
and burned them. Do-gooder!
The well-meant holocaust became
a mist of venom, sowing itself along
the sculptured hollows of his overalls,
braceleting wrists and collarbone—
a mesh of blisters spreading to a shirt
worn like a curse. For weeks
he writhed inside it. Awful.
                      High art
with a stiff neck: an upright Steinway
bought in Chicago; a chromo of a Hobbema
tree-avenue, or of Millet's imagined peasant,
the lark she listens to invisible, perhaps
irrelevant: harpstrings and fripperies of air
congealed into an object nailed against the wall,
its sole ironic function (if it has any)
to demonstrate that one, though he may
grunt and sweat at work, is not a clod.
Beethoven might declare the air
his domicile, the winds kin, the tornado
a kind of second cousin; here,
his labor merely shimmers—a deracinated
album leaf, a bagatelle, the "Moonlight"
rendered with a dying fall (the chords
subside, disintegrate, regroup
in climbing sequences *con brio*); there's
no dwelling on the sweet past here,
there being no past to speak of
other than the setbacks: typhoid
in the wells, half the first settlers
dead of it before a year was out;
diphtheria and scarlet fever
every winter; drought, the Depression,
a mortgage on the mortgage. High art
as a susurrus, the silk and perfume
of unsullied hands. Those hands!—
driving the impressionable wild with anguish
for another life entirely: the Lyceum circuit,
the doomed diving bell of Art.

                                        Beethoven
in his workroom: ear trumpet,
conversation book and pencil, candlestick,
broken crockery, the Graf piano
wrecked by repeated efforts to hear himself—
out of a humdrum squalor the levitations,
the shakes and triplets, the *Adagio*
molto semplice e cantabile, the Arietta
a disintegrating surf of blossom
opening along the keyboard, along the fencerows
the astonishment of sweetness. My father,
driving somewhere in Kansas or Colorado,
in dustbowl country, stopped the car
to dig up by the roots a flower
he'd never seen before—a kind
of prickly poppy most likely, its luminousness
wounding the blank plains like desire.
He mentioned in a letter the disappointment
of his having hoped it might transplant—
an episode that brings me near tears,
still, as even his dying does not—
that awful dying, months-long, hunkered,
irascible. From a clod no plowshare
could deliver, a groan for someone
(because he didn't want to look
at anything) to take away the flowers,
a bawling as of slaughterhouses, slogans
of a general uprising: *Freiheit!*
Beethoven, shut up with the four walls
of his deafness, rehearsing the unhearable
semplice e cantabile, somehow reconstituting
the blister shirt of the intolerable
into these shakes and triplets, a hurrying
into flowering along the fencerows: dying,
for my father, came to be like that
finally—in its messages the levitation
of serenity, as though the spirit might
aspire, in its last act,
                                        to walk on air.

Three   Heartland

The fulcrum of America is the Plains, half sea half land.   CHARLES OLSON

There is no Middle West. It is a certain climate, a certain landscape; and beyond that, a state of mind of people born where they do not like to live.
GLENWAY WESCOTT

THE QUARRY

Fishes swam here through the Eocene
too many fathoms up
to think of without suffocation. Light-years
of ooze foreshortened into limestone
swarm with starfish
remoter than the antiquated
pinpoints of astronomy
beneath the stagecoach laboring,
when the thaws came, through mud
up to the hubs. Midsummer's welling bluestem
rose so high the wagons, prairie schooners
under unmasted coifs of canvas,
dragged belly-deep in grass
across the sloughs.
              No roads,
no landmarks to tell where you are,
or who, or whether you will ever find a place
to feel at home in: no alpine
fastness, no tree-profiled pook's hill,
the habitat of magic: only waves
of chlorophyll in motion, the darkened jetsam
of bur oaks, a serpentine of willows
along the hollows—a flux
that waterlogs the mind, draining southeastward
by osmosis to the Mississippi,
where by night the body of De Soto,
ballasted with sand—or was it armor?—
sank into the ooze, nudged by the barbels,
as it decomposed, of giant catfish. Others,
in a terrain as barren
as the dust of bones, kept the corrupt
obsession going: Gold—greed for the metal
most prized because by nature it's
least corruptible. Flushed finally
out of the heartland drainpipe,
the soft parts of De Soto's body filtered
into the capillaries of the delta.   Will
some shard of skull or jawbone, undecomposed,
outlast his name, as the unquarried starfish
outlast the seas that inundated them?
                    Think back
a little, to what would have been

without this festering of lights at night,
this grid of homesteads, this hardening
lymph of haste foreshortened into highways:
the lilt and ripple of the dark,
birdsong at dusk augmented by frog choirs
already old before the Eocene; the wickiups
now here, now there, edged westward
year by year, hemmed in or undermined,
done in finally by treaties. The year
the first land office in the territory opened,
when there were still no roads
other than wagon tracks, one Lyman Dillon,
starting at Dubuque, drove a plow southwestward
a hundred miles—the longest furrow
ever, straight into the belly of the future,
where the broken loam would soon
be mounted, as on a howdah, by
a marble capitol, the glister
of whose dome still overtops
the frittered sprawl of who we are,
of where we came from,
with its stilted El Dorado.

THE WOODLOT

Clumped murmuring above a sump of loam—
grass-rich, wood-poor—that first the plow,
then the inventor (his name plowed under
somewhere in the Patent Office) of barbed wire,
taught, if not fine manners, how at least to follow
the surveyor's rule, the woodlot nodes of willow,
evergreen or silver maple gave the prairie grid
what little personality it had.
                      Who could
have learned fine manners where the air,
that rude nomad, still domineered,
without a shape it chose to keep,
oblivious of section lines, in winter
whisking its wolfish spittle to a froth
that turned whole townships into
one white wallow? Barbed wire
kept in the cattle but would not abrade
the hide or draw the blood
of gales hurled gnashing like seawater over fences'
laddered apertures, rigging the landscape
with the perspective of a shipwreck. Land-chained,
the blizzard paused to caterwaul
at every windbreak, a rage the worse
because it was in no way personal.
                        Against
the involuted tantrums of spring and summer—
sackfuls of ire, the frightful udder
of the dropped mammocumulus
become all mouth, a lamprey
swigging up whole farmsteads, suction
dislodging treetrunks like a rotten tooth—
luck and a cellarhole were all
a prairie dweller had to count on.
                        Whether
the inventor of barbed wire was lucky
finally in what he found himself
remembering, who knows? Did he
ever, even once, envision
the spread of what he'd done
across a continent: whale-song's
taut dulcimer still thrumming as it strung together
orchard, barnyard, bullpen, feedlot,

windbreak: wire to be clambered over,
crawled through or slid under, shepherded—
the heifers staring—to an enclosure
whose ceiling's silver-maple tops
stir overhead, uneasy, in the interminably
murmuring air? Deep in it, under
appletrees like figures in a ritual, violets
are thick, a blue cellarhole
of pure astonishment.
                              It is
the earliest memory. Before it,
I/you, whatever that conundrum may yet
prove to be, amounts to nothing.

IMAGO

Sometimes, she remembers, a chipped flint
would turn up in a furrow,
pink as a peony (from the iron in it)
or as the flared throat of a seashell:
a nomad's artifact fished from the broth,
half sea half land—hard evidence
of an unfathomed state of mind.

Nomads. The wagon train that camped
and left its name on Mormon Ridge.
The settlers who moved on to California,
bequeathing a laprobe pieced from the hide
of a dead buffalo, the frail sleigh
that sleeps under the haymow, and a headstone
so small it might be playing house,
for the infant daughter, aged two days,
no name, they also left behind.

Half sea half land: the shirker propped
above her book in a farmhouse parlor
lolls with the merfolk who revert to foam,
eyeing at a distance the lit pavilions
that seduced her, their tailed child,
into the palaces of metamorphosis. She pays
now (though they do not know this)
by treading, at every step she takes,
on a parterre of tomahawks.

A thirst for something definite so dense
it feels like drowning. Grant Wood
turned everything to cauliflower,
the rounded contours of a thunderhead,
flint-hard. He made us proud:
though all those edges might not be quite
the way it was, at least he'd tried.

"But it has no form!" they'd say to
the scribbler whose floundering fragments
kept getting out of hand—and who, either
fed up with or starved out of
her native sloughs, would, stowed aboard
the usual nomadic moving van, trundle her
dismantled sensibility elsewhere.

Europe, that hodgepodge of ancestral
calamities, was hard and handsome, its rubble
confident, not shriveling on the vine,
as here, like an infertile melon—the Virgin
jejune in her grotto of cold plaster, half sick
of that sidelong enclave, the whispered "Cathlick."

Antiquity unshrouds on wimpling canvas,
adjunct of schoolhouse make-believe: the Italy
of urns and cypresses, of stairways
evolving toward a state of mind
not to be found except backstage
among hunchbacks and the miscreants
who control the scenery, flanked
by a pair of masks whose look, at even
this remove, could drill through bone:
the tragic howl, the comic rictus,
eyeholes that stare out of the crypt
of what no grownup is ever heard to speak of
but in the strangled tone whose lexicon
is summed up in one word: *Bankrupt.*

Bankrupt: the abysm of history,
a slough to be pulled out of
any way you could. Antiquity, the backward
suction of the dark, amounted to a knothole
you plugged with straw, old rags, pages
ripped from last year's Sears Roebuck catalog,
anything, to ward off the blizzard.

Not so, for the born-again, the
shuddering orifices of summer.
On prayer-meeting night, outside
the vestibule among multiple
bell-pulls of Virginia creeper,
the terrible clepsydra of becoming
distils its drop: a luna moth, the emblem
of the born-again, furred like an orchid
behind the ferned antennae, a totem-
garden of lascivious pheromones,
hangs, its glimmering streamers
pierced by the dripstone burin of the eons
with the predatory stare out of the burrow,

those same eyeholes. Imago
of unfathomable evolvings, living
only to copulate and drop its litter,
does it know what it is, what it has been,
what it may or must become?

THE LOCAL GENIUS

SPACE (spelled large) the central fact:
thus Charles Olson. For Glenway Wescott,
the state of mind of those who never liked
to live where they were born—all that
utilitarian muck down underfoot,
brown loam, debris of grassroots packed
thicker than anywhere else on the planet—
soil, so much of it that the central fact

must be, after all, not SPACE but DIRT,
forever present as the sense of guilt
washday alone can hope to expiate.
With what Will Voss of Davenport
invented, the Maytags of Newton built
a dynasty on getting rid of it.

STACKING THE STRAW

In those days the oatfields'
fenced-in vats of running platinum,
the yellower alloy of wheat and barley,
whose end, however gorgeous all that trammeled
rippling in the wind, came down
to toaster-fodder, cereal
as a commodity, were a rebuke
to permanence—to bronze or any metal
less utilitarian than the barbed braids
that marked off a farmer's property,
or the stoked dinosaur of a steam engine
that made its rounds from farm to farm,
after the grain was cut and bundled,
and powered the machine that did the threshing.

Strawstacks' beveled loaves, a shape
that's now extinct, in those days were
the nearest thing the region had
to monumental sculpture. While hayracks
and wagons came and went, delivering bundles,
carting the winnowed ore off to the granary,

a lone man with a pitchfork stood aloft
beside the hot mouth of the blower,
building about himself, forkful
by delicately maneuvered forkful,
a kind of mountain, the golden
stuff of mulch, bedding for animals.
I always thought of him with awe—

a craftsman whose evolving altitude
gave him the aura of a hero. He'd come down
from the summit of the season's effort
black with the baser residues of that
discarded gold. Saint Thomas of Aquino
also came down from the summit
of a lifetime's effort, and declared
that everything he'd ever done was straw.

Four Triptych

PALM SUNDAY

Neither the wild tulip, poignant
and sanguinary, nor the dandelion
blowsily unbuttoning, answers
the gardener's imperative, if need be,
to maim and hamper in the name of order,
or the taste for rendering adorable
the torturer's implements—never mind
what entrails, not yet trampled under
by the feet of choirboys (sing,
my tongue, the glorious battle),
mulch the olive groves, the flowering
of apple and almond, the boxwood
corridor, the churchyard yew,
the gallows tree.

GOOD FRIDAY

Think of the Serengeti lions looking up,
their bloody faces no more culpable
than the acacia's claw on the horizon
of those yellow plains: think with what
concerted expertise the red-necked,
down-ruffed vultures take their turn,
how after them the feasting maggots
hone the flayed wildebeest's ribcage
clean as a crucifix—a thrift tricked out
in ribboned rags, that looks like waste—
and wonder what barbed whimper, what embryo
of compunction, first unsealed the long
compact with a limb-from-limb outrage.

Think how the hunting cheetah, from
the lope that whips the petaled garden
of her hide into a sandstorm, falters,
doubling back, nagged by a lookout
for the fuzzed runt that can't
keep up, that isn't going to make it,
edged by a niggling in the chromosomes
toward these garrulous, uneasy caravans
where, eons notwithstanding, silence
still hands down the final statement.

Think of Charles Darwin mulling over
whether to take out his patent on
the way the shape of things can alter,
hearing the whir, in his own household,
of the winnowing fan no system
(it appears) can put a stop to,
winnowing out another little girl,
for no good reason other than
the docile accident of the unfit,
before she quite turned seven.

Think of his reluctance to disparage
the Wedgwood pieties he'd married into,
his more-than-inkling of the usages
disinterested perception would be put to:
think how, among the hard-nosed, pity
is with stunning eloquence converted

to hard cash: think how Good Friday
can, as a therapeutic outlet, serve
to ventilate the sometimes stuffy
Lebensraum of laissez-faire society:

an ampoule of gore, a mithridatic
ounce of horror—sops for the maudlin
tendency of women toward extremes
of stance, from virgin blank to harlot
to sanctimonious official mourner—
myrrh and smelling salts, baroque
placebos, erotic tableaux vivants
dedicated to the household martyr,
underwriting with her own ex votos
the evolving ordonnance of murder.

The spearpoint glitters in the gorge:
wonder, at Olduvai, what innovator,
after the hunting cat halfway sniffed out
remorse in the design of things,
unsatisfied perhaps with even a lion's
entitlement, first forged the iron
of a righteousness officially exempt
from self-dismay: think, whatever
rueful thumbprint first laid the rubric
on the sacerdotal doorpost, whose victim,
knowing, died without a murmur,
how some fragment of what shudders,
lapped into that crumpled karma,
dreams that it was once a tiger.

EASTER MORNING

a stone at dawn
cold water in the basin
these walls' rough plaster
imageless
after the hammering
of so much insistence
on the need for naming
after the travesties
that passed as faces,
grace: the unction
of sheer nonexistence
upwelling in this
hyacinthine freshet
of the unnamed
the faceless

Five Watersheds

MARGINAL EMPLOYMENT

The Duc de Berry usually wore a robe
the color of the Mediterranean, and listed
two pots of salts of cobalt
along with apes and dromedaries,
a tooth of Charlemagne, another
from a narwhal, and a charred snippet
from the mantle of the prophet,
among his choicest curios.

Though unacquainted with the works
of Marx, he added value
to the hours of no one knows
how many lapidaries, couturiers,
embroiderers of passementerie
with gilt and pearls, and wielders
in gold leaf of the minutest
marginal punctilio. The progress
of his *Très Riches Heures*
is burdened with a fossil gilding
not only of the lily but also of the even
finer flower of the grass, which goes

clothed nowadays in common purple—
nerve-nets of tressed fertility,
marginal fan-vaultings scintillating
with a sequin rain: out of what matrix
of pounded relics, what impastos'
thickened blood and mire, the scandal
of such squandered ornament, no less
than any artifice uniquely crafted
for an emperor's enjoyment, escapes
our mere totting-up. The earth's hours
are weightier, for all this lightness,
than the sum of human enterprise's
tumbledown fiascos, and the burden
of the oceans' robe, unlike the air
it takes the color of, is more ponderous
than greed, although
it flows, it flows, it flows.

TEPOZTLÁN

The Aztecs, conquering, brought Huitzilopochtli
and ceremonial slitting the heart out; Cortés,
a.k.a. Son of the Sun, along with new weapons,
El Señor and the Virgin of the Remedies,
· introduced heaven and hell (which the Tepoztecans
never quite took hold of); the gringos
arrived with sanitary arrangements
and a great many questions.
                Autonomy
climbed down from the plane empty-handed,
carrying only introspection and a few
self-canceling tropisms, innocent
of history as any peasant, to travel,
all in a day, from upland maguey fields'
clumped pewter prongs through treetop regions
where songbirds bright as parrots flashed
uncaged, living free as fishes; alongside
churches of ice-cream-tinted stone
carved like a barbed music, and vendors
of a poisoned rainbow — *helados, refrescos,*
nopals, papayas, mangos, melons all swarming
with warned-against amoebas — down
through villages smelling of pulque,
jasmine and dysentery; past haciendas
torpid with dust, the dogs owned by nobody,
the burros, whether led or tethered, all
long-suffering rancor, the stacked coffins
waiting, mainly child-size (fatality,
part jaguar, part hummingbird, part
gila monster, alive and well here,
clearly needs children); through the daily
dust-laying late-afternoon rainstorm,
in cadenced indigenous place-names
the drip of a slow waterfall,
or of foliage when the rain stops —
arriving, just after sundown,
at the town of Tepoztlán.
                Autonomy,
unaware that in some quarters
the place was famous, saw hanging
cliffs dyed a terrible heart-color
in the gloaming light; a marketplace

empty of people; a big double-towered
church whose doors stood open. No one
inside but a sexton in white *calzoni,*
sweeping up a litter that appeared
to be mainly jasmine: so much fragrance,
so much death, such miracles—El Señor,
glitter-skirted, casketed upright in glass—
such silence . . . until, for no known reason,
overhead the towered bells broke out
into such a pounding that bats, shaken
from their hooked-accordion sleep
by the tumult, poured onto the dark,
a river of scorched harbingers
from an underworld the Tepoztecans
don't altogether believe in.
       They speak
on occasion of Los Aires, or, in their
musical Nahuatl, of *Huehuetzintzin,*
the Old Ones. Who knows what ultimately
is, and what's mere invention? Autonomy,
encapsuled and enmembraned hitherto
by a deaf anxiety, left Tepoztlán
marked, for the first time ever,
by the totally unlooked-for—by a
halfway belief that from out there,
astoundingly, there might be,
now and then, some message.

REMEMBERING GREECE

For Peter Kybart

At noon in this blue cove of the Atlantic
a stiff breeze gets up, exactly as you've seen
it do off Delos. Poseidon, to whose unease
mumbling Delphi purported to assign some meaning,

is quiescent here. Snoring under northern shores,
the Earth-Disturber has hardly more than whimpered
since, enrobed in thickening catastrophes of ice,
the drowned once-mountaintops of this red granite

all but suffocated in his bath—today so blue,
it halfway dislocates itself to the Aegean
and becomes, if only in the way events can weigh
upon events, the bloodied bath of Agamemnon.

THE RESERVOIRS OF MOUNT HELICON

The monks are dying out at Hosios Loukas.
At Great Vespers the celebrant,
singing alone in a cracked ancient voice
while I hug the stall, sole auditor,
keeps losing his place in the chant-book's
stiff curled parchment. Having come by taxi
all the way from Delphi (the driver waits
outside, in no hurry) to be mowed down by a tsunami
of Greek voices, I experience only
the onset of an urge to giggle.
                                    The mosaics
are hardly up to the postcards; tourists,
now that there's a highway, arrive
by the busload. But the ride up—
wet appletrees' cusp-studded wands
aped by the unlikely topside hue of crows
braking and turning just below eye level—
is worth it, and so are the plane trees
that grow here: huge as churches,
they might go back a thousand years, be older
than Hosios Loukas, whose hermitage this was,
be older even than Luke the painter
of seraphic epiphanies. He'd have found it
strange here: the light all muzzy silver,
Helicon green and vast across a mist-
hung gorge, these plane trees
so palpably, venerably pagan—
but I think he might have liked it.
                                    Waiting
outside for the vesper bell, I fell into
conversation with a monk—one of fifteen
now remaining, he told me—who spoke a kind
of English learned, and since largely forgotten,
during a sojourn in Brooklyn. They'd been building
a bridge then, he recalled, across the Hudson;
he supposed it must be finished by now.
I told him, in a faint voice, yes,
it had been finished—and looked out, whelmed
into vertigo by gulfs spanned for a moment
by so mere a thread, across a gorge
already half-imaginary with distance
toward the improbable, the muse-haunted
reservoirs of Mount Helicon.

TRASIMENE

Tourmaline plashing in a noose of reeds,
Lake Trasimene is being slowly strangled
in ecology, no respecter of the Quattrocento.
How could that sheeted
opacity be looked at, after Arezzo,
except as the filtered tint,
wet lake-hue into fresco, Piero
della Francesca laid like rain
over sky, drapery, the roofs of houses?
How, after Perugia, after the Louvre
and the Uffizi, can the Umbria
of Perugino be seen, five centuries later,
except as he pre-empted it?—as space
looking inward, transparency set breathing
to commend an attitude: Madonna,
head drooping like a tulip, among donors.
Fashions in felicity play hide and seek
with decor; reigning apostolates
shrink to a simper. It's the lake's
look that breathes here,
infinity's eutrophic emerald
that won't keep either.

RAIN AT BELLAGIO

For Doris Thompson Myers

I

The omnipresence of the sound of water: rain
on the graveled walks, the lakeside terraces,
the red pantiles of Bellagio.

At Paestum we had not heard it.
An acreage of thyme, winnowed by sea breezes.
A line of blue out past the silted harbor—
unauthenticated because unheard,
a scene one might have dreamed.

At Herculaneum, a stoppage of the ears.
Cicadas mute, an oleander stillness.
Rancor of cypresses. Impacted fire.
Effete ribaldry strangling in hot mud
up to the nostrils. Water stricken
from the ledgers of memory.

At Naples, human noise inundating the bayfront,
lapping at castles' elephantine hooves, rampaging
tenement ravines. Once in the night
I woke and knew it had been raining—
not from the sound but from the smell, as though
an animal had left its spoor.

Under an aspect less clement, the trickle
of sewers, the vine-patched bombholes,
bambini with no underpants, gnarled women
wearing the black of perpetual resignation,
might have figured more gravely than as a condiment,
garlic for a week of living well.

II

Aboard the *wagons-lits* we drank Est! Est! Est!,
leaned tipsily out of windows, behaved
as though we owned the railway car, owned
the platform as it receded, owned even, overhead,
the diminution to a half-perceived scintilla

of the stars, after the manner of the young who travel
Europe, garnering experience in pairs.

We passed the Apennines asleep, and woke in a country
where the color of the olive trees was rainy.
Gray rain muddying the emerald of ricefields,
blurring, across the flood plain of the Po, the vague
geometry of poplars on the march—a part
of some interminable uprising.

At Milan a drizzle, the boulevards inlaid
with dun-colored patines, the slough of plane trees.
A car sent from the villa, behind whose steamed windows
we talk as freely as though the driver had no ears.
Glimpsing, through sheets of rain, the first gray-green,
narrow windings of Lake Como,
the red pantiles of Monza and Lecco,
the little farms, the villa walls
sequestering unimagined pleasures. Vineyards.
Terraces. The starred darkness of lemon trees
through the downpour. Gravel under our shoes,
a footman holding an umbrella. All as in
that terrifying place where no one is admitted
whose taste is not impeccable.

III

Servants. The butler's practiced deference,
the liquid glance unerring as a falcon's—
a lisp in the shrubbery, a blur of wingbars
and he's placed you. On the hall table
tuberoses' opening racemes purport a sadness
the equal of Elysium. Massed carnations
in a cushioned bedroom, a bath overlooking
the flutter of chaffinches, cypresses'
columned melancholy, the lacquered foliage
of magnolias seen from the balcony, are no refuge
from the surveillance of chambermaids, scathing
as a penitent's examination of conscience.
The scuffed suitcase cannot escape: as soon as
your back is turned, they have
already unpacked it.

Out on the lake a white traghetto, moving
almost without pause from one shore to the other,
a punctual amphibious spider, skeins
into one zigzag the descending
clatter from the campaniles of Bellagio,
of Varenna and Cadenabbia, as though reining
the fragments of experience into one process—
being-and-becoming fused, a single scheme.

The rustle of descending silk (these shores
being mulberry country), the curtains drawn
against the prerogative of the chambermaids,
behind closed doors, having had our tea,
conspiratorially, two high-church Episcopalians, we begin
to read aloud the office of Compline.

The damask weave of luxury, the arras
of melodrama. A wailing about the eaves.
Confidences wading like a salvage operation
toward an untidy past: the admirer
who had in fact been a bricklayer,
who wore dirty undershirts; the rue
of not-yet-dealt-with gaffes, chagrins
and false positions, tinder
for the scorn of maître d's, the pained
look of a host whose taste is impeccable:
hazards of a murderous civility, the beast
snared in a nightmare of living well.

IV

Cocktails in the salotto, underneath a portrait
of the late owner, a distiller's heiress
of dim but cultivated beauty, whose third spouse
left her title to an extinct principality. The villa,
acquired by caprice, became her favorite household.
Though in the way of moral character not much
is to be expected, *noblesse oblige:* the servants—
eighty of them altogether—must be provided for.
Emissaries of those foundations into which
the larger fortunes have unavoidably been siphoned
were circuitously whispered to; and so, the times

being what they have become, the princeliest
of the seventeen bedrooms, stripped
of its cushier urgings to dalliance,
is now a conference room—this week
for a conclave of jurisprudes, the week after
for experts in the field of public health
concerning the eradication of malaria.

Reclamation of the land: the labor gangs,
the overseers, the seasonal migrations,
the Lombard plain at last made habitable,
a source of fortunes: irrigated water meadows,
ricefields, wheat, mulberries, the channeled music
of the Po, the Oglio, the Adda, the Ticino. Vineyards.
Landed estates. Walled properties above Lake Como,
for the view. A rural proletariat whose fortunes
and miseries go unrecorded.

V

In her declining years the Principessa
was to be seen leaning, as she made her rounds
nuzzled in sable against the lake damp,
on the arm of her butler.

The indispensable tyranny of servants.
Gardeners, kitchen maids, woodcutters, grooms,
footmen. Private secretaries.
Confessors. Archbishops.
Above the fever trap of the Maremma
the ritual complicity: in castle towers
the secret stair, the cached aconite,
the hired assassin.

Fiefdoms. Latifundia. The wealth of nations.
The widening distance between rich and poor,
between one branch and another of the tree of misery.
A view of lakeside terraces
to sell one's soul for.

VI

Among the company at dinner, Professor B.,
reputedly the best mind in Italy,
who speaks no English; also Professor d'E.,
who speaks it more exquisitely than any native—
slim, fair, elfin, author of a legal treatise
no one (he says) has read.
      —Then I will read it.
      —Oh, but really it is very dull.
The weather in Italy, he says, is changing.
Now that charcoal is no longer burned
extensively, the forests have grown up again,
forests draw moisture—*Ecco!*

Flooding along the Po, the Adige, the Ticino.
Dykes giving way at Ferrara, inundations
at Rimini, the beetfields of Ravenna
already under water. On the flood plain,
the mosaics of Sant' Apollinare in Classe
ripple as though drowned—redemption
envisioned as a wall of water.

VII

What does a place like this not offer?
Flawless cuisine, a first-rate cellar,
mountain footpaths laced with wild cyclamen
and maidenhair; topiary, sunken gardens,
wood nymphs and a dying slave in marble; even,
when nothing short of total solitude
will do, a hermitage.

My friend is twenty,
blond as Lucrezia Borgia, her inclinations
nurtured with care since childhood.
She speaks three languages and has had
six proposals. Since January
her existence has been an exercise
in living like a Principessa. Her father
still cannot fathom what has happened.
He points, appealing, to a letter

on the hall table, overhung
by the tuberoses' extravagant love-death,
addressed to an abbess.

And will she be free to leave if she should wish to?
He, for one, does not believe it. They will wear her down
in that enclosed community, those Anglican Benedictines.
She will become nothing other than a model prisoner.
That, as he understands it, is the long and short
of what what they call *formation* amounts to.

One might have said by way of a response (but did not)
that living under vows, affianced to a higher poverty,
might likewise be an exercise in living well.

VIII

Her last evening amounts to an exercise in prevarication.
Where precisely she is going, and why, she has
given up explaining. Dinner is a banquet. Afterward,
half sozzled on red wine followed by champagne
followed by Strega, we're in raincoats,
climbing into a villa car with a pair
of half-fledged jurisprudes. A halt
somewhere along the way, the rain slackening
and closing in again like trees in a landscape,
to snitch grapes from a vineyard. We arrive
at the farewell party pretending we're bacchantes.

Antique U.S. jazz on a portable phonograph.
Liqueurs. Chocolates. My friend dancing
the cha-cha-cha, engaging in mock flirtations
with a moody Italian, then with a cheerful one
whose profession entails the proliferation of supermarkets.
    —But how *can* you?
    —And why isn't what's good for your country
      good also for Italy?

A prolonged huddle with the cheerful one. Emerging,
they announce they have an announcement:
they have decided to get married
for about a week. At midnight,

trying for a departure, we find the door
locked against us, the key hidden prettily
in somebody's décolletage. Everybody
is going away tomorrow. We say goodbye
to the jurisprudes, the young footman
standing expressionless beside the door.

IX

The pang of bells, through rain-filled dark,
at every hour. Half slumber,
feeble morning light. At seven, booted
and raincoated, we're plunging through the wet
to board the traghetto—the only passengers,
along with a truckload of Italian beer—for Cadenabbia
and early communion at the English church.

A port, a buoy, a rudder: hymnbook similes
capsize in the act of kneeling
and receiving the substance of such controversy,
cataclysms from the winepress of the glaciers,
whatever it is that knows itself only
in the sense of being carried,
all the bridges out, surrounded
by the rush of moving water—total
self-abandonment perceived as living well.

A rush for the landing, the water rushing alongside,
down gutters, over cobblestones. In one hour
the level of the lake has risen astoundingly.
Aboard the traghetto, a priest
wears a violet-lined biretta
and buckles on his shoes.

Seeing how the picturesque outlives its meaning.

X

Punctually at three in the afternoon, our luggage
waits by the door, the car stands in the rain,
its motor running. Bathos of tuberoses

on the hall table, the butler's formal bow,
the footman holding an umbrella. Gravel
under our shoes. Behind the steamed windows
confidences interspersed with silences.
At Milan, dim through fatigue, a watershed:
for the rest of our lives, we will be traveling
in opposite directions. Behind us, limestone
and chestnut mountainsides, streaming, release
their increment of moisture: rain, glacier melt,
the wine of change. Ahead of us,
spilling across the lap of Italy, the tributaries
of the Po—the Adda, the Oglio, the Sesia—
mingle and descend toward Ferrara,
toward Rimini and Ravenna: uncontrollable
as rumor, as armies set in motion,
the sound of water.

XI

Sometimes since, in dreams I find myself obliged
to assume, without previous instruction, control
of a plane I have no memory of boarding. I wake
without ever having learned the outcome. Or,
in another region, I find myself
face to face with the transparent strata
of experience, the increment of years,
as a wall of inundation, the drowned mosaic
glimmering above the flood plain. Waking,
I hear the night sounds merge, a single rustle
as of silk, as though becoming might amend,
unbroken, to one stilled, enclosing skein.

XII

At the Abbey, between the shored-up Norman church
and the trefoiled oak of the pilgrim hostel,
running liquid and garrulous through a life of silence,
cushioned and tended between banks of tamed wildflowers,
the sound of water: indivisible, unstilled,
unportioned by the bells that strike the hours.

Six   Hydrocarbon

OR CONSIDER PROMETHEUS

In 1859 petroleum was discovered in Pennsylvania. Kerosene, petroleum, and paraffin began rapidly to replace whale oil, sperm oil, and spermaceti wax. . . . Consider whaling as FRONTIER, *and* INDUSTRY. *A product wanted, men got it: big business. The Pacific as sweatshop . . . the whaleship as factory, the whaleboat the precision instrument. . . .* CHARLES OLSON, *Call Me Ishmael*

I

Would Prometheus, cursing on his rock
as he considered fire, the smuggled gem
inside the weed stem, and the excesses
since his protracted punishment began,

have cursed the ocean's copious antidote,
its lapping, cold, incessant undulance
plowed to shards by wheeling porpoises,
hydrogen-cum-oxygen fanned up in mimicries

of hard carbon, diamond of purest water,
the unforbidden element crosscut by fire,
its breakup the absolving smile of rainbows?
Or, considering leviathan, whose blameless

progenitors turned from the shore, from its
seducing orchards, renouncing the prehensile
dangle of a brain all eyes and claws,
twittering fishhook strategies of grasp

and mastery, for immersion among moving
declivities, have envied the passivity
whose massive ease is no more than his own
tormented rectitude, immune from drowning?

II

How would the great cetaceans, Houyhnhnm
intelligences sans limbs, ungoaded by
the Promethean monkeyshines that gave us
haute cuisine, autos-da-fé and fireworks,

dining al fresco off cuttlefish and krill,
serving up baleen-strained plankton, whose
unmanipulative ears explore Olympian parterres
of sonar, devise the ringing calculus

of icebergs, compute the density of ships
as pure experience of hearing—how
would these basking reservoirs of fuel,
wax and glycerine have read the trypots

readied for their rendering into tallow
for a thousand candles? How, astronomers
of the invisible, would they have tracked
the roaring nimbus of that thieving

appetite, our hunger for the sun, or
charted the harrowing of jet and piston
pterodactyls, robots fed on their successor,
fire-drinking vampires of hydrocarbon?

THE ANNIVERSARY

SEPTEMBER 1, 1939

Night after night of muffled
rant, of tumefying apprehension
impended like a marriage
all through the summer—larger
even, for one as yet without
consensual knowledge, than
the act of love.

The weather that last weekend
at the Crescent Beach Hotel
went bad. Lake Okoboji, under
a tarpaulin of overcast (bare
springboard, all the rowboats
idle) turned pale, then
darkened to gunmetal.

A lolling weekend foursome,
unwelcomed as wet weather,
tainted the family dinner hour
with a scurrilous good humor
as of having, without compunction,
already seen how far the arson
in our common nature
would choose to go.

The meaning of the evening newscast,
no news, confirmed the reluctant

off-color miracle that had
made the summer pregnant.
Ultimatums had brought forth
their armored litter; Poland
had witnessed even now,
in darkness, the beginning
of the burning.

THE ANNIVERSARY

Rain roared down all night,
unstoppable as war, onto
the stricken porches of
the Crescent Beach Hotel.
Lightning through the downpour
repeatedly divebombed the water
like an imagined lover.

Arson, a generation's habitual
dolor, observes its anniversary,
its burning birthday, its passage
from an incendiary overture
to what the ignorance of that
September, of this September
minus forty, would
consent to know.

LETTERS FROM JERUSALEM

Engines of burning took him there
and brought back the first postcard,
a view of Jerusalem. The high air
swam with domes, their drowned gilding
glimmering like live fish scales.
The sky at night was an aquarium
of light-years whose distances
at noon, converging, turned the desert
        to burning glass.

The kibbutzim aren't quite, he admits,
what he'd expected. The Talmud
couldn't care less about anybody's
happiness. But is that (he writes)
even important? Perhaps the true
arrival is always inward? He walks
the hills, the clogged bazaars,
everywhere. He is learning Hebrew.
        Immerse, immerse—

inward but also downward. He sees
time impend, the weather changing.
Clouds mass on the horizon; daylight
shrinks backward to the Maccabees'
last reckoning. In secret, from
the squalid rigor of the Yeshiva
and his unheated room, he flees
with Saint-Exupéry into regions
        of wind, sand and stars.

Immersion, thirst for roots, the passion
of expecting less: he asks now (he writes)
no more than to be here as a witness.
He begins even to dream in Hebrew:
locutions bend as though half in,
half out of water. But the watershed
that waits is made of fire: a cherub
in the doorway poses the blazing
        conundrum of the Jews

whose Biblical injunction is: if he stays
he must go into the army. The 'sixties
subversive pacifist he was must unadopt
that arrogance or lose Jerusalem.
A bush burned once; volcanoes
tutored the patriarchs; Elijah
was taken up in rafts of flame.
From Moscow, rumors arrive of new
      pogroms. He stays.

The latest letter, with no date, begins
Shalom! Tomorrow his leave ends,
then back to the desert. Tanks are less
accommodating even than the Talmud
to a divided mind. The promised land
more and more is dense with engines.
Converging overhead, in skies that swam,
the distances grow predatory and explode
      with burning seraphim.

BERCEUSE

Listen to Gieseking playing a Berceuse
of Chopin—the mothwing flutter
light as ash, perishable as burnt paper—

and sleep, now the furnaces of Auschwitz
are all out, and tourists go there.
The purest art has slept with turpitude,

we all pay taxes. Sleep. The day of waking
waits, cloned from the phoenix—
a thousand replicas in upright silos,

nurseries of the ultimate enterprise.
Decay will undo what it can, the rotten
fabric of our repose connives with doomsday.

Sleep on, scathed felicity. Sleep, rare
and perishable relic. Imagining's no shutter
against the absolute, incorrigible sunrise.

THE DAHLIA GARDENS

There are places no history can reach.   NORMAN MAILER, *Armies of the Night*

Outside the river entrance, between the Potomac
and the curbed flowerbeds, a man walks up and down,
has been walking this last half hour. November leaves
skip in the wind or are lifted, unresisting,
to mesh with the spent residue of dahlias'
late-summer blood and flame, leached marigolds,
knives of gladioli flailed to ribbons:
parts of a system that seems, on the face of it,
to be all waste, entropy, dismemberment;
but which perhaps, given time enough, will prove
to have refused nothing tangible,
                                    enjambed
without audible clash, with no more than a whiplash
incident, to its counterpart, a system
shod in concrete, cushioned in butyl, riding
chariots of thermodynamics, adept with the unrandom,
the calculus of lifting and carrying, with vectors,
clocks, chronicles, calibrations.
                                    File clerks
debouch into the dusk—it is rush hour; headlights
thicken, a viscous chain along the Potomac—
from concentric corridors, five sides
within five sides, grove leading on to grove
lit by autonomous purrings, daylight
on demand, dense with the pristine,
the dead-white foliage of those archives
that define and redefine with such precision,
such subtleties of exactitude, that only
the honed mind's secret eye can verify
or vouch for its existence, how the random
is to be overcome, the unwelcome
forestalled, the arcane calamity
at once refused, delineated and dwelt on. Where,
as here, triune Precaution, Accumulation
and Magnitude obtain, such levitations
and such malignities have come, with time,
to seem entirely natural—this congeries
being unquestionably the largest
office building in Christendom.

                    The man alone
between blackened flowerbeds and the blackening
Potomac moves with care, as though balanced
astride the whiplash between system and system—
wearing an overcoat, hatless, thinning-haired,
a man of seemingly mild demeanor
who might have been a file clerk
were it not for his habit of writing down
notes to himself on odd scraps of paper,
old bills, the backs of envelopes, or in a notebook
he generally forgets to bring with him,
and were it not for the wine jug
he carries (the guard outside the river entrance,
as he pauses, has observed it, momentarily puzzled)
cradled close against his overcoat.
                              By now file clerks,
secretaries, minor and major bureaucrats, emerging
massively through the several ports of egress,
along the ramps, past the walled flowerbeds,
which the lubrications and abrasions of routine,
the multiple claims of a vigilant anxiety,
the need for fine tuning, for continual
readjustment of expectation, have rendered
largely negligible, flow around him.
He moves against the flux, toward the gardens.
Around him, leaves skip in the wind
like a heartbeat, like a skipped
heartbeat

            if I were a dead leaf
            thou mightest bear

                    He shivers,
cradling the wine jug, his heart beating strangely;
his mind fills up with darkness

                overland, the inching caravans
                the blacked-out troop trains
                convoys through ruined villages
                along the Mekong

                        merging
with the hydrocarbon-dark, headlight-inflamed Potomac

the little lights   the candles
flickering on Christmas eve
the one light left burning
in a front hallway   kerosene-
lit windows in the pitch dark
of back-country roads

His mind

plunges like a derrick
into that pitch dark as he uncorks the wine jug
and with a quick gesture not unlike
a signing with the cross (but he is a Quaker)
begins the anointing of himself with its contents,
with the ostensible domestic Rhine wine
or chablis, which is not wine—which
in fact is gasoline.

tallow, rushlight, whale oil, coal oil,
gas jet: black fat of the Ur-tortoise
siphoned from stone, a shale-tissued
carapace: hydrocarbon unearthed
and peeled away, process by process,
in stages not unlike the stages
of revelation, to a gaseous plume
that burns like a bush, a perpetual
dahlia of incandescence, midway
between Wilmington and Philadelphia
gaslight, and now these filamented
avenues, wastelands and windows
of illumination, gargoyles,
gasconades, buffooneries of neon,
stockpiled incendiary pineapples,
pomegranates of jellied gasoline
that run along the ground, that cling
in a blazing second skin
to the skins of children

Anointing the overcoat, and underneath it the pullover
with one elbow out, he sees, below the whiplash threshold,
darkness boil up, a vatful of sludge, a tar pit,
a motive force that is all noise: jet engines,
rush-hour aggressions, blast furnaces,
headline-grabbing self-importances

the urge to engineer events
compel a change of government,
a change of heart, a shift
in the wind's direction—lust
after mastery, manipulations
of the merely political

Hermaphrodite of pity and violence, the chambered
pistil and the sword-bearing archangel,
scapegoat and self-appointed avenger, contend,
embrace, are one. He strikes the match.
A tiger leap, a singing envelope goes up,
blue-wicked, a saffron overcoat of burning

> *in the forests of the night*
> *make me thy lyre*

Evolving
out of passionless dismemberment,
a nerveless parturition, green wheels'
meshed intercalibration with the sun

A random leaf, seized by the updraft, shrivels
unresisting; fragments of black ash
drift toward the dahlia gardens

from dim tropisms of avoidance,
articulated, node upon internode,
into a scream, the unseen filament
that never ends, that runs
through all our chronicles

a manifesto flowering like a dahlia
into whole gardens of astonishment—
the sumptuous crimson,
heart's dark, the piebald
saffron and scarlet riding
the dahlia gardens of
the lake of Xochimilco:

Benares, marigold-garlanded
suttee, the burning ghats
alongside the Ganges: at

the An Quang pagoda, saffron
robes charring in fiery
transparency, a bath of burning

Scraps of charred paper, another kind of foliage,
drift toward the dahlia gardens

a leaf
thou mightest bear

The extravaganza
of a man afire having seized, tigerlike, the attention
it now holds with the tenacity of napalm, of the homebound
file clerks, secretaries, minor and major bureaucrats,
superimposing upon multiple adjustments,
the fine tuning of Precaution and Accumulation,
the demands of Magnitude, what the concentric
groves of those archives have no vocabulary
for dwelling on, the uniformed man of action,
in whom precaution and the unerring impulse
are one, springs forward to pound and pummel,
extinguishing the manifesto as decently as possible.
                                        Someone,
by now, has sent for an ambulance.

The headlights crawl, slowed by increasing density,
along the Potomac, along the diagonal thoroughfares,
along the freeways, toward Baltimore, toward Richmond,
toward Dulles and toward Friendship Airport, the airborne
engines' alternating red
and green, a pause and then again a red,
a green, a waking fantasy upborne
on a lagoon of hydrocarbon, as
the dahlia gardens ride the lake of Xochimilco.
While the voiceless processes of a system
that in the end perhaps will have
refused nothing tangible, continue neither
to own nor altogether to refuse the burning filament
that runs through all our chronicles, uniting
system with system into one terrible mandala,
the stripped hydrocarbon
burns like a bush, a gaseous plume
midway between Wilmington and Philadelphia.

THE BURNING CHILD

After a few hours' sleep, the father had a dream that his child was standing beside his bed, caught him by the arm and whispered reproachfully: "Father, don't you see I'm burning?" FREUD, *The Interpretation of Dreams*

Dreamwork, the mnemonic flicker
of the wave of lost particulars—
whose dream, whose child, where, when, all lost
except the singed reprieve, its fossil ardor
burnished to a paradigm of grief,
half a century before the cattle cars,
the shunted parceling—*links, rechts*—
in a blaspheming parody of judgment
by the Lord of burning: the bush, the lava flow,
the chariot, the pillar. What is, even so,
whatever breathes but a reprieve, a risk,
a catwalk stroll between the tinder
and the nurture whose embrace is drowning?

The dream redacted cannot sleep; it whimpers
so relentlessly of lost particulars, I can't
help thinking of the dreamer as your father,
sent for by the doctors the night he said the *Sh'ma*
over the dim phoenix-nest of scars
you were, survivor
pulled from behind a blazing gas tank
that summer on the Cape, those many years
before we two, by a shuttlecock-and-battle-
dore, a dreamworklike accretion of nitwit
trouvées, were cozened into finding how
minute particulars might build themselves
into a house that almost looks substantial:
just as I think of how, years earlier,
the waves at Surfside on Nantucket, curveting
like herded colts, subsiding, turned
against my staggering thighs, a manacle
of iron cold I had to be pulled out of. Drowning,
since, has seemed a native region's ocean,
that anxiety whose further shores are lurid
with recurrences of burning.

The people herded from the cattle cars
first into barracks, then to killing chambers,
stripped of clothes, of names, of chattels—all those
of whom there would remain so few particulars:
I think of them, I think of how your mother's
people made the journey, and of how
                                        unlike
my own forebears who made the journey,
when the rush was on, aboard a crowded
train from Iowa to California, where,
hedged by the Pacific's lunging barricades,
they brought into the world the infant
who would one day be my father, and
(or the entire astonishment, for me, of
having lived until this moment would
have drowned unborn, unburied without
ever having heard of Surfside) chose
to return, were free to stay or go
back home, go anywhere at all—
                                        not one
outlived the trip whose terminus was burning.

The catwalk shadows of the cave, the whimper
of the burning child, the trapped
reprieve of nightmare between the
tinder and the nurture whose
embrace is drowning.

WHAT
THE
LIGHT
WAS
LIKE

(1985)

Ay, on the shores of darkness there is light,
And precipices show untrodden green.
KEATS, *To Homer*

One   The Shore

A BAROQUE SUNBURST

struck through such a dome
as might await a groaning Michelangelo,
finding only alders and barnacles
and herring gulls at their usual squabbles,
sheds on the cove's voluted
silver the aloof skin tones
of a Crivelli angel: a region,
a weather and a point of view
as yet unsettled, save for the lighthouse
like a Venetian campanile, from whose nightlong
reflected angelus you might suppose
the coast of Maine had Europe
on the brain or in its bones, as though
it were a kind of sickness.

THE AUGUST DARKS

Stealth of the flood tide, the moon dark
but still at work, the herring shoals
somewhere offshore, looked for
but not infallible, as the tide is,
as the August darks are—

stealth of the seep of daylight, the boats
bird-white above the inlet's altering
fish-silver, the murmur of the motor
as the first boat slips out
ahead of daylight

into the opening aorta, that heaving
reckoning whose flux informs the heart-
beat of the fisherman—poor,
dark, fallible-infallible
handful of a marvel

murmuring unasked inside the ribcage,
workplace covert as the August darks are,
as is the moon's work, masked within
the blazing atrium of daylight,
the margin of its dwindling

sanguine as with labor, but effortless:
as is the image, far out, illusory
at the dark's edge, of the cruise ship
moving, seemingly unscathed by effort,
bright as a stage set

for the miming of the tiara'd swan's danced
dying, the heartbeat's prodigies of strain
unseen, the tendons' ache, the blood-
stained toe shoes, the tulle
sweat-stained, contained

out where the herring wait, beyond
the surf-roar on the other side of silence
we should die of (George Eliot
declared) were we to hear it. Many
have already died of it.

LOW TIDE AT SCHOODIC

Force, just here, rolls up
pomaded into vast blue curls
fit for the Sun King, then crumples
to a stuff of ruffs and kerchiefs
over ruined doorposts, the rubble
of an overthrow no one remembers
except through cooled
extrapolation—tunnels
underneath the granite,
the simmering moat, the darkened sill
we walk on now,
prowling the planar windowpanes of tidepools
for glimpses of kelp's ribboned whips,
the dead men's fingers.
      Boulders
smothered in a fur of barnacles
become a slum, a barrio
of hardened wigwams, each
(notwithstanding a seeming armor
that invites, when added to the fate
of being many, the hobnails
of a murderous indifference)
holding an entity no less
perishably tender than any
neonate delivered, red
and squalling, in the singular.
      Spruces,
turreted above the ledge,
lodge in the downdraft
of their precarious stairwells
a warbler who, all nerves tuned to
alarums, dapper in a yellow domino,
a noose of dark about his throat,
appends his anxious signature—
a wiry wheeze,
a blurred flute note.

BERTIE GOES HUNTING

For Mary Jo Salter and Brad Leithauser

Dear beast, luxurious of pelt,
moon-orbed possessor of the
screen-door-unlatching paw,
the lurk that twitches in
   the haunch at every

piebald quiver of out-in-the-
open; past the fern-flanked
porchside boundary, a froth
of goldenrod and timothy
   absorbs his predatory

crouch-and-spring, quick-
silver underside of memory,
the lunge-evoking, paradisal
rustle of the underbrush, the
   just-missed quarry:

his vanishings into a history
so dense with molecules, so
chary of the traceable, you
never quite believe the ata-
   vism's only temporary—

that à la the silver lizards
Robert Frost purported to have
seen cascading down the
mountainside in slush-time,
   this time the furry

entity you knew, if not quite
yet dissolved into a dew, will
have surrendered to the texture
of that habitat, the slither
   of its understory.

Yet when you call the name you've
given him, that like a skipped
stone skims the surface of what-
ever's out there, something,
   primed to be ready for a

game of shake-and-bake, a fondling
session, with the inevitable risk
of being laughed at—is it habit,
is it altogether voluntary?—
      brings him in a hurry.

CLOUDBERRY SUMMER

First ventured into
in mid-July, the bog's sodden hollow
muffled the uproar of the shore
it hunkered in the lee of. Wrung residues
of sphagnum moss steeped in self-
manufactured acids stained the habitat's
suffusing waters brown,

to feed the red-
haired, hair-trigger sundews' mazy glint,
the ground-level pseudo-pomegranate
drowning dens of pitcher plants. Sheer dearth,
a poverty of nitrogen, they tell us,
is what turned this vegetation predatory
as the blood-craving

blackflies and
mosquitoes it has evolved its several
macabre ways of preying on. Bog
laurel and lambkill distil a nectar and a
petty poison of their own. Rancor
is rarely simple, least so in the dank
sector of organic

chemistry. Likewise
its lack, as in these strangely sallow-
tinged, blandly baked-apple-
flavored thimble nubbins, singly borne, no
more than inches from the bog's
sour surface. Could so odd a crop
be edible? Yes,

it could. Called
hayth- (but spell it *heath*) berries by
the populace Down East, they're
known and relished as cloudberries farther north.
Here, they figure as subarctic strays—
pale-jeweled morsels of seed and sweetness
for some ravenous

small mammal to
wring a minim's undiluted, untainted
pleasure from, the distillation
of a boreal summer's luminous, perfervid,
snow-ringed haven. And a rare thing
pleasure is too, even for the mammal who
in effect invented

and then lost no
time polluting it, in ways the wretchedest
den-fouling lemming would surely
find astonishing. A thing still rarer (or so
for me it was) than that cloud-
berry summer is what in June, not quite a
summer later,

would prove on
bemused observation to be a thriving
cloudberry spring: revisited, the
bog's sunken floor a dapple of such countless,
singly borne, close-to-the-
ground corollas, each of a whiteness
so without a flaw

I thought, for
half a second, *Snow.* But no. Some new
species, then? A moonflake
guelder rose? I stooped to look. A clue
appeared: the stem beneath each
flower bore a paired leaf-clasp, its
halves consisting

of two pale,
wizened infant claws; and as the wavering
appendage of a single barnacle
is multiplied, on observation, to a kind of choir
(what are they doing? Merely
seizing any passing thing that may be
edible), thereby

tending to unhand
one's sense of balance, I swam, immersed
in undersurfaces, the filling tide-
pool of surprise. Days later—all those claws
by now mere greenery, the whiteness fallen—
the whole unstable, illusory van of pleasure
had moved on.

GOOSEBERRY FOOL

The gooseberry's no doubt an oddity,
an outlaw or pariah even—thorny
and tart as any
kindergarten martinet, it can harbor
like a fernseed, on its leaves' under-
side, bad news for pine trees,
whereas the spruce
resists the blister rust
it's host to. That veiny Chinese
lantern, its stolid jelly
of a fruit, not only has
no aroma but is twice as tedious
as the wild strawberry's sunburst
stem-end appendage: each one must
be between-nail-snipped at both extremities.

Altogether, gooseberry virtues
take some getting
used to, much as does trepang,
tripe à la mode de Caen,
or having turned thirteen.
The acerbity of all things green
and adolescent lingers in
it—the arrogant, shrinking,
prickling-in-every-direction thorn-
iness that loves no company except its,
or anyhow that's what it gets:
bristling up through gooseberry ghetto sprawl
are braced thistles' silvery, militantly symmetrical
defense machineries. Likewise inseparably en-
tangled in the disarray of an
uncultivated childhood, where gooseberry bushes (since
rooted out) once flourished, is
the squandered volupté of lemon-
yellow-petaled roses' luscious flimflam—
an inkling of the mingling into one experience
of suave and sharp, whose supremely im-
probable and far-fetched culinary
embodiment is a gooseberry fool.

Tomorrow, having stumbled into
this trove of chief ingredients
(the other being very thickest cream)
I'll demonstrate it for you. Ever since,
four summers ago, I brought you,
a gleeful Ariel, the trophy
of a small sour handful,
I've wondered what not quite articulated thing
could render magical
the green globe of an unripe berry.
I think now it was simply
the great globe itself's too much to carry.

THE SPRUCE HAS NO TAPROOT

Cats, as a rule, don't take to travel
any better than the lobed, immobile
lichen whose tenure in the rock's
bleak niches, though it lacks
roots, is all but fanatical.

Likewise the cinquefoil: though nebulous
of flower head and petal
as a yard of dotted Swiss,
it keeps, under the froufrou, a profile
low as any fugitive's. The strawberry's

red skeins crisscross the gravel
with such rigor you might suppose
it knew the habitat to be untenable
unless tied down. So do the rootstocks
of the rose its cousin, whose colonies

along the coast rise as they widen
into a mimic mountain.
Depth isn't everything: the spruce
has no taproot, but to hold on
spreads its underpinnings thin—

a gathering in one continuous,
meshing intimacy, the interlace
of unrelated fibers
joining hands like last survivors
who, though not even neighbors

hitherto, know in their predicament
security at best is shallow.
Whoever fancies an uprooted fragment
of the coast of Maine might settle into
a New York apartment—foolish,

unnatural whim!—discovers what
must have possessed the cat
when, rather than go through
one more uprooting, she hid out,
a fugitive fanatic who

instead preferred to starve and stiffen.
Found too late, according to her wish
what's left of her is now in-
extricable from the ground. Every
day for weeks, half a can of Figaro

flavored with liver or tunafish
waited out there for her. Every night
for weeks, some mobile opportunist
slipped in from the forest
to banquet from her dish.

WHAT THE LIGHT WAS LIKE

For Louise Dickinson Rich and the family of Ernest Woodward

Every year in June—up here, that's the month for lilacs—
        almost his whole front yard,
with lobster traps stacked out in back, atop the rise
        that overlooks the inlet
would be a Himalayan range of peaks of bloom,
        white or mauve-violet,

gusting a turbulence of perfume, and every year the same
        iridescent hummingbird,
or its descendant, would be at work among the mourning cloaks
        and swallowtails, its motor loud,
its burning gorget darkening at moments as though charred.
        He kept an eye out

for it, we learned one evening, as for everything that flapped
        or hopped or hovered
crepuscular under the firs: he'd heard the legendary
        trilling of the woodcock,
and watched the eiders, once rare along these coasts,
        making their comeback

so that now they're everywhere, in tribes, in families
        of aunts and cousins,
a knit-and-purl of irresistibly downy young behind them, riding
        every cove and inlet;
and yes, in answer to the question summer people always ask,
        he'd seen the puffins

that breed out on 'Tit Manan, in summer improbably clown-faced
        behind the striped scarlet
of Commedia dell' Arte masks we'll never see except in
        Roger Tory Peterson's
field guide, or childish wishful thinking. There was much
        else I meant to ask about

another summer. But in June, when we came limping up here
        again, looking forward
to easing up from a mean, hard, unaccommodating winter,
        we heard how he'd gone out
at dawn, one morning in October, unmoored the dinghy
        and rowed to his boat

as usual, the harbor already chugging with half a dozen
    neighbors' revved-up craft,
wet decks stacked abaft with traps, the bait and kegs stowed
    forward, a lifting weft
of fog spooled off in pearl-pink fleeces overhead with the first
    daylight, and steered,

as usual, past first the inner and then the outer bar, where in
    whatever kind of weather,
the red reef-bell yells, in that interminable treble, *Trouble,*
    out past where the Groaner
lolls, its tempo and forte changing with the chop, played on
    by every wind shift,

straight into the sunrise, a surge of burning turning the
    whole ocean iridescent
fool's-gold over molten emerald, into the core of that
    day-after-day amazement—
a clue, one must suppose, to why lobstermen are often
    naturally gracious:

maybe, out there beside the wheel, the Baptist spire
    shrunk to a compass-
point, the town an interrupted circlet, feeble as an apron-
    string, for all the labor
it took to put it there, it's finding, out in that ungirdled
    wallowing and glitter,

finally, that what you love most is the same as what you're
    most afraid of—God,
in a word; whereas it seems they think they've got it licked
    (or used to), back there
in the Restricted Area for instance, where that huge hush-
    hush thing they say is radar

sits sprawling on the heath like Stonehenge, belittling every
    other man-made thing
in view, even the gargantuan pods of the new boat hulls you
    now and then see lying,
stark naked, crimson on the inside as a just-skinned carcass,
    in Young's boatyard,

even the gray Grange Hall, wood-heated by a yardarm of stovepipe
      across the ceiling.
Out there, from that wallowing perspective, all comparisons
      amount to nothing,
though once you've hauled your last trap, things tend to wander
      into shorter focus

as, around noon, you head back in: first 'Tit Manan lighthouse,
      a ghostly gimlet
on its ledge by day, but on clear nights expanding to a
      shout, to starboard,
the sunstruck rock pile of Cranberry Point to port; then
      you see the hamlet

rainbowed, above the blurring of the spray shield, by the
      hurrying herring gulls'
insatiable fandango of excitement—the spire first, then
      the crimson boat hulls,
the struts of the ill-natured gadget on the heath behind them
      as the face of things expands,

the hide-and-seek behind the velvet-shouldered, sparse
      tree-spined profiles,
as first the outer, then the inner bar appears, then the scree-
      beach under Crowley Island's
crowding firs and spruces, and you detect among the chimneys
      and the TV aerials,

yours. But by midafternoon of that October day,
      when all his neighbors'
boats had chugged back through the inlet, his
      was still out; at evening,
with half the town out looking, and a hard frost
      settling in among the alders,

there'd been no sign of him. The next day, and the next,
      the search went on,
and widened, joined by planes and helicopters from as
      far away as Boston.
When, on the third day, his craft was sighted
      finally, it had drifted,

with its engine running, till the last gulp of fuel
    spluttered and ran out,
beyond the town's own speckled noose of buoys, past
    the furred crest of Schoodic,
vivid in a skirt of aspens, the boglands cranberry-
    crimson at its foot,

past the bald brow the sunrise always strikes first, of
    the hulk of Cadillac,
riding the current effortlessly as eiders tied to water
    by the summer molt,
for fifty miles southwestward to where, off Matinicus,
    out past the rock

that, like 'Tit Manan, is a restricted area, off limits for
    all purposes but puffins',
they spotted him, slumped against the kegs. I find it
    tempting to imagine what,
when the blood roared, overflowing its cerebral sluiceway,
    and the iridescence

of his last perception, charring, gave way to unreversed,
    irrevocable dark,
the light out there was like, that's always shifting—from
    a nimbus gone berserk
to a single gorget, a cathedral train of blinking, or
    the fogbound shroud

that can turn anywhere into a nowhere. But it's useless.
    Among the mourning-cloak-
hovered-over lilac peaks, their whites and purples,
    when we pass his yard,
poignant to excess with fragrance, this year we haven't
    seen the hummingbird.

Two   The Hinterland

BLACK BUTTERCUPS

In March, the farmer's month
for packing up and moving on, the rutted
mud potholed with glare, the verb *to move*
connoted nothing natural, such as the shifting
of the course of streams or of the sun's
position, sap moving up, or even
couples dancing. What the stripped root, exhumed
above the mudhole's brittle skin, discerned
was exile.
           Exile to raw clapboard,
a privy out in back, a smokehouse
built by the pioneers, no shade trees
but a huddle of red cedars, exposure
on the highest elevation in the township,
a gangling windmill harped on by each
indisposition of the weather,
the mildewed gurgle of a cistern
humped underneath it like a burial.
                   Menace
inhabited that water when the pioneers,
ending their trek from North Carolina, farther
than Ur of the Chaldees had been from Canaan,
settled here and tried to root themselves:
four of the family struck down on this farm
as its first growing season ended. Menace
still waited, literally around the corner,
in the graveyard of a country church,
its back against the timber
just where the terrain began to drop (the creek
down there had for a while powered a sawmill,
but now ran free, unencumbered, useless)—
that not-to-be-avoided plot whose honed stones'
fixed stare, fanned in the night
by passing headlights, struck back
the rueful semaphore:
There is no safety.
                I was ten years old.
Not three miles by the road that ran
among the farms (still less if
you could have flown, or, just as unthinkable,
struck out across country, unimpeded
by barbed wire or the mire of feedlots)

the legendary habitat of safety
lay contained: the memory
of the seedleaf in the bean, the blind
hand along the bannister, the virgin sheath
of having lived nowhere but here. Back there
in the dining room, last summer's
nine-year-old sat crying on the window seat
that looked into the garden, rain
coursing the pane in streams, the crying
on the other side and it one element—and sits
there still, still crying, knowing
for the first time forever what it was
to be heartbroken.
             The look of exile
foreseen, however massive or inconsequential,
hurts the same; it's the remembered
particulars that differ. How is one to measure
the loss of two blue spruces, a waterfall
of bridal wreath below the porch, the bluebells
and Dutchman's-breeches my grandmother
had brought in from the timber
to bloom in the same plot with peonies
and lilies of the valley? Or, out past
the pasture where the bull, perennially
resentful, stood for the menace of authority
(no leering, no snickering in class),
an orchard—or a grove of willows
at the far edge of the wet meadow
marking the verge, the western barrier
of everything experience had verified? We never
thought of going there except in February,
when the sap first started working up
the pussywillow wands, the catkins
pink underneath a down of eldritch silver
like the new pigs whose birthing coincided,
shedding their crisp cupolas' detritus
on the debris of foundering snowbanks
brittle as the skin of standing ponds
we trod on in the meadow, a gauche travesty
of calamity like so many entertainments—
the nuptial porcelain, the heirloom crystal
vandalized by wanton overshoes, bundled-up
boredom lolling, while the blue world reeled
up past the pussywillow undersides of clouds

latticed by swigging catkins soon to haze
with pollen-bloat, a glut
run riot while the broken pond
unsealed, turned to mud
and, pullulating, came up buttercups
lucent with a mindlessness as total
as the romp that ends up wet-mittened,
chap-cheeked, fretful beside the kitchen stove,
later to roughhouse or whine its way
upstairs to bed.
          Night froze it up again
for the ten thousandth time, closing the seals
above the breeding ground of frogs, the Acheron
of dreadful disappointed Eros
stirring up hell—the tics,
the shame, the pathological ambition,
anxiety so thick sometimes that nothing
breeds there except more anxiety,
hampering yet another generation, all
the sodden anniversaries of dread:
black buttercups that never see daylight
or with lucent chalices drink of the sun.
Did we then hear them moving
wounded from room to room? Or in what shape
was it we first perceived it—the unstanched
hereditary thing, working its way
along the hollows of the marrow,
the worry taking root within like ragweed,
the noxious pollen flowering into
nothing but sick headaches
passed down like an heirloom? When,
under the same roof the memory of
a legendary comfort had endowed
with what in retrospect would seem
like safety, did the rumor
of unhappiness arrive? I remember waking,
a February morning leprous with frost
above the dregs of a halfhearted snowfall,
to find the gray world of adulthood
everywhere, as though there never
had been any other, in that same house
I could not bear to leave, where even now
the child who wept to leave still sits
weeping at the thought of exile.

WITNESS

An ordinary evening in Wisconsin
seen from a Greyhound bus—mute aisles
of merchandise the sole inhabitants
of the half-darkened Five and Ten,

the tables of the single lit café awash
with unarticulated pathos, the surface membrane
of the inadvertently transparent instant
when no one is looking: outside town

the barns, their red gone dark with sundown,
withhold the shudder of a warped terrain—
the castle rocks above, tree-clogged ravines
already submarine with nightfall, flocks

(like dark sheep) of toehold junipers,
the lucent arms of birches : purity
without a mirror, other than a mind bound
elsewhere, to tell it how it looks.

FROM A CLINIC WAITING ROOM

I write from the denser enclave of the stricken,
eight stories up, a prairie *gratte-ciel*.
Above the valley floor, the bell tower
of a displaced Italian hill town listens, likewise
attentive to the mysteries of one Body.
If the two salute, it must be as monks do,
without gesture, eyes lowered
by the force of gravity. Between them,
down among the car parks, tree shapes
stripped twig-bare appear to bruise
with tenderness, illusory as sea anemones.
There is no wind. For days
the geese that winter in the bottomland
have been the one thing always on the move,
in swags of streaming fronds, chiaroscuro
sea blooms, their wavering V-signs
following the turnings of one body.
Where are they going?
                            Down in the blood bank
the centrifuge, its branched transparent siphons
stripping the sap of Yggdrasil
from the slit arm of the donor, skims
the spinning corpuscles, cream-white
from hectic red. Below the pouched pack
dangled like a gout of mistletoe, the tubing
drips, drips from valve to valve to enter,
in a gradual procession, the cloistered
precincts of another body.
                             Sunset, its tinctured
layerings vivid as delirium, astonishing
as merely to be living, stains the cold
of half a hemisphere. The old
moon's dark corpus, its mysteries
likewise halfway illusory, tonight sleeps slumped
on the phosphorescent threshold of the new.

A CURFEW

Fever, the clang in the beleaguered pumproom
muffled with Tylenol, banked under icepacks,
rising while outside snow fell, a seeming flux
of strict constructions, the vapors' mimic
of turmoil among the leucocytes—mass panic,
blocked corridors, the riddlings of dispersal:
Why? If meaning is a part of any system,

what laws apply? To Alfred Wallace, burning
on his bed in the Moluccas, the malarial shimmer,
parting, whispered "Malthus": accident, disease,
war, famine certified as a severe epiphany, a random
elegance unfeeling as the Snow Queen's hex, the filter
of the future of the species. The stoic laughter
of Democritus: Nothing truly is except the atom,

the Whole a sieve of particles, its terrors
loomed of shadows' cumber. Along the thoroughfares
of Warsaw martial law, the day my brother died,
serried the pallid Baltic sun with roadblocks;
a curfew overtook the solstice. This winter, would
the sun turn round again for the gregarious gamble
of Solidarność? My brother dead, I cried over the news.

He'd looked into the murk of so much turmoil,
flux and rigor, unbought *pietàs* of the suicidal,
such jigsaw-fault-line fracturings of seeming
entity, fears of the action of God knew what laws
laid down by God knows who among the shadows
of the cave, the cloakroom or the bedroom—listening,
head down, eyes impassive, musing, feeling his way

along the pillared halls of withheld judgment—
and still, like a despairing small-hour phone call,
they trailed him down the fever's passageways
into the pumproom of delirium. "I think I won't
go to the office for a while," he murmured. "From
now on, just a few private patients." The snow fell,
the fever guttered, and the streets of Warsaw froze.

The thinnest of osmotic boundaries contain what once
was called the soul; the universal laws, the flux
of Heraclitus, packed yin-and-yangwise into the globule
of the infinitesimal, are now coöpted for a game of jacks,
taws toyed with by the hubris of a species whose petulant
chevaux-de-frise infest the globe with roadblocks,
a raging mimic of the universe's grand indifference.

URN-BURIAL AND
THE BUTTERFLY MIGRATION

Rest for the body's residue:
boxed ashes, earth pocket
under its lifted flap of turf
roofed by a black circumference
of Norway spruce, an old settler
now among old settlers, in their
numb stones' cooled silicates
the scar of memory benighted
alone articulate.

O friable repose of the organic!
Bark-creviced at the trunk's
foot, ladybirds' enameled herds
gather for the winter, red pearls
of an unsaid rosary to waking.
From the fenced beanfield,
crickets' brisk scrannel
plucks the worn reed of
individual survival.

Mulleins hunker to a hirsute
rosette about the taproot; from
frayed thistleheads, a liftoff
of aerial barbs begins; milkweed
spills on the wind its prodigal,
packed silks—slattern gondolas
whose wrecked stalks once
gave mooring to the sleep of
things terrestrial:

an urn of breathing jade, its
gilt-embossed exterior the
intact foreboding of a future
intricately contained, jet-
veined, spangle-margined,
birth-wet russet of the air-
traveling monarch emerging
from a torpid chrysalis. Oh,
we know nothing

of the universe we move through!
My dead brother, when we were
kids, fed milkweed caterpillars
in Mason jars, kept bees, ogled
the cosmos through a backyard
telescope. But then the rigor
of becoming throttled our pure
ignorance to mere haste
toward something else.

We scattered. Like the dandelion,
that quintessential successful
immigrant, its offspring gone
to fluff, dug-in hard-scrabble
nurtured a generation of
the mobile, nomads enamored
of cloverleafs, of hangars, of
that unrest whose home—*our*
home—is motion.

Here in the winds' terrain, the
glacier-abraded whetstone of their
keening knives, anvil of thunder,
its sabbaths one treacherous
long sob of apprehension, who
will rein in, harpoon or anchor
rest for the mind? Were the dead
to speak, were one day
these friable

residues to rise, would we hear
even that airborne murmur? Listen
as the monarchs' late-emerging
tribes ascend; you will hear
nothing. In wafted twos and threes
you may see them through the window
of a southbound Greyhound
bus, adrift across the
Minnesota border;

or in flickering clots, in dozens
above the parked cars of the
shopping malls of Kansas—this
miracle that will not live to
taste the scarce nectar, the
ample horror of another summer:
airborne marathon, elegiac
signature of nations who
have no language,

their landless caravans augment
among the blistered citadels
of Oklahoma; windborne along
the Dallas–Fort Worth airport's
utopian thoroughfares, their
hovering millenniums become
a mimic force of occupation,
a shadeless Vallombrosa,
forceless, autonomous.

O drifting apotheosis of dust
exhumed, who will unseal
the crypt locked up within
the shimmer of the chromosomes,
or harvest, from the alluvial
death-dance of these wrecked
galaxies, this risen residue
of milkweed leaf and honey,
rest for the body?

THE COOLING TOWER

By night a laddered diagram
seen from the windows of this
bedroom town—rayflowers of dread
ascending and descending—
identifies the cooling tower,
insomniac vision

revealed by day as a grayed
obese archangel, its twiddled
dirk of ash and rhinestone
a metronomic rerun of some
half-obliterated last
nightmare of Eden

in the West: O Abendland, O
astral monochrome, steam-plume
whose throttled howl deploys
above the cooling tower
a pillared, effortless
volume of milkweed.

The air is windless. Harmless
outside the moat and continent of
power, the tabernacled rods'
implosive marrow, an aureole
of bright particulars let fall
falls unregarded,

such an excess as to be all but
sorrowless: the sumac's roadside
flares, used-car lots bannered as
for a gala, street maples' tattered
circus-tent extravaganza
sifting unnumbered

relics, emblems of the everywhere
expendable: O Abendland, astral
insomniac, prophetic hulk of the
unuttered: by whom, should your
hot hour arrive, will all the dreams
of Adam be remembered?

A NEW LIFE

Autonomy these days—surprise!—is moving up
in the corporate structure. She's thrown over
the old laid-back lifestyle, repudiated its
green-haired prophets, and gotten married

(pre-Raphaelite red velvet, a sheaf of roses,
hair falling in two long blond tresses). She's
now at home on a rural route, its row of mailboxes
a mile and a half from the Freeway. Not-quite-

two-year-old Autonomy Junior spends long days
with the sitter, can count up to five, and sees
the world moving past so fast, he delivers daily
not slow words but quick, predicated word-clusters.

Up before dawn three days out of five, at the
bathroom mirror Autonomy swiftly, with brush and
hairdryer, concocts a frame for her face of that
temporal gold, like the gilding of the aspens

in the Rockies, like every prototypical true
blonde who began as some other color; puts on
her boardroom clothes—flounced denim with
boots and weskit, or spiked sandals and pallid

executive knit—to drive off into the just-
stirred mother-of-pearl of the day, the velour
of hoarfrost's transient platinum on the blacktop
of a piece with the pristine pale upholstery

of the brand-new Brougham—into the ductile
realm of the Freeway, that reentry into the mystery
of being betweenwheres, alone in the effortless
anteroom of the Machine, of the Many. The Company

these days is paying her way to an earlybird
course in Econ at the University. At eight-
thirty, while her wedded bedfellow, in the other
car, the red Toyota, drops off their offspring

with the sitter, her class over, she'll be taking
the Freeway again to headquarters. These days
she's in Quality Circles, a kind of hovering
equipoise between Management and not-Management,

precarious as the lake-twinned tremor of aspens,
as the lingering of the ash-blond arcade of foliage
completing itself as it leans to join its own inversion.
Whatever fabrication, whatever made thing

she is thus vertiginously linked to, there's no
disconnecting the image of Autonomy contained but
still moving—toward what is unclear—up through
the heady apertures of the Gross National Product,

from that thing, the ambiguous offspring of the Company—
through whose dense mansions, burbling with unheard
melodies of the new, her pal and bedfellow is moving up too.
Evenings, while he heads for *his* course at the University,

she collects the not-yet-two-year-old from the sitter,
kicks off her stiltwalker's footgear, peels away
the layers of the persona she takes to Quality Circles,
and slides into irontight jeans, the time-honored

armor of mellowing out; picks up yesterday's litter
around the playpen, puts together a quick concoction
via the microwave oven, and resumes—her charge,
all the while, voluble at her hip or underfoot—

the improbable game of move-and-countermove-between-
mother-and-child. Whether, back at headquarters,
back there in the winking imaginary map that leaps
from the minds of the computer programmers, there's

a mother-lode of still smarter bombs, the germ
of an even cleverer provocation to instability
within the neutron or of God knows what other, yet
inviolate speck at the core of the cosmos, who knows—

or whether playing at mothering, the mirage of a
rise into ethereal realms of the managerial—of
hoarfrost at dawn along the edge of the Freeway,
the hurtled ease of finding oneself betweenwheres,

alone in the evolving anteroom of the Machine, of
that artifice of the pursuit of happiness—will be,
as the green-haired prophets of punk would have it,
a total, or only a partial
                              apocalyptic freakout.

HIGH CULTURE

The geranium and the begonia
bloom with such offhand redundance
we scarcely notice. But the
amaryllis is a study in

disruption: everything routine
gives way to the unsheathing
of its climbing telescope—
a supernova of twin crimson

tunnels, porches of infinity
where last week there was nothing.
Months of clandestine preparation
now implode in pollen

that will never brush a bee,
fueling the double-barreled velvet
stairwell of its sterile pistils
with a tapered incandescence

that's already short of breath
and going blind before a
week is out. Such show
of breeding, such an excess

of cultivation, all but asks us
to stop breathing too until
it's over. I remember
how, the night the somewhat

famous violinist came to supper,
the whisper of the gown she
put on just before the concert
filled the parlor of the farmhouse

with things it had no room for—
the slave marts of the East,
the modes of Paris, the gazing
ramparts of the stratosphere.

Three   Voyages:

A Homage to John Keats

Cowslip and shad-blow, flaked like tethered foam
Around bared teeth of stallions, bloomed that spring
When I first read the lines, rife as the loam
Of prairies, yet like breakers cliffward leaping!
    . . . My hand
            in yours,
                    Walt Whitman . . .

                        HART CRANE, *The Bridge*

Chaff, straw, splinters of wood, weeds, and the sea-gluten,
Scum, scales from shining rocks, leaves of salt-lettuce, left by the tide,
Miles walking, the sound of breaking waves the other side of me,
Paumanok there and then I thought the old thought of likenesses,
These you presented to me you fish-shaped island . . .

                        WALT WHITMAN, *Sea Drift*

Perhaps my whisper was already born before my lips,
the leaves whirled round in treelessness
and those to whom we dedicate our life's experience
before experience acquired their traits.

                        OSIP MANDELSTAM *(Moscow, January 1934)*

. . . a haggling of wind and weather, by these lights
Like a blaze of summer straw, in winter's nick.

                        WALLACE STEVENS, *The Auroras of Autumn*

MARGATE

Reading his own lines over, he'd been
(he wrote) in the diminished state of one
"that gathers Samphire dreadful trade."
Disabled Gloucester, so newly eyeless
all his scathed perceptions bled together,
and Odysseus, dredged up shipwrecked
through fathoms of Homeric sightlessness—

"the sea had soaked his heart through"—
were the guides his terror clutched at.
Now all of twenty-one, he'd written nothing
of moment but one bookish sonnet: "Much have
I traveled . . ." Only he hadn't, other
than as unrequited amateur. How clannish
the whole hand-to-hand, cliffhanging trade,

the gradual letdown, the hempen slither,
precarious basketloads of sea drift
gathered at Margate or at Barnegat:
along Paumanok's liquid rim, the dirges,
nostalgia for the foam: *the bottom of
the sea is cruel*. The chaff, the scum
of the impalpable confined in stanzas,

a shut-in's hunger for the bodiless
enkindlings of the aurora—all that
traffic in the perilous. That summer,
orphaned of sublimity, he'd settled for
the way an oatfield's stalks and blades
checquered his writing tablet with their
quivering. But after, back in Hampstead,

the samphire-gatherer's mimic god-deliverer
still bled metonymy: an ordinary field of
barley turned to alien corn's inland sea-
surfaces, and onto every prairie rolling,
sans the samphire trade's frail craft, un-
basketed, undid the casement of the homesick,
stared once more, and called an image home.

TEIGNMOUTH

Even in mild Devon, that spring, the lung-
destroying English climate was one long
dank rampage: high winds, trees falling
onto the roads, stagecoaches overturning,

day upon day of drumming, streaming rain
swollen to weeks, the sun a half-believed-in
pagan god above the azure of the Mediterranean.
At night he'd lie in bed (he wrote) and listen

to it with a sense of being drowned and rotted
like a grain of wheat. He very nearly hated
Tom because he coughed so; then his raw mood
froze as he saw his brother cough up blood.

His writing plodded. By now *Endymion* bored him.
His letters joked of waterspouts and rattraps. Rhyme,
that light-fingered habit, ran down and went grim:
beyond an untumultuous fringe of foam,

he'd seen, once the weather eased, into a maw
of rot, a predatory core of dying. Melodrama
mildewed the sources of romance: the basil grew
rank from her dead lover's skull for Isabella.

What might still flower out of that initiation
to the sodden underside of things — those Eleusinian
passageways that seem (he wrote) only to darken
as the doors of new and vaster chambers open —

he could no more than guess at. On May Day
he looked from the window of a single stanza
leaning toward Theocritus and the blue Bay
of Baiae (read Naples). Not yet twenty-three,

he'd presently begin to resurrect, to all but
deify the issue of his own wretched climate —
primroses, cress and water-mint, great wet-
globed peonies, the grape against the palate:

an *annus mirabilis* of odes before the season
of the oozing of the ciderpress, the harvest done,
wheatfields blood-spattered once with poppies gone
to stubble now, the swallows fretting to begin

their windborne flight toward a Mediterranean
that turned to marble as the mists closed in
on the imagination's yet untrodden region—
the coal-damps, the foul winter dark of London.

THE ELGIN MARBLES

For Frederick Turner

Openings. Winandermere and Derwentwater.
The Elgin Marbles. That last evening
at the Crown in Liverpool, with George
and his new wife, imagination failed

   —and still fails: what can John Keats
   have had to do with a hacked clearing
   in the Kentucky underbrush? How could
   Mnemosyne herself, the mother of the Muse,
   have coped with that uncultivated tangle,
   catbrier and poison ivy, chiggers,
   tent caterpillars, cottonmouths,
   the awful gurglings and chirrings
   of the dark?

                  Turning his back
against the hemp and tar, the
creaking tedium of actual departure,
the angry fogs, the lidless
ferocity of the Atlantic—epic
distances fouled by necessity—
he left them sleeping, George
and his Georgiana, so much wrapped up
in being newly wed they scarcely knew
they had no home now but each other,
he took up his pack (a change of
clothes, pens, paper, the *Divine
Comedy* in translation—he knew no
Italian yet, or Greek) and headed north,
on foot, with his friend Brown. Rain
held them up a day, but on
the twenty-sixth of June (a letter
to his brother Tom records) they came
in sight of Winandermere. He stared,
then slowly swore, "This—
must—beat—Italy."

                   Imaginary
   Italy, the never-never
   vista, framed, of Stresa

on Lago Maggiore, to badger
an imagination starved for charm,
for openings, living on cornpone,
coonskin, literary hand-me-downs,
and hating everything in sight.

Hyperbole:
a vista, as he put it, to make one forget
what tended to cut off, refining what he called
the Sensual Vision into—he fumbled for
an image—a sort of North Star, open-
lidded, steadfast. Winandermere:
the Italy he'd never seen, though in
imagination he already lived there:
his mind's America. Bright star.
Made one forget the creak, the tar,
the lunging hulk, homesick, sea-
sick, of the Atlantic.

Or almost did.
Next day, at Helvellyn (mist about its foot
so thick he never saw it, the Nag's Head
flea-infested) he invoked,
in an acrostic on Georgiana's name, Odysseus
stormed at sea, and after
Derwentwater and Lodore made weak amends
with fact by conjuring a doggerel prospect
"where furrows are new to the plow."
After Skiddaw—a ten-mile hike,
made fasting, having gotten up
at four—they took a coach
for Scotland.

The tomb of Burns.
Pinched lives. Bad food. A fog
of whisky. The cold, pale, short-
lived, primeval summer. He was tired now,
homesick for another kind of grandeur:
Lord Elgin's windlass-lowered metopes ("A sun—
a shadow of a magnitude," he'd written
of the space they opened). Scotland
seemed—the epithet broke from him—
anti-Grecian. Admitting prejudice,

he repented, tried whisky-toddy,
wrote a ballad, saw the poverty, grew somber
as he thought of Burns, observing his imagination
had been southern too; caught a cold
he couldn't shake, grew peevish,
cut short his tour. In Hampstead,
Tom had been coughing blood again.

                        Another
summer gone, Tom worse, his own sore throat
recurring, *Endymion* stillborn, picked over
by the vultures. Well,
they were partly right; the rest he wouldn't
think about. Now, primed on *Lear,*
Milton, Gibbon, Wordsworth, he'd set himself
to re-imagining an epic grandeur, such as
(if it arrived at all) came battered
and diminished, fallen like Lucifer,
or else dismantled, fragmentary, lowered and
transported, piece by piece, like the heroic
torsos, the draperied recumbent hulks Lord Elgin
took down from the Parthenon.

                           —Behold,
in the back settlements, the rise
of Doric porticoes. Courthouse
spittoons. The glimmer of a classic
colonnade through live oaks. Slave
cabins. Mud. New Athenses, Corinths,
Spartas among the Ossabaws and
Tuscaloosas, the one no less
homesick than the other for
what never was, most likely,
but in some founder's warped
and sweating mind.

                         Ruin alone,
in a bad time, had seemed to him
grand enough. But then, out of the
still unimagined West, that welter
of a monument to hardship, stirrings
of another sort: Georgiana
was to have a child.

                        Precarious
domestic comfort, a firelit
ring of faces' bright cave
in the Kentucky wilderness: the wonder
of it! Not quite two years
since, in lodgings he and George and Tom,
three orphaned, homeless brothers
had moved into, he'd invoked
just such an image: small, busy flames
playing through fresh-laid
coals, a refuge hollowed from
the gloom of London in November. Now,
out of that solitude, a child,
another Keats, to be the bard of what
John Keats himself could never quite
imagine: he turned the fantasy
into a lullaby, went back
to reconstructing such an inlet
to severe magnificence
as a god might enter. "I think
I shall be among the English
poets after my death." There,
he'd said it.

                    The evening of
October twenty-fourth (a date that,
once again, would go on record),
walking from Bedford Row to Lamb's
Conduit Street, he met the enigmatic
Mrs. Isabella Jones, and walked her home.
Her sitting room a trove of bronze,
books, pictures, music (an Aeolian
harp, a linnet): rich and somber—moonlight
through diamond panes, a Turkish carpet—
was the way he'd re-imagine it. A
prior contretemps seemed to require
some move. Tactfully declining to
be kissed, however, she released him
to a state of mind that was—
he discovered, walking home
astonished—infinitely
better:
                    He was free.
He could imagine anything at all,

needed no home, would never marry—not
though the carpet there were silk,
the curtain made of morning cloud, with windows
that opened on Winandermere. The roaring
of the wind, he wrote (hyperbole again, but
never mind) would be his wife, the stars
seen through the windows would be his children.
A perfect solitude. A thousand worlds thrown open.
He was as happy as a man could be—or would be,
he conscientiously amended, if Tom were better.

Bright star. Winandermere. A week
from now, he would be twenty-three.

CHICHESTER

There would have been the obligatory tour
of the cathedral. Stone under boot heels,
the great, numbed ribcage chilled-to-the-bone
cold. The aisles of sculptured effigies stone
dead. Tom dead at the beginning of December.
It was January now. Buried at St. Stephen's
Coleman Street. The bare spire, the leafless
trees. The church bells' interminable reminder.
One Sunday evening, hearing them, he'd dashed
off—with Tom there in the room, timing him—
a sonnet "In Disgust of Vulgar Superstition."
Here, the recurrent chatter of those great
metal tongues would have brought it back,
setting his memory on edge again. *Poor Tom.*
The scene out on the heath forever lurking
in his mind. Back in October he'd underlined
the words: Poor Tom. Poor Tom's a-cold.

His friends meant well, had kept him occupied.
Visits. A play. Dragged him down to Sussex
for a prizefight. Mrs. Isabella Jones, with
new notions for him to write about. Miss
Brawne: beautiful, elegant, graceful, silly,
fashionable and strange. He'd set down the
words with care. It was important to keep
things accurate. A minx—he'd called her
that, and also ignorant, monstrous in her
behavior, flying out in all directions, calling
people such names. Hair nicely arranged.
Loved clothes. Eighteen years old. Down here,
best not to think very much about her. Brown
playing the fool, putting on an old lady's
bonnet. At night, old dowager card parties.
As always, the anxiety about getting down
to work. No progress with the epic since Tom
died. Isabella Jones urging him to try another
romance. Why not, she'd said, the legend
of St. Agnes' Eve? A girl going to bed . . .

He must have whistled at the notion that struck
him now. And then blushed. Or vice versa. A
girl going to bed on St. Agnes' Eve—that very
night, or near it—without supper, so as to

dream of the man she was to marry. Imagine
her. Imagine . . . He blushed now at the
audacity. But the thing had taken hold:
St. Agnes' Eve. A girl going to bed . . .
On the twenty-third of January, they walked
thirteen miles, to a little town called (of
all things) Bedhampton. The house they stayed
in there still stands. Out of the frozen
countryside they'd passed through, once his
numb hands had thawed, he had what he needed
to begin: the owl, the limping hare, the
woolly huddle inside the sheepfold. Even
the owl a-cold. *Poor Tom.* The cold stone
underfoot, the sculptured effigies. How
they must ache. His own numb fingers. How
the Beadsman's hands must ache. Paid to hold
a rosary for the souls of others richer and
more vicious. The stones he knelt on cold.
The girl's bedchamber cold, the bed itself
too, until the girl—blushing, he saw her
kneel—had warmed it. He saw it all.

He saw it: saw the candle in the icy draft
gone out, the little smoke, the moonlight,
the diamond panes, the stained-glass colors
on her as she knelt to say her silly prayers.
Saw her, smelled her, felt the warmth of the
unfastened necklace, the brooch, the earrings,
heard the rustle as the dress slid down;
backed off, became the voyeur of a mermaid.
Discovered, while she slept, that the sheets
gave off a sachet of lavender. Admired but
did not taste the banquet his senses had
invented, and whose true name was Samarkand.
He was in fact too excited to eat. What is
a poet to do when he stumbles onto such
excitement? He was not sure. He was also
somewhat embarrassed. Later he'd declare,
hotly, that he wrote for men, not ladies
(who are the ones who dream such things),
that he'd despise any man who was such a
eunuch as not to avail himself . . . It was
the flaw, as he must have known. He'd
imagined it all. He'd imagined it all.

For ten days that lush, decorated stanza,
with its shut casements and dying fall,
had been the room he lived in. He'd
imagined it all; his senses had seduced
an entire posterity into imagining what
had never happened. His own virgin vision,
of a solitude that needed no wife, had been
seduced by that imaginary place, that stanza,
where nothing at all had happened. The minx
who was eighteen, beautiful, silly, strange
and fond of clothes, and who had never lived
there, was real. The cold outside was real.
Dying was real, and the twitch of the old
woman's palsy. The effigies were real,
and the stones in the churchyard at St.
Stephen's Coleman Street. *Poor Tom.*

HE DREAMS OF BEING WARM

The April he'd invoked from the despond
of February (when his sore throat
came back)—its hillsides starred
by an upended firmament of daisies—
found him straining at particles of
light in a great darkness, bright-eyed
underfoot with scurryings of purpose:
the alert stoat, the quivering fieldmouse,
the lowlife fracases he'd seen erupting
in the streets of London—instinct in
the bud, the blood stirred in a poor
forked creature battered by the same
mischances, subject to the same
          inclement weather.

On the eleventh day of April he
shook the hand of Coleridge, and
felt warmed. But the low mood that
had hampered him continued. *Hyperion,*
he knew now after a final try—*Apollo
shrieked—and lo! from all his limbs
celestial* . . . would not be completed.
How could he not think with irony of
that *celestial?* The foreign sun-god,
aloof familiar of the Muse, once-blazing
luminary now a mere pinprick, remote
among the other stars—himself left
shivering, abandoned to the merciless
catarrhs of London. Infernal visions
drew him: not now that scathing splendor,
the lyre, the paean, the white glare
of sunstruck marble, but the wailing
shades, the cranes' cry, the starlings
interminably circling: imagined torments
          of felicity remembered.

April in hell, a courteous reception
to the circle of the lustful: the dream
he'd had came back as pure enjoyment.
Welcomed by Francesca, late of Rimini,
into the storm of starlings, joined
to another solely by a kiss, for what
had seemed an aeon's celestial levitation,

he had been happy: in the midst of all
that cold and darkness, *he was warm.*
April in hell: a firmament upended
to a stirred greensward of treetops
that, tiptoe, he felt expanding into
secret zodiacs of blossom. And then
   woke. And shivered.

Outside, it was raining. He stayed in
all day, attempting in a sonnet—"Pale
were the lips I kissed"—to summon
back the dream. Damp, half-charred
firewood brought in from the rain,
it wouldn't kindle—until, on the
twenty-first of April, in an aubade
set to the starved meter of a ballad,
he harpooned the levitating kiss, and
quartered it. (Why *four* kisses?—Because,
he quipped, the Muse needs reining in.
Suppose I had said seven?) So adieu,
Francesca, late of Rimini. Farewell,
imaginary region of the headlong; even
your lusts cannot (it seems) delude so well
as the received morality would have it.
Dream of being warm, farewell.
Exposure on a cold hillside,
   good morning.

April long gone, the sedges dead
and withered: wake, poor fool, to agues
of the morning after—to having been,
from your brief *saison en enfer,*
locked out, the ecstasy aborted,
masked Melancholy's sable domino
torn off, the Muse herself disclosed,
in the strict morning light, as an
unforthcoming warden: no comfort,
only carnage underfoot, a cutthroat
cunning prowling the streets of
London—and waking, one among
the many, from dim dreams, harbored
numberless as vermin, of being warm,
to freezing on this houseless,
   flowerless hillside.

THE ISLE OF WIGHT

Toward the end of April, for an idyllic
 week, the rain stopped, and on the third
of May he wrote, "O there is nothing like
 fine weather, health, Books, a contented
Mind . . ." The ballad's nightmare hillside
 turned, on a burst of bloom, into a picnic:
Psyche, poor butterfly-winged, put-upon immortal,
 last met with in the cold of that starved bedrock,
translated, bless her, to shameless daylit *al
fresco,* the flowery upheaval of the marriage bed.

Reclaimed thus for Eros, what had he to offer?
 Rash promises, no more. He'd build (he wrote)
a sanctuary purely of the mind, in some far-
 off, untrodden region, with a window in it
left open every night, not now to frame
 the stars (if any) but to admit a visitor
prohibited the homelier usages of daylight.
 A sanctuary of the mind, no more. That summer,
cooped with a Bacchic leopard on the Isle of Wight,
 he'd wish he'd never offered it house room.

"Ask yourself my love whether you are not
 very cruel to have so destroyed my freedom,"
he wrote—hyperbole such as he'd often laughed at.
 But now he'd let this hot sprite in, the gloom
of sundown brought home, night after night,
 to that room he said was like a coffin,
no ornate access such as had beguiled him—
 no casement triple-arched as on the night,
long gone, those lovers fled into the storm:
 the framework of escape had shut him in.

His sore throat had come back in June; he saw
 still no prospect of a settled income,
could not live with her but could not now sue
 love for a retraction. Shut up with phantom
rivals in that little room at Shanklin,
 where was the old, wild pleasure of a window
opening on a view of water?—Sealed off like a poem
 he might have written once but couldn't now—
its magic casements closed against the spume
 and spindrift of a serpentine illusion.

Illusion, snared in a brisk running couplet,
    was his new preoccupation—the dazed lamé
of its phosphorescent moons, its shivering scarlet
    and skewered emeralds a weird trophy
hung among the totems of his own ambivalence:
    he almost yearned, he'd written at the start,
for metempsychosis as an insect—for just three
    butterfly-winged summer days' intensity. *Delight,*
he'd called it: poor worn-out word. Poor Psyche,
    poor feeble suffix of doubtful provenance!

WINCHESTER:
THE AUTUMN EQUINOX

Salubrious air, free of the low fogs that were
(he wrote) like steam from cabbage water;
past scrubbed stoops and ram's-head-knockered
doors, a daily walk through the cathedral yard
down to the river: how beautiful
the season was—ay, better than
the chilly green of spring, the warmed hue
of grainfields' harsh stubs turned pictorial
with equinoctial bloom, the tincture of
the actual, the mellow aftermath of fever:
purgatorial winnowings, the harvest over.

Seamless equipoise of crossing: Nox,
primordial half-shape above the treadle,
the loomed fabric of the sun-god's ardor
foreshortened, with a roar as if of earthly
fire, all twilit Europe at his back,
toward the threshold of the west: *in me*
thou seest such twilight, in me thou seest
the glowing of such fire as after sunset
floods the west's unentered spaces. Black gates
shut against the sunrise; north and south, a mist
of nothing: the opening was to the west.

The opening of the West: what Miltonic
rocketry of epithet, what paradigm
of splendor in decline, could travel,
and survive, the monstrous region (as he'd
later depict it) of dull rivers poured
from sordid urns, rank tracts unowned
by any weed-haired god he'd ever heard of,
that had fleeced his brother George? "Be careful,"
he wrote, "of those Americans"—meaning
mainly a certain Audubon, of Henderson,
Kentucky. "I can not help thinking Mr. Audubon

has deceived you. I shall not like the sight
of him . . . You will perceive," he'd also
written, "it is quite out of my interest to
come to America. What could I do there? How

could I employ myself?" John James Audubon,
whether swindler or merely incorrigibly careless,
might carve a kind of wonder, a fierce, frightful
elegance, out of the houseless openings,
the catbrier-hammock deadfalls of that
unfenced paradise. But what could Milton,
from whom he'd set himself to learn, have done

to clear a path either for grandeur or
for simple ruth to enter? Look homeward—
where? What images, what language, fossil
child of all the dislocations of antiquity,
could clear that threshold? *Like the mild moon
who comforts those she sees not, who knows not
what eyes are upward cast,* Moneta, Shade
of Memory, Admonisher, when called upon—
whereon (he wrote) *there grew a power within me
of enormous ken*—showed only splendor fallen.
His peace made with the diminishments of autumn,

he now declared the second epic of the sun-
god's fall abandoned.
                    Hampstead: Fever
and passion. A comedy. A sonnet. In letters,
now and then a cry of protest. The rest
is posthumous.

VOYAGES

On April twenty-seventh, 1932, Hart Crane
walked to the taffrail of the *Orizaba,*
took off his coat, and leaped. At seventeen,
a changeling from among the tire-and-rubber

factories, steel mills, cornfields of the Ohio
flatland that had absent-mindedly produced him,
on an enthralled first voyage he'd looked into
the troughed Caribbean, and called it home.

Back where he'd never been at home, he'd once
watched the early-morning shift pour down South Main—
immigrant Greeks eager to be Americans—
and then tried to imagine Porphyro in Akron

(Greek for "high place"): the casement, the arras,
the fabricated love nest, the actual sleet storm,
the owl, the limping hare, the frozen grass,
Keats's own recurring dream of being warm—

who'd been so often cold he looked with yearning even
into blacksmiths' fires: "How glorious," he wrote
of them, shivering (with Stevens) to see the stars put on
their glittering belts: of what disaster was that

chill, was that salt wind the imminence? The cold-
a-long-time, lifetime snow man did not know.
Beside the Neva, Osip Mandelstam wrote of the cold,
the December fog-blurs of Leningrad. O to throw

open (he wrote) a window on the Adriatic!—a window
for the deprived of audience, for the unfree
to breathe, to breathe even the bad air of Moscow.
Yet on the freezing pane of perpetuity,

that coruscating cold-frame fernery of breath,
harsh flowerbed of the unheated rooms of childhood,
even from the obscurity that sealed it off, his breath,
his warmth, he dared declare, had already settled.

The dream of being warm, its tattered cargo
brought too late to Italy, a mere dire fistful
of blood (*the sea had soaked his heart through*):
the voyage, every voyage at the end is cruel.

In February 1937, from exile to flatland
Voronezh, a kind of twin of Akron, Mandelstam
wrote, in an almost posthumous whisper, of round
blue bays, of sails descried—scenes parted from

as now his voyage to the bottom of a crueler
obscurity began, whose end only the false-haired
seaweed of an inland shipwreck would register.
Untaken voyages, Lethean cold, O all but unendured

arrivals! Keats's starved stare before the actual,
so long imagined Bay of Naples. The mind's extinction.
Nightlong, sleepless beside the Spanish Steps, the prattle
of poured water. Letters no one will ever open.

Four   The Metropolis

THE REEDBEDS
OF THE HACKENSACK

Scummed maunderings that nothing loves but reeds,
Phragmites, neighbors of the greeny asphodel
that thrive among the windings of the Hackensack,
collaborating to subvert the altogether ugly
though too down-to-earth to be quite fraudulent:
what's landfill but the backside of civility?

Dreckpot, the Styx and Malebolge of civility,
brushed by the fingering plumes of beds of reeds:
Manhattan's moat of stinks, the rancid asphodel
aspiring from the gradually choking Hackensack,
ring-ditch inferior to the vulgar, the snugly ugly,
knows-no-better, fake but not quite fraudulent:

what's scandal but the candor of the fraudulent?
Miming the burnish of a manicured civility,
the fluent purplings of uncultivated reeds,
ex post cliché survivors like the asphodel,
drink, as they did the Mincius, the Hackensack
in absent-minded benediction on the merely ugly.

Is there a poetry of the incorrigibly ugly,
free of all furbishings that mark it fraudulent?
When toxins of an up-against-the-wall civility
have leached away the last patina of these reeds,
and promised landfill, with its lethal asphodel
of fumes, blooms the slow dying of the Hackensack,

shall I compare thee, Mincius, to the Hackensack?
Now Italy knows how to make its rivers ugly,
must, ergo, all such linkages be fraudulent,
gilding the laureate hearse of a defunct civility?
Smooth-sliding Mincius, crowned with vocal reeds,
coevals of that greeny local weed the asphodel,

that actual, unlettered entity the asphodel,
may I, among the channels of the Hackensack—
those Edens-in-the-works of the irrevocably ugly,
where any mourning would of course be fraudulent—
invoke the scrannel ruth of a forsooth civility,
the rathe, the deathbed generations of these reeds?

BURIAL IN CYPRESS HILLS

For Beverly and Lloyd Barzey

Back through East Flatbush, a raw grave
littered by the trashing of the social contract,
to this motel of the dead, its plywood and acrylic
itching gimcrack Hebrew like a brand name.

Her case botched by a vandal of a Brooklyn doctor,
she'd readied everything, had all the old snapshots
sorted, down to the last mysterious interior
obliterated in the processes of coming clear.

Surprising, the amount of privacy that opens,
for all the lifetime rub of other people,
around a name uncertified by being in the papers—
one mainly of the bilked, who never formed a party—

and how unhandsome the nub of actual survival.
Nobody is ever ready for the feel of the raw edge
between being and nothing, the knowledge
that abrades the palm, refusing to lie easy.

Yet something in the way the sun shines even now,
out in the open, on that final nugget, makes
bereavement blithe. The undertaker's deputy,
getting the latest lot of mourners into cars,

barks like a sergeant, as though even limbo must
be some new sort of boot camp. "Brooklyn people"—
one of the cousins sums it all up, without rancor:
a way of doing business, part of the local color.

Burial in Cypress Hills, a place whose avenues
are narrower than anywhere in Brooklyn: dark-
boled gateposts crowded elbow to elbow,
the woodlot of innumerable burial societies,

each pair of verticals dense as a tenement
with names, or as a column in the *Daily Forward*.
Whoever enters here to take up residence
arrives an immigrant, out of another country.

The cortege, one of many, inches forward, no more
to be hurried than at Ellis Island. On foot now,
we find the yellow cellar hole, a window into clay,
without a sill, whose only view is downward.

Time, for the gravediggers, is unarguably money:
the cadence of their lifted shovelfuls
across the falling phrases of the Kaddish
strikes on a rarely opened vein of metal

whose pure ore rings like joy, although that's not
the name we've been conditioned into giving it.
Around us, flowering trees hang their free fabric,
incorporeal as the act of absolution. At our feet

an unintended dandelion breaks the hasp
of the adjoining plot's neglected ivy
to spend ungrudgingly its single
fringed medallion, alms for the sun.

THE GODFATHER
RETURNS TO COLOR TV

The lit night glares like a day-glo strawberry,
the stakeout car beside the hydrant is full of feds,
and the ikon of our secret hero(ine?), atop the
feckless funnypaper mesa we try to live in, is that
poor dumb indestructible super-loser Krazy Kat.

O Innocence, spoiled Guinea Brat!—after whose
fits of smashing and screaming, O Holy Mother,
All-American Girl, I need you, I want
to protect you: after that one sunstruck
glimpse, on a Sicilian mountainside,

of virgin stupidity, its sensual lockbox
so charged with possibilities of being
that we too tremble at the thought of nakedness,
of marriage, we too burn to build a shrine for,
raise armies to protect a property that history

godfathered dumb. I told you: DON'T ASK
QUESTIONS ABOUT MY BUSINESS! While the old
bull in a new world, who's lost respect,
too-big pants bunched underneath the belly, stumbles
expiring past the staked tomato vines,

and the grandchild thinks for a minute he's
only playing, we *know* he is, admiring
Marlon Brando in a show of weakness. But the blood
isn't all ketchup, or the weekend all football, nor
do all commodities survive in lighted shrines.

O Italy! Imagine Eros reinvented on that hillside
as Giovanni di Paolo did—a passeggiata
where men and women walk into the day ungoaded,
unprotected, unenshrined—while we make do, stranded
on this day-glo mesa, with its epicene cartoon.

REAL ESTATE

Something there is that doesn't
love a Third Avenue tenement,

that wants it gone the way the El
went. Façade a typical example

of red-brick eclectic, its five dozen
windows half now behind blank tin,

scrollwork lintels of strange parentage,
fire escapes' curling-iron birdcage,

are an anomaly among high-rise elevators,
besieged by Urban Relocation (Not A

Governmental Agency). Holdout tenants
confer, gesticulating, by storefronts

adapted only to an anxious present—Le
Boudoir, Le Shampoo, Le Retro (if passé

is chic, is chic passé?). One gelded
pawnshop, until last week, still brooded,

harboring, among tag ends of pathos,
several thirty-year-old umbrellas.

Regularly twice a day, the lingering wraith
within stepped out to shake her dustcloth.

That's done now. She advertised a sale.
Still nothing moved. Finally, a U-Haul

truck carted everything off somewhere.
Hail, real estate! Bravo, entrepreneur!

A SCAFFOLD

The lumbering chords that open
    a Beethoven sonata,
the autumnal thump of cordwood
    Baudelaire, with a

premonitory shiver, heard unloaded
    in a Paris courtyard;
the offstage axe precipitately ringing down
    the cherry orchard

before the trunks are packed: what woke us,
    cleaving the usual
matutinal cacophony, inexorable as a
    wrecker's ball, was all

of these: the *choc funèbre* of a hard-
    hat hammerklavier,
the latest demolition crew whose live-
    lihood requires, before

they can ring down, irrevocably as
    a scuttled stage set,
the tenement whose last holdouts have been
    pried out like crabmeat—

I watched their banished chattels go,
    the sick pianoforte
with its jangled nerves, the purblind allegori-
    cal museum copy—

the raising of a scaffold (Baudelaire,
    his ear infallibly
tuned to foreboding, was already there
    to hear that echo),

a sidewalk arcade, a makeshift footing
    for the executioners,
a floor for a cowcatcher crèche, a flange
    made of dismantled doors,

a coffin (Baudelaire, needless to say, was
    also on hand to hear
it put together, blow added to blow,
    shudder to shudder)

for the last remains of rooms—
    the beams, the falling
lath and plaster—whose only crime was
    hanging on too long.

VACANT LOT WITH TUMBLEWEED AND PIGEONS

The rooms gone, hallways and stairwells
air, the cornices and fire escapes
where troops of sunning pigeons spun
from common-garden opalescence
the transience of some other thing
more rich and strange, two summers
and a winter solstice since

a dozen dumpsterloads of rubble dis-
embodied what had once seemed settled
here, effaced: the ricepaper
of the first December snowfall
inscribed with a not-yet-uprooted
tumbleweed's whip-limber pyramid,
spare, see-through, symmetrical,

an evergreen in one dimension, each
brushed-in, accidental grass-stroke
beside it letter perfect. Two
summers and a winter solstice
since their perching places went,
pigeons still arrive from somewhere,
and as in a liturgy retrace,

descending yet again the roofless
staircase of outmoded custom, the
soon-to-be-obliterated stations
of nostalgia—as though the air
itself might wince at the stigmata
of the dispossessed, the razed,
the *triste,* the unaccounted-for.

RINGING DOORBELLS

that night for Gene
McCarthy at the edge
of Little Italy
turned into
an olfactory
adventure: after

the mildew, after
the musts and fetors
of tomcat and cockroach,
barrooms' beer-reek,
the hayfield whiff
of pot, hot air

of laundromats
a flux of borax,
the entire effluvium
of the polluted
Hudson opened
like a hidden

fault line, and from
a cleft between the
backs of buildings
blossomed, out of
the dark, as
with hosannas,

the ageless,
pristine, down-
to-earth aromas
of tomorrow's
bread from
Zito's Bakery.

TOWNHOUSE INTERIOR WITH CAT

For Joan and Dean McClure

Green-gold, the garden leans into the room,
the room leans out into the garden's
hanging intertwine of willow. Voluptuous
on canvas, arum lilies' folded cream
rises on its own green undertone. The walls
are primrose; needlepoint-upholstered
walnut and, underfoot, a Bokhara heirloom
bring in the woodwind resonance of autumn.
Mirrored among jungle blooms' curled crimson
and chartreuse, above the mantel, diva-throated
tuberoses, opening all the stops, deliver
Wagnerian arias of perfume.
                        The kettle
warbles in the kitchen; we take our teacups
downstairs to where the willow harbors,
improbably, a ring of mushrooms. Tulips
and rhododendrons have almost done blooming;
laced overhead, neighboring locust trees
discard their humid ivory.
                         But where's
the favorite with the green-gold headlamps?
She's perverse today; declines, called out
of hiding, to recall past tête-à-têtes
of sparring hand-to-paw; claws up a tree;
patrols a wall. We see her disappear
into her own devices. Cornered later
under the gateleg table, tail aloof,
she flirts, an eloquence of fur, but won't
be wooed or flattered. The look she gives
me, when she looks—the whole green-gold,
outdoor-indoor continuum condensed
to a reproachful pair of jewels—is wild
and scathingly severe.

TIME

It may be we are in the last days.
Seven hundred years ago to the week,
on the eleventh of December, the kingdom of Wales went under.
Today, the sixth day of the twelfth month of the nineteen hundred
    eighty-second year, according to the current reckoning,
there are roses the size of an obsolete threepenny bit—
one fingernail-pink, the other minute, extravagant crimson—
flanked by masses of sweet alyssum
and one time-exempt purple pansy
on the site of what was formerly the Women's House of Detention
at the triangular intersection of Tenth Street with Greenwich and
    Sixth Avenues,
just back of the old Jefferson Market courthouse
whose tower clock, revived, goes on keeping time.
And I think again of October violets,
of their hardy refusal to adhere to conventional expectation—
so hardy that I've finally ceased to think of it as startling,
this phenomenon which, in fact, I devoted myself in October to
    looking for—
a tame revenant of the blue fire-alarm of the original encounter
    with the evidence,
among the dropped leaves and superannuated grass of the season
    of hickory nuts,
that neither time nor place could be counted on to remain
    self-sufficient,
that you might find yourself slipping back toward the past at any
    moment,
or watch it well up in artesian springs of anachronism,
with the prospect of being drowned in that aperture's abrupt blue,
in that twinkling of an eye, at any moment.
It was November, or near then, I found violets massed at the foot
    of the foundations of the castle of Chepstow,
at the edge of Wales—not any longer, as once, covert, fecklessly
    undermining
that sense of fitness, so fragile that at any moment of one's
    childhood
whatever sense of continuity has not ebbed or been marked for
    demolition
may break like an eggshell, and be overrun from within by the
    albumen of ruin—
their out-of-season purple not any longer hinting at something, but
    announcing it with a flourish:

TIME

the entire gorgeous, intractable realm of the forgotten,
the hieratic, the heraldic, the royal, sprung open
at the gouty foot of that anachronism
on the fringes of a kingdom that went under
at or near the downward slope of the thirteenth century. I have seen
the artesian spring of the past foam up at the foot of the castle of
    Chepstow
on a day in November, or thereabouts. I have seen a rose the size of
    a perfectly manicured crimson fingernail
alive in a winter that does not arrive, though we plunge again
    toward the solstice.

HOMER, A.D. 1982

For Irving Kizner and his class at Hunter College

Much having traveled in the funkier realms of Ac-
ademe, aboard a grungy elevator car,
deus ex machina reversed, to this ninth-floor
classroom, its windows grimy, where the noise of traffic,
πολυφλοίσβοιο-θαλάσσης-like, is chronic,
we've seen since February the stupendous candor
of the *Iliad* pour in, and for an hour and a
quarter at the core the great pulse was dactylic.

We've seen the clash, from those great halls, of light and dark,
the sullen campfires of a brooded-over choler,
Odysseus, rising, sway his peers with storms of logic,
the spurned priest of Apollo shrink along the shore,
and Hector's baby, shadowed by the plumes of war
as we are, pull back from his own father with a shriek.

Five   Written in Water

THE HICKORY GROVE

Flint-skinned, bone-hued
loot from the till of fall—
its draperies all a heap,
the latch left open—
you'll need a hammer
and a brace of nutpicks
to get at the meat of
these obdurate nuggets,

clench-kin to the KEEP OUT
that drives home what matters
is whose woods these are:
a category of autonomy
ignored by squirrels, nor
can the shambling seasons
be neatened and shut into
watertight compartments

such as memory, that burrower,
will undermine with awe,
out there in the bare-
boled, frost-bitten-eared,
enormous silences of winter:
or, alarmingly, the ramrod
shagbarks stirred, up over-
head, into one green-gold

churn of things opening and
unfolding—leaf clusters big
as wheatsheaves cascading
out of casqued sheathings
too extravagant to figure
as a source of income—the
inner burnish of all that
scrap satin such as is un-

amenable to the hard arts
of bronze, of mining and
smelting—or of pouring
an ingot of metaphor so
dazzling, some day some
critic, come round to see
these woods, will post a
sign that says PROPRIETOR.

LOSING TRACK OF LANGUAGE

The train leaps toward Italy, the French Riviera
falls away in the dark, the rails sing dimeter
shifting to trimeter, a galopade to a galliard.
We sit wedged among strangers; whatever
we once knew (it was never much) of each other
falls away with the landscape. Words
fall away, we trade instead in flirting
and cigarettes; we're all rapport with strangers.
The one with the yellow forelock that keeps falling
and being shaken back again, syncopating
the dimeter-trimeter, galopade-into-galliard,
is, it seems, Italian—recently a pilgrim
to the Vaucluse, where Petrarca,
to the noise of waterfalls, measured out
his strict stanzas, little rooms
for turmoil to grow lucid in, for
change to put on more durable
leaves of bronze, a scapular of marble.

A splutter of pleasure at hearing the name
is all he needs, and he's off
like a racehorse at the Palio—plunging
unbridled into recited cadenzas, three-beat
lines interleaving a liquid pentameter.
What are words? They fall away into the fleeing
dark of the French Riviera, as once a shower
of bloom, *una pioggia di fior,* descended
into the lap of the Trecento: her hair
all gold and pearl, the grass still warm
as when she sat there, six centuries
gone by; that squandered heartbeat
(the black plague took her, young) now
fossilized as bronze, as carved laurel.
Whatever is left of her is language;
and what is language but breath, leaves,
petals fallen or in the act of falling, pollen
of turmoil that sifts through the fingers?

—*E conosce* (I ask it to keep the torrent
of words from ending, to keep anything
from ending, ever) *anche Sapphò?* Yes,
he knows, he will oblige. The limpid pentameter
gives way to something harsher: diphthongs
condense, take on an edge of bronze. Though
I don't understand a word, what are words? Do these
concern one Timas, led before she was married
(or so one leaf of what's left would have it)
to the dark bedroom of Persephone, for so long
nowhere at home, either here or there, forever
returning and falling back again
into the dark of these ten thousand years?
The train leaps toward Italy; words fall away
through the dark into the dark bedroom
of everything left behind, the unendingness
of things lost track of—of who, of where—
where I'm losing track of language.

WRITTEN IN WATER

From a woman's dream of being,
at her age, still deemed desirable,
preserved—the quivering reliquary
of the dew of decades snared
among the fernery—till morning,

to wake in winter to this antic
glare—the Snow Queen's frore
boudoir, the numbed orthography
of being seen, its milkweed
smithereens turned every which way—

is still to listen for the seep
within the crypt, the mirror-
drip of stalactites, blind milk
of perpetuity whose only witness
is the viewless salamander.

A CURE AT PORLOCK

For whatever did it—the cider
at the Ship Inn, where the crowd
from the bar that night had overflowed
singing into Southey's Corner, or

an early warning of appendicitis—
the remedy the chemist in the High Street
purveyed was still a dose of kaopectate
in morphine—the bane and the afflatus

of S.T.C. when Alph, the sacred river,
surfaced briefly in the unlikely
vicinity of Baker Farm, and as quickly
sank again, routed forever by the visitor

whose business, intent and disposition—
whether ill or well is just as immaterial—
long ago sunk Lethewards, a particle
of the unbottled ultimate solution.

I drank my dose, and after an afternoon
prostrate, between heaves, on the
coldly purgatorial tiles of the W.C.,
found it elysium simply to recline,

sipping flat ginger beer as though it were
honeydew, in that billowy bed,
under pink chenille, hearing you read
The Mystery of Edwin Drood! For whether

the opium was worth it for John Jasper,
from finding being with you, even sick
at Porlock, a rosily addictive picnic,
I left less likely ever to recover.

THE SACRED HEARTH FIRE

Some sort of road does go up there,
they'll tell you, but unless you're
exceptionally good at maps, it's better

to go by the public footpath, rocks
and all—tree-root-contorted hummocks,
the rhododendron-filtered lilt of brooks

you never see until the footbridge,
brown water gabbling a liquid passage
underneath, and then there's the church

you've come to look at—its valley tucked
fast against a steep slope cassocked
in a murk of oaks, an apron pocket-

ful of sun. The church is very old and tiny,
surplices are laid out for next Sunday,
and the starch-smooth interior cube's as though

a whitewashed sea chapel had been lifted
up here (having been deftly introverted)
from the glare of Mýkonos. Nothing could,

though, be more un-Greek than the choir
stalls' gnarled wood-sorrel quatre-
foils—as English as to be famished for

a cup of tea. Which, as you'll have heard,
there's a lady hereabouts who can provide.
Asked, one of two men studying the underside

of a stalled car just where the road dwindles
to its dead end, says, "Well, there's Mrs.
Cook. She's deaf. Don't know if she's

there. Better knock loud"—with a gesture
toward the slope above the church tower:
a chimneyed cottage of a stone the color,

approximately, of a Cox's orange pippin,
a twirl of smoke above a steep small garden,
moss roses, gooseberry bushes, a carillon

of fuchsia trees, the gate open and then
a flight of flagstones, the door open
too, as though unaware one might walk in

and claim, on having crossed the threshold,
merely by the walking in, the unguarded
mysteries of an entire existence. Elated

almost to the brink of fear—how can
the act of entering not alter, and ruin
in altering, what one loves for having been

until this instant wholly uninfected
by oneself?—you pause, and at the threshold
of possession, you observe the sacred

coal fire on the grate, the elbowed
stovepipe, the meal dish and the bed
of a household animal; the sideboard

in the adjoining room, a reredos
of snapshots, postcards, mementos
from all over, the unself-conscious

showpiece of a lifetime that must
have—otherwise why, as you paused
just now, that tremor of an unforced

happiness?—been happy. She appears,
small, quick but unhurried. There's
a hearing aid under the wreathed hair's

bright blond gone hay-color. Yes, she can
give you tea. Since the day's fine,
will you have it here in the garden?

She lays it all out on a tablecloth,
brings biscuits and a book to autograph,
as visitors coming up by the footpath

have been doing all these years—people from
all over, depositing an unwitting perfume
of far climates along with the humdrum

"Thanx for the nice cuppa." You venture
that the church down there made you, for
a minute, think of Greece. From her

vague nod you see she hasn't followed.
The church, you say again—it's splendid.
Now she does. She tells you she was married

in it back in 1914, has lived here, in this
same cottage, ever since. Her husband's
just now ill and in hospital. No one knows

exactly what the matter was. "He's better?"
"I hope he is"—said with such composure
you're relieved, as though one might be sure

the bourn of age would prove on opening
to have inurned the blessedness of dying—
only not yet, Lord, it takes some growing

into, still. Time meanwhile to admire
the fuchsia trees, a memento (minus their
attendant hummingbirds) of the steep sea air,

the sun and fog of northern California.
She nods, with no surprise. "A lady
here who comes from California told me

it was very like. She came here for a
visit, and stayed on. She has the pottery
up there"—deferring to a building of the

same apple-colored stone, but surer
of its tone, in being new, than either
this cottage, with its sacred spire

of coal smoke, or the whitewash-walled
landmark down below. "But"—lest you should,
at this intelligence, rush up only to find

no one—"she's not there now." You have
just now not the least wish to think of
pots, or anything that might be craf-

ted in a day and given to a kiln to harden—
that oven smelling of no substance so in-
dispensable as home-made bread. To go in

for pots—to be so earthbound and so
fired-up at once—seems somehow crazy:
to be forever whacking at the clay,

forever trying out its character
with switches of local weeds, forever
making things whose function's either

merely to contain some other thing,
coffinlike, or to stand idle, wearing
the smirk of one content with being

well turned out, a calculated object.
No. No object. Better a process. No, not
that either. No process but the unshaped

accretion, the watershed, the accidental
bloom that won't survive the kiln—
being, totally untainted by the will:

only the doing without making so very
much of what one does will do—with no
particular design for giving shape to any-

thing at all, even the outlines of one's
own experience: asking for no consequence
other than those decades of sentiments

in the pages of a guest book: the whole
of what at last is no more durable
than crumbling soil, the common, friable,

finally intangible, that may come up again
as gooseberries or go down drowning un-
der the sound of brooks. Just now, one

might be tempted to drop everything, to
settle into an acquaintance with the clay,
and so put down one's roots here like the lady

from California. "Here I am!" A young
woman—or possibly one not young,
merely vivid and lissome—is rushing

up, is leaving, in leaning, a flying kiss
above the cheek and the wreathed hair of Mrs.
Cook. That, Mrs. Cook says as she vanishes,

is the lady who has the pottery.
The world is full of mystery.
A creature half California poppy,

half hummingbird, could hardly come from
any other place. But pots? Perhaps
her husband (if she has one) or some
      minion makes them.

LET THE AIR CIRCULATE

spaces between
archetypal openings   the aperture
seen through binoculars   carved by the lone boatman's
arm athwart the tiller   the schooner's traveling
house of air   split like a nutshell   or a bivalve's domicile
jalousies   belfries   cupolas   floor-through
apartments   let the air circulate   spaces between (sixteen
floors up and still rising)   scaffolded pourers
of reinforced concrete   by the motorized   wheelbarrowful
silhouetted   (a hardhatted frieze)   make of them
something unwittingly classical

clamdiggers
wading mudflats   bending in attitudes
older than   the names of anything   spaces between
things looked at   or unlooked at   beatitudes
of the unaware they're   being looked at
eiders flying   straight as a die   to wherever they're going
triglyph and metope   of air   let the light pass
let the air circulate   let there be intervals
for moving   apart   for
coming back together

the antipodal
the antiphonal   the gradual
the totally unexpected   the counted on   as infallible
the look of   from a particular   window
an island   in profile
the fish-spine   silhouette   of a particular
spruce   intersecting at nightfall   the unaltering interval
of 'Tit Manan light   opening up   folding into
itself   fading   brightening   an orbiting
sidereal buttercup

ARCHAIC
FIGURE

(1987)

FOR PETER KYBART, HOWARD MOSS,
AND MARY JO SALTER

The ancient consciousness of women, charged with
suffering and sensibility, and for so many ages dumb,
seems, in them, to have brimmed and overflowed . . .

VIRGINIA WOOLF
in *The Common Reader*
on the heroines of George Eliot

One   Hellas

ARCHAIC FIGURE

Headless in East Berlin, no goddess
but a named mere girl (Ornithe, "Little Bird")
out of the rubble, six centuries underneath
    the plinth of what we quaintly call

Our Time, informs the foaming underside
of linden boulevards in bloom, sweet hide
laid open onto—sterile as an operating table,
    past the closed incision of the Wall—

the treeless reach of Alexanderplatz,
paved counterpart of the interior flatland,
halfway across the globe, we'd left behind:
    projection, factor, yield, the quantifiable

latitude; malls, runways, blacktop; tressed
cornsilk and alfalfa, drawn milk of the humdrum
nurture there were those of us who ran away from
    toward another, earlier, bonier

one, another middle of the earth, yearned-
for stepmotherland of Hölderlin and Goethe:
sunlight and grief, the cypress and the
    crucifix, the vivid poverty

of terraced slopes, of bread, wine, olives,
fig and pomegranate shade we stumbled into,
strolling the sad northern drizzle, in
    the uprooted Turks' quasi-bazaar,

as here, among uprooted artifacts, we've come
upon this shape's just-lifted pleats, her
chitoned stillness the cold chrism of a time
    that saw—or so to us it seems—

with unexampled clarity to the black core
of what we are, of everything we were to be,
have since become. Who stands there headless.
    Barbar, she would have called us all.

THE OLIVE GROVES OF THASOS

Thronging the warped treadmill
of antiquity, the silver-polled
assemblies, knothole-
tunneled, generations-old

abeyances, posthumous postures
and contortions of a common
weathering, their burled stupor
pierced and cloven

by fierce threnodies of
daybreak, penetrable,
root-cooled in dazzlements
of unquarried marble,

these wards of turbulence
beneath the shaken
shrines of the acropolis,
delivering a gray-green

annual glut of worry-
beads that blacken
in October, after the summer
people have all gone,

when from the villages along
the shore, where in the evenings
we watched the fishing
boats go out in strings

of three, in trinities,
from each of whose sterns
there bloomed a mimic
trinity of lanterns,

linked in a ring, as
darkness fell, to frame
a single, cyclic reënactment
of the timeless; and from

the plane-tree-dimmed, cool-
all-summer refuge
of hill villages above the
tideline of gray foliage;

from the middle villages
the buses pass through, their
hens, their dust and oleanders,
their voluble cafés no more

than islets in the vast,
single surf of olive
groves that circumscribe,
that are the chief live-

lihood and artifact of
Thasos—the whole populace
turns out, with tarpaulins and
poles, to bring in the harvest

of these trees: of this time-gnarled
community of elders—so many-
shaped, so warped, so densely
frugal, so graceful a company,

what more can we say, we who have
seen the summer boats go out,
tasted the dark honey, and savored
the oil-steeped, black, half-bitter fruit?

ANO PRINIOS

Transport was what we'd come in search of.
A hill village where no bus goes—
we caught a lift there in a pickup truck,
hopped down onto cobblestones. Dank plane trees,
root, branch and foliage, engulfed the square.
The mountain slope behind spoke, murmurous,
in tongues of torrents. In what was actually
someone's living room, a small bar at the back,
two men sat by the window, drinking coffee.
We asked for ouzo. Olives on a bed of herbs
came with it, and feta, freshly made.
What next? Conversation halted, stumbling,
drew repeated blanks. The woman of the house
sat half-retired, hands busy, needle-glint
releasing a slow rill of thread lace.
What it was for—a tablecloth, a baby's
christening robe perhaps—I tried to ask,
she tried to tell me, but the filament fell short.
The plane trees dripped. The old man,
the proprietor, moved in and out. A course
we hadn't asked for—two fishes, mountain trout
they must have been, served on a single plate—
was set between us: seasoned with leeks,
I could not guess what else, the ridged
flesh firm and delicate.
Later, as I came from the latrine,
the old man, intercepting, showed me
the rooms we might have slept in—hangings
vivid over whitewash, the blankets rough.
A disappointed avarice—how could we, savoring
a poverty rarer than any opulence, begin
to grasp how dear our fickle custom was?—
gloomed, hurtful as a bruise, on
our departure: the rooted and the footloose
each looking past the other, for something missed.
A scruple over how to deal with matters so
fundamental, and so unhandsome, restrained me,
for two years and more, from writing
of what happened in between: how happiness
asperged, redeemed, made the occasion
briefly articulate. One of the coffee-drinkers,
having vanished, came back in. He brought,

dripping as from a fountain, a branch just severed
from some fruit tree, loaded with drupes
that were, though still green, delectable.
Turning to the woman, I asked what
they were called in Greek. She answered,
"Damaskēno." Damson, damask, damascene:
the word hung, still hangs there,
glistening among its cognates.

TEMPE IN THE RAIN

What leaf-fringed legend haunts
this sodden loess of picnics,
sardine-tin litter dripped on
by unmythic fig and laurel—
what latterday pursuits,
   what struggle

to escape the tourist traps,
what souvenir-stall
indignities beside the
footbridge, what coffee bar
depopulated by a sudden
    summer downpour?

To this running anachronism,
the giggling, gray-green
roar that fills a gorge
(sweet Thames! run softly)
old books refer to as the
    vale of Tempe,

the tributaries writhe,
sidle, and defy connection
with the roadside spring, high
up, at which two days ago the
bus made an unscheduled
   stop (we

all got out, washed fruit, filled
bottles, drank from our hands,
found a marsh-marigold in
bloom) or with, above the plain
of Thessaly (Peneus shimmering
   like the Python

Apollo slew, and having slain,
fled here to undo the pollution)
the crazy pinnacles of silt
compacted, cracked open, rain-
and-wind-sanded, where hermit
   monks hole up in

precarious balconies aswarm with
reptilian slitherings, with
gilding, martyrdoms and demons,
with the bong of bells to deafen
and the smell of flame-warmed
      beeswax to sweeten

a side trip Spenser never
contemplated; nor did Keats,
on whose account I've just
jumped off the bus, in this
unseasonable summer rain, to
      find no trace

here of Apollo in pursuit,
mad for the green, leaf-
slippery virginity of Daphne,
but rather, in a hollow under
Mount Olympus' obliviously
      pagan shoulder,

this shrine warmed by a
fragrant sweat of brown beeswax—
where, since some memorial
piety seems called for, before
the ikon of another virgin,
      I've lit a taper.

OLYMPIA

The marble stumps, the plundered archeology of games—
the foot race, the hippodrome, the chariot on the racetrack;
the fox-and-geese-track in the schoolyard snow; the footprints
of the weasel and the fleeing fieldmouse, the quick pickpocket,
dexterity of hand embellishing the margins of disorder;
Harpo Marx's scamp-as-saint, a voiceless kosher Mozart;

the katydid-faced TV hockey goalie, who never heard of Mozart,
all vicious equanimity on ice: what's to enjoy but games?
Baseball, weekend football orgies, a day off at the racetrack,
that spinoff of the heavy Greeks' reverberating footprints.
(What culture, pre- or post-gunpowder, spawned the pickpocket?)
Games, the last prop as stunned civility trips into disorder:

Berlin in '36, then Buchenwald's drill sergeants of disorder.
What's to be done, then, with the equanimity of Mozart?
Mandelstam and friends converting into chanting-games
the wording of a ration book, till the vagaries of the racetrack
ran him down: his widow gathering up the filched footprints
of his racing mind, raffish and incorrigible as a pickpocket.

When heavy breathing plays the superhero, the pickpocket
at his quick work acts the antihero—a slight disorder
in the bronze of monuments, like the dexterity of Mozart,
sick with overwork, converting even hackwork into games.
How far such insolent hilarity is from the racetrack
of dead earnest, bent on obliterating misplaced footprints!

The marble retrospect, the paleozoology of footprints
taken over by the guided tour, the masher, the pickpocket,
the frog-pond *brek-ek-ek-ex ko-ax ko-ax,* the slight disorder
of what's unplanned, ad hoc, or made up on the spot: Mozart
dashing off a bawdy letter, Mandelstam with *sotto voce* games
tweaking the management until it drove him off the racetrack.

The heavy Greeks were deadly serious about their racetrack.
Since Pelops won there by a trick, the solemn footprints
of mythology have not been done with boding. The pickpocket
and the masher remain the faithful guardians of disorder;
they keep their equanimity, although they never heard of Mozart.
A pest on heavy breathing! *À bas* civility! Long live the games!

THERMOPYLAE

Where the bay flashed, and an unrecorded number
of the Persian troops, whip-flicked into the spear-
clogged hourglass of the pass, were impaled and fell
screaming from the precipice to drown, the mirror

clogs: geography too gathers dust, though busloads
of us (sandaled Germans mostly), hankering for
an attar or a foothold, a principle that still
applies, a cruse of oil, a watershed no rain erodes,

find small inkling of what was staved off here,
or saved. A calcined stillness, beehives, oleanders,
polluted air, the hung crags livid; on the little hill
(beneath, the bay flashed as men fell and went under

screaming) where a stone lion once stood in honor
of that grade-school byword of a troop commander
Leonidas, we ponder a funneled-down inscription: Tell
them for whom we came to kill and were killed, stranger,

how brute beauty, valor, act, air, pride, plume here
buckling, guttered: closed in from behind, our spears
smashed, as, the last defenders of the pass, we fell,
we charged like tusked brutes and gnawed like bears.

LEAVING YÁNNINA

The lake like glass, like space
framed in a verdigris of reeds:
the arrow-pointed threadpulls
of small boats that scarcely
flaw the surface,
the mosque a floating
waterlily-garden of the air
upended on a minaret.
                              Last night
as, thrusting past the public square,
the strut of a platoon in khaki
cut through the burble and
meander of the *volta,*
the warm whiff, from
souvlaki stalls, of burning meat
took on a hint of carnage.
                              This morning
in the little archeological museum, time
lies still: the earrings,
the arrowpoints, the spearheads
no one will ever flee again
through time
or space: some latent source
stands open like a room.

DODONA: ASKED OF THE ORACLE

The female body, its creases and declivities
leading to the sacred opening, the hollow
whose precincts, here, neither seduce nor threaten:
bee-hum, birdsong, side-oats' leaning awns,
the blowing grasses (one vivid
lizard flickers on gray stone,
is gone); the drifting
down of poplars; harebells,
convolvulus. The triumph-song,
far off, of strutting cocks
no threat, merely ridiculous. Olympus
a mountain range away: huge valleys
charged with gargantuan
foreshadowings, new-minted
laser glints of force.
                  From such bluster
was this once a place of refuge? Before Dione,
the dim earlier consort, gave place
to bitchy Hera (who for her nagging
had, of course, good cause),
was there a season when
the unraised voice, attuned
to civic reticence by whisperings
among totemic oak leaves,
might gain a hearing?
                  Or did that wounded,
melismatic howl, heard now from
the taxicab cassette, or filtered
through the heat of the debate
above the tric-trac—whether
of shaman, priest, muezzin
or lying, half-self-deceived seducer—
countervail: this siren
tremor, male, ancient,
mindless, that raises
Armageddons from within the doddering
sheep run of politics—this echo
of recesses deeper, even, than
the archetypal cleft of sex?

Two   The Mirror of the Gorgon

*. . . the myriad tribes of the dead came thronging up with a wondrous cry,
and pale fear seized me, lest august Persephone might send forth upon me
from out the house of Hades the head of the Gorgon, that awful monster.*
HOMER, *The Odyssey, XI, 631–635* (translated by A. T. Murray)

MEDUSA

The tentacles, the brazen phiz whose glare
stands every fibril of the mind on end—
lust looked at backward as it were,
an antique scare tactic, either self-protection
or a libel on the sex whose periodic
blossom hangs its ungathered garland
from the horned clockwork of the moon:
as cause or consequence, or both, hysteric
symptoms no doubt figure here. She'd been
a beauty till Poseidon, in a flagrant
trespass, closed with her on Athena's temple floor.

The tide-rip torrents in the blood, the dark
gods not to be denied—or a mere indiscretion?
Athena had no time at all for talk like this.
The sea-god might be her old rival, but the woman
he'd gone to bed with was the one who paid.
A virginal revenge at one remove—there's none more
sordid or more apt to ramify, as this one did:
the fulgent tresses roiled to water-snake-
like writhe, and for long lashes'
come-hither flutterings, the stare
that hardens the psyche's soft parts to rock.

The female ogre, for the Puritan
revisionists who took her over, had a new
and siren sliminess. John Milton
put her at the gate of hell, *a woman to
the waist, and fair; but ended foul, in
many a scaly fold, voluminous and vast*—
whose name indeed was Sin. And in the den
of doctrine run amok, the armored glister
of a plodding Holiness revealed her
as likewise divided but, all told, *most
loathsome, filthy, foul, and full of vile disdain.*

The Gorgon, though, is no such Manichean tease,
no mantrap caterer of forbidden dishes,
whose lewd stews keep transgression warm.
The stinging jellyfish, the tubeworm,
the tunicate, the sea anemone's
whorled comb are privier to her mysteries:

her salts are cold, her home-
land Hyperborean (the realm that gave us
the Snow Queen and the English gentleman),
her mask the ravening aspect of the moon,
her theater a threshing floor that terror froze.

Terror of origins: the sea's heave, the cold mother
of us all; disdain of the allure that draws us in,
that stifles as it nurtures, that feeds on
what it feeds, on what it comforts, whether male
or female: ay, in the very tissue of desire
lodge viscid barbs that turn the blood to coral,
the heartbeat to a bed of silicates. What surgeon
can unthread those multiplicities of cause
of hurt from its effect; dislodge, spicule by spicule,
the fearful armories within; unclench the airless
petrifaction toward the core, the geode's rigor?

PERSEUS

His errand took him to the brink of Ragnarok,
past the last pillar of the charted world, where rain-
worn prototypes of animals and men,
extinct long since, preserved the evidence
of rookeries whose motive force went dark,
sealed shut by that grimace: eroded
stumps of horror antedating even
Odysseus, for whom the Gorgon's head
harrowed with unmanning fear the corridors
of Tartarus, that feeding trough of nightmares,
where every look breeds dread: unstared-down landmark,
last, first and most primitive of portents.

He came armed with an adamantine kris
Hermes had lent him, plus certain items gotten
(as so often happens when crusading zeal
sets forth) by means not over nice: prodigious
sandals' heavier-than-air device, the cowl
of a purloined intelligence, the pouch of blackmail
extorted from the Graeae, a triplet sisterhood
tied to an economy of scarcity (one tooth and one
eye among them, intercepted as they slid
from hand to hand); and above all indispensable,
the shield Athena gave, whose burnished metal
served as an intervening mirror of the Gorgon.

Like any other prospector for the hard,
the heavy, the hideously toxic,
he knew the risk he ran: he could not look
except at one remove at what he'd vowed to take
and hustle out: that head, struck
bleeding from its trunk, whose clotted
dreadlocks and gagged, staring scowl became
the badge and totem of what no one can
encounter and survive: among dredged glisten-
ings of seaweed, the unfledged millennium —
the branched, ineradicable stem of time,
whose cold coils wind about the moon's inexorable clock.

And even as he fled, the undiplomatic
pouchful safely stowed, two angry other
Gorgons in pursuit (as any Greek will caution,

mischiefs tend to come in triplicate),
the stem he'd lopped, already pregnant by Poseidon,
gave birth to Chrysaor, precocious warrior
whose cumbering falchion would overhang
the ungrazed field, the unturned furrow of the future,
and to unbridled Pegasus, the winged fraternal twin
who kicked at Helicon, and from whose hoofprint sprung
the mirror flash among the cromlechs—one wet
eyeblink in the antediluvial dark.

HIPPOCRENE

I came to the puddle. I could not cross it. Identity failed me. We are nothing, I said, and fell.   VIRGINIA WOOLF, *The Waves*

The cold spring
of an intense depression,
moon-horror-struck posthumous
offspring of Medusa,
harbinger of going under,
of death by water.

Though above the pillars
of ruined Sounion the air
is calm, the white-lipped,
violet-hued flowerbed
of drowning, fraying
at the rim,

lies sleek with signals
of unbeing: the cold hoofprint's
doorway into nothing
metamorphosing from a
puddle in a courtyard,
the huge irruption

of blank seas the psyche
cannot cross: the terror-
twinning muse, the siren
and the solace: done and
undone by water—whether
beyond the stormy

Hebrides, the voyage
out, the long-looked-forward-to
excursion to the lighthouse:
the Ouse closing over;
a fin, far out. The waves
break on the shore.

ATHENA

Force of reason, who shut up the shrill
foul Furies in the dungeon of the Parthenon,
led whimpering to the cave they live in still,

beneath the rock your city foundered on:
who, equivocating, taught revenge to sing
(or seem to, or be about to) a kindlier tune:

mind that can make a scheme of anything—
a game, a grid, a system, a mere folder
in the universal file drawer: uncompromising

mediatrix, virgin married to the welfare
of the body politic: deific contradiction,
warbonnet-wearing olive-bearer, author

of the law's delays, you who as talisman
and totem still wear the aegis, baleful
with Medusa's scowl (though shrunken

and self-mummified, a Gorgon still): cool
guarantor of the averted look, the guide
of Perseus, who killed and could not kill

the thing he'd hounded to its source, the dread
thing-in-itself none can elude, whose counter-
feit we halfway hanker for: aware (gone mad

with clarity) we have invented all you stand for,
though we despise the artifice—a space to savor
horror, to pre-enact our own undoing in—
living, we stare into the mirror of the Gorgon.

THE NEREIDS OF SERIPHOS

*. . . Here Perseus left Danaë, and when after a successful voyage he
returned with Medusa's head, and found King Polydectes making
love to Danaë, he forthwith turned him and all the Seriphiotes into
stones.* J. T. BENT, *The Cyclades* (1885)

Sealed up in fright, the wedding party turned
to rock: the way they used to tell it,
one look at whatever the eye-catching
widow's son had brought back from
whatever place he'd gone—out west,
or was it somewhere back east they said?—
had done it. But pin anybody down,
you find evasions, hearsay, a mere blur
of allegation.
        And as for all that
weathered-clean economy, that fluted-pillared,
clear-eyed residue of myth—listen a minute
to the nineteenth-century traveler: "Of
all the towns in the Greek islands, Seriphos
will remain fixed in my mind as the
most filthy. The main street is a sewer
into which all the offal is thrown, and
it is tenanted by countless pigs. . . ."
                      The mire,
the stink of pigsties, of privies, of
the chamber pot upstairs, of soured milk,
mildew, kerosene, the purgatorial Lysol.
Yes. All this we know. Down there among
said-to-be-domesticated beasts—
the boar, the fenced-in bull, green drool
from bovine lips, green ooze of cowflops—
that we are animals, mire-born,
mud-cumbered, chilled and full of fear,
we know.
          "The houses opening upon
this street were black holes, where sat families
shivering around charcoal fires. . . ." The discomforts
of Seriphos or of my own New Providence
(so called, an act of piety and resolution),
the terrors everybody knows about
and no one speaks of: God. Dying.
Getting caught. The telephone at midnight.
Fire. Tornadoes.

Horse Poseidon.
An old woman comes hobbling in, crossing herself
lest the stranger cast on her the evil eye.
His query has to do with certain
survivals of belief—in Nereids,
to be precise. Closing her eyes,
she groans, then mutters, "I know nothing."
It had all happened years ago, of course.
Michael Kapuzacharias had been digging
near the church (here once again she
vehemently crosses herself) on what
had been a very calm, still day,
when suddenly a whirlwind came. They found him
lying senseless, and in that state
carried him home to his family. Of course.
The nineteenth-century traveler evinces
no surprise. All one, those whirlwinds—
Nereids, Harpies, whatever, such as carried
off the daughter of Pandareus.
Of course.

But in landlocked New Providence
(so called), a place of fright as yet
uncertified, Greek myth being merely
Guido Reni in a frame above the blackboard,
the elements are otherwise accounted for.
Thus, on the third day of June, 1860,
the meetinghouse was lifted from its foundation
by a wind wrapped in a cloud (as an eyewitness
by the name of A. M. Mulford would describe it)
of a dark purplish color, changing,
as it approached, to a white mist
so thick he could not see the fence
some thirty feet away. Whereupon (he wrote)
the wind began to blow with a fearful,
hollow, roaring sound . . .

A place of fright,
rebuilt with stained glass and a belfry, where
the sessions that, each Sunday morning, passed
for worship, were chilled still further
by the presence of a well-off farmer's wife,
witheringly millinered, gowned, beaded,
vitrified; but in whose Gorgon look
nobody chose to speak of having met with

the evil eye—or with anything more notable
than the fatuity of those who'd rise above
the herd. The mire. The torpor.
         No Nereids.
No Gorgons, "monstrous females with huge teeth
like those of swine"—thus Bulfinch,
nineteenth-century burnisher of myth,
who mentions "an ingenious theory . . .
that the Gorgons and the Graeae were only
personifications of the terrors of the sea."
Only. *Only!* (Shipwreck. Fear death by water,
whirlwind, waterspout, tornado.) No Nereids.
No Harpies. Bulfinch recycled to a tedious,
sapless anthology. Guido Reni, master
of those who prettify, auroral in a frame
above the blackboard in fifth grade. No mire.
No stink. The pig-tusked Gorgon
decertified, sealed up in fright
of the unmentionable:
         Cancer. The
lurid budding of the menses. Having
your underpants fall down in public.
The epidemic that strikes down the young
before the name of what it was is known.
Exposure. Rape. Abortion. The mute
gropings of the wedding night
locked up in fright. Fright
locked in for life. Mere allegation.
Headed west, they say. Or was it
east? Nobody knows the story.

SERIPHOS UNVISITED

The Nereids have departed. A century
of progress, as some once quaintly
termed it, has passed that island by.

Though, come summer, others of the Cyclades
will swarm with topless Nordic beauties,
Seriphos has still so few amenities,

is still so nil in terms of monuments,
the *Guide Bleu* hands it a two-sentence
detour (damaged frescoes). Poverty and silence,

rust stains, juttings of suicidal rock,
an anchorage too far off the beaten track,
according to Durrell. He sends us back

to old J. T. Bent, the classic indefatigable
traveler, who's told us everything we'll
ever know of pig-thronged, dank-hovel-

holed-up-in Seriphos, summer or winter.
For rural mid-America, the housing's better;
the price of pork is up, pigs grow fatter

faster, are still pigs. Against tornadoes, still
no remedy. Sundays, the tone in the split-level,
L-plan ranch-style shrine is newly evangelical.

What else is new? Psychoanalysis.
The crabgrass rootstocks of the middle class—
O thou great Sameness of our works and days!—

absorb the spread of a small, still conclusion:
progress, a century and more of it, has gotten
us nowhere. New world or old, beneath the skin

there's no true novelty. The fossil trait you
thought you'd shed looms in the rear-view
mirror. An unprecedented analgesic brew

dilutes the touted California honey.
Our meat is pulverized mythology. The
Nereids of consequence have passed us by.

PERSEUS AIRBORNE

. . . Thereafter, Perseus was driven by warring winds all over the vast expanse of sky. . . . Three times he saw the frozen north, three times, borne southwards, he beheld the claws of the Crab. . . .
    OVID, *Metamorphoses, Book IV* (translated by Mary M. Innes)

What lay beyond those blowing beaches,
that heaving barrier, was still unmapped:
the wind-scoured moors of Patagonia,
the blizzard whiteouts of the Antarctic,

vast scarfed screechings at the center
of a Caribbean air mass; the norther,
the chinook, El Niño; gale force in wait,
the lurking possibility of wind shears:

even for a son of Zeus the Thunderer
(who'd impregnated his mother Danaë,
in a daring raid, with pollen-gold),
to be airborne entails a daunting,

a radical insouciance. The B-52s
panting in tandem, not-quite-new-fangled
coursers of the Sun, howl up from grasslands
that were terra incognita once: beyond

the last temptation, the untaken leap
they now rehearse, rehearse, rehearse.

ATLAS IMMOBILIZED

Hulk grown monumental with refusal,
intolerable landlock under the stars
he cannot shift, cannot rescind, cannot
look up into the cave of—

delirium, myopic rockface, the towering
quagmires of infinity
shrunk to a hairshirt—
what ultimatum

binds this certitude upon his back
that once set in place, nothing can alter?
Is even the moon's seeming to loiter,
a half-hearted voyeur,

mere robotry? The wedding party
garroted inside the skull, the
psyche's well-heeled, wall-
to-wall captivity,

the conversation pit a desert: airborne
murder overhead in squadroned
follicles, mad seed of the
purely theoretical,

orbiting as talks continue, with the usual
handwringing: thrones, dominations, powers
adhering to the same unshakable
proposition: nothing

truly is except what overcomes. No
rapprochement: the moon looks in,
moves off again: Orion's
mitered studs once more

abrade the hemisphere. Are all these
rigors fixed, the single step
untakable, the postures of the
conversation pit unfree

to bend, to make amends? Were all
that's still locked up in fright
to shriek, might not some warden, even
yet, unforge the key?

Three   A Gathering of Shades

"I'm very brave, generally," he went on in a low voice: *"only today I happen to have a headache."*   LEWIS CARROLL, *Through the Looking-Glass*

GEORGE ELIOT COUNTRY

For Gordon Haight (1901–1985)

From this Midland scene—glum slagheaps,
barge canals, gray sheep, the vivid overlap
of wheatfield and mustard hillside like
out-of-season sunshine, the crabbed silhouette
of oak trees (each joint a knot, each knot
a principled demurral—tough, arthritic, stubborn
as the character of her own father)—fame,
the accretion of a Pyrrhic happiness, had
exiled her to London, with its carriages
and calling cards, its screaming headaches.

Griff House—dear old Griff, she wistfully
apostrophized it—in those days still intact,
its secrets kept, has now been grafted to a
motel-cum-parking-lot beside the trunk road,
whose raw, ungainly seam of noise cuts through
the rainy solace of Griff Lane: birdsong,
coal smoke, the silvered powderings of
blackthorn, a flowering cherry tree's
chaste flare; the sludge-born, apoplectic
screech of jet aircraft tilting overhead.

The unmapped sources that still fed nostalgia
for a rural childhood survive the witherings
of retrospect: the look of brickyards,
stench of silk mills, scar of coal mines,
the knife of class distinction: wall-enclosed,
parkland-embosomed, green-lawned Arbury Hall,
fan-vaulting's stately fakeries, the jewel-
stomachered, authentic shock of Mary Fitton and
her ilk portrayed, the view of fishponds—school
and role model of landed-proprietary England.

Born in the year of Peterloo, George Eliot
had no illusions as to the expense of such
emoluments. Good society (she wrote), floated
on gossamer wings of light irony, required no less
than an entire, arduous national existence,
condensed into unfragrant, deafening factories,
cramped into mines, sweating at furnaces, or
scattered in lonely houses on the clayey or chalky
cornland . . . where Maggie Tulliver, despairing
of gentility, ran off to join the gypsies.

Violets still bloom beside the square-towered
parish church where Mary Anne was christened;
the gashed nave of Coventry fills up with rain
(another howling doodlebug of fright hurls itself
over); the church from which, refusing to commit
the fiction of a lost belief in One True Body,
she stayed away, upholds the fabric in which her
fictions, perdurable now, cohere like fact: Lydgate
still broods, Grandcourt still threatens, and
in Mrs. Transome disappointment turns to stone.

MEDUSA AT BROADSTAIRS

A seaside place so tranquil
her very mind might drift, grow indolent,
become a tidepool: the articulate spine,
its resolutions and attenuations—all
acquired at such a price—
sweetly let go.

This couldn't last, of course. It never did.

On Saturday the 10th, H.S. came down—
to whom she'd cheerfully agreed
(and let the fact be widely known)
that she was not attached.

No use. The unwanted love-child of a note
she evidently handed him survives. The stored-up
spikenard of ardor in its ungainly vessel—
whole forests of it, bending and shimmering—
again refused. Aged thirty-three
and still so quick to feel, so soon
a rigid gazingstock.

Night terrors. The huge claustrophobia of childhood
starting up again: the dried shriek,
the claw about the windpipe.

Medusa, whether stinging jelly with no backbone
or stare of fury petrified,
in wait: the obscure cold pool
where Hetty, unlikely early offspring of George Eliot—
mindless, adorable, the smoldering dark girl
who must, her fatuous ardor ditched,
be done away with—will not be brave enough
to drown herself, to have it over:

The motions of a little vessel without ballast
(she'd write): the horrors
of this cold, and darkness, and solitude,
out of all human reach, becoming greater
every minute . . . The bitter waters spread,
the Arthur Donnithornes, the Stephen Guests
ride by: John Chapman, Herbert Spencer:

"If you become attached to someone else"
(she ignominiously writes) "then I must die."

There will be more: the sudden cold
about the knees, the inundated threshold,
Maggie Tulliver awake, borne outward
by (recurring nightmare of her childhood)
the actual surge: the same dark girl
grown tall and mindful, whose excesses
must be done away with, drowned.

George Eliot is not yet, Hetty Sorel not yet,
nor Maggie Tulliver, except (If you
become attached to someone else . . .)
in aching embryo. Only
long-faced, brainy Marian, prone
to hysterics. Back in London,
the usual observances—four walls
closing in, headache that lasts an age—
are sure to follow.

HIGHGATE CEMETERY

Laid in unconsecrated ground, a scandal
still—note how good Gerard Hopkins
recoiled from what a queer, awkward girl,
frail-shouldered, massive, rickety,
volcanic, out of an unconsecrated
attachment, a marriage that was
no marriage (one would have added,
till opprobrium intervened, *but
something better*) to a pockmarked
lightweight of a drama critic,
saw blossom: this domestic improbability,
this moonflower: they were happy.

Happiness: *that*—as it always has been—
was the scandal. As for the uninhibited
pursuit of same, gone merrily
amok, by now, among the lit-up
purlieus of a game show (died
of a conniption, beaming): time
spared her that, though not the cold shoulder,
the raw east wind, fog, the roar that issues
from the other side of silence; not headache,
kidney stone, the ravages of cancer—or
of grief foreseen, met with, engulfed by,
just barely lived through.

Nature (she'd written, years before) *repairs
her ravages, but not all. The hills
underneath their green vestures bear
the marks of past rending.* Johnny Cross,
younger by two decades, a banker,
athletic, handsome, read Dante with her,
fell in love; repeatedly, distressingly,
spoke of marriage, was at last accepted.
Another scandal—in the eyes of devotees
who looked on marrying at all with horror
as for the breathing fishbowl of appearances.
Grotesque, my dear. An episode in Venice,
on their honeymoon (who knows what makes any
of us do what we do?) was somehow weathered.
Then, in six months, she was dead.

At Highgate, the day she was buried,
a cold rain fell, mixed with snow. Slush
underfoot. Mud tracked inside the chapel.
Her brother Isaac, more than twenty years estranged
(a ravage never healed), was there
among the mourners—hordes of them,
the weather notwithstanding. Edith Simcox,
crazed with devotion to this woman who'd been,
in her ill-favored way, so beautiful, arrived
with a nosegay of violets, wandered off distracted
into the dusk, came to herself finally
at a station she didn't recognize,
somewhere in Hampstead.

In rain-wet May, not quite a century later—
cow parsley head-high, the unkempt
walks a blur, faint drip of birdsong,
ivy taking over—the stone is hard to find.
Herbert Spencer, a creature of exemplary
good sense, however ill-equipped
for rapture, lies buried not far off,
his monumental neighbor a likeness
of Karl Marx, egregious in granite—
godfather of such looked-for victories
over incorrigible Nature, his memory red
with nosegays ribboned in Chinese.

MARGARET FULLER, 1847

In this her thirty-seventh year, the Italy
she'd discerned already smoldering,
through some queer geological contortion,
beneath a New World crust, abruptly ceased
to be a metaphor. She was in Rome,
and from her lodgings on the Corso
she watched as things began to happen:
the torchlit procession to the Quirinal,
the flung-out embrace of Pio Nono
from his balcony seeming (at least)
to give the upheaval in the streets his blessing.

By September, in Florence, in Milan,
more demonstrations: that second spring
she'd once despaired of, the kernel
lying dormant in the husk no longer,
the shattered chrysalis, the tidal
concourse in the streets and through the bloodstream
one and the same. Angelo Ossoli, whom
she'd met by chance—the faintly scandalous
perennial adventure that awaits a woman,
of whatever age or status, in such a place—
was now her lover. Without the cause he'd drawn

her into—a mutilated Italy made whole,
at peace within, left to itself at last,
the hated foreign uniforms gone home—
she'd once again have kept her head,
perhaps: remained unconscionably chaste,
seen the admirer she'd somehow led on
pull back bewildered as, her self-esteem
gone numb, she worked at being noble.
Not now. Not in this place. The furnace
that had scathed her solitude burned with the torches,
glowed in the votive banks lit by the faithful.

The two of them went frequently to Mass;
on long excursions into the countryside
inhaled the reek of grapes still on the vine,
observed the harvest. The violets and roses
that still bloomed made her bedroom sweet
all through November. "I have not been so well,"

she wrote her mother, "since I was a child, nor
so happy ever." *Nor so happy ever.* Short of money,
she lived now in one room, on fruit, bread,
a little wine; saw few acquaintances,
dissembled, as she'd so often done, even with those.

The mild days shrank. A season ended.
Nor so happy ever. In mid-December
a cold, steady rain began. Increasingly
the high-walled towers along the Corso
shut out the daylight. *Since I was a child:*
then there had been terror
in the night, as now: she'd wake
alone to find herself back in Nantasket,
where she'd dreamed her mother dead,
re-dreamed her best friend's body lying
on hard sand, until the waves reclaimed it,

drowned. Brave metaphor of tides became,
lodged in that sullen dark, a heaving
succubus of mud. The street-corner
flower vendors disappeared.
Lamplit all day, the stale cul-de-sac
she could not leave now stank of charcoal
and the chamber pot. Migraine, a vengeful
ever-since-childhood doppelgänger,
returned, with a new kind of nausea:
the body so little of her life had ever
found sweetness in, life for its own inexorable

purposes took over. "A strange lilting lean
old maid," Carlyle had called her—though
not nearly such a bore as he'd expected.
What would Carlyle, what would straitlaced
Horace Greeley, what would fastidious
Nathaniel Hawthorne, what would all Concord,
all New England and her own mother
say now? An actuality more fraught
than any nightmare: terrors of the sea,
of childbirth, the massive, slow,
unending heave of human trouble.

Injustice. Ridicule. What did she *do?*
it would be asked (as though that mattered).
Gave birth. Lived through a revolution.
Nursed its wounded. Saw it run aground.
Published a book or two.
And drowned.

GRASMERE

For Lois Squires

Rainstorms that blacken like a headache
where mosses thicken, and the mornings
smell of jonquils, the stillness
of hung fells thronged with the primaveral
noise of waterfalls—contentment
pours in spate from every slope; the lake fills,
the kingcups drown, and still it rains,
the sheep graze, their black lambs bounce
and skitter in the wet: such weather
one cannot say, here, why
one is still so happy.

Cannot say, except it's both so wild
and so tea-cozy cozy, so snugly
lush, so English.

A run-into-the-ground complacency nonetheless
is given pause here. At Dove Cottage
dark rooms bloom with coal fires; the backstairs
escape hatch into a precipitous small orchard
still opens; bedded cowslips, primroses,
fritillaries' checkered, upside-down
brown tulips still flourish where
the great man fled the neighbors:
a crank ("Ye torrents, with
your strong and constant voice, protest
the wrong," he cried—i.e., against the Kendal-
to-Windermere railway). By middle age a Tory,
a somewhat tedious egotist even (his wild
oats sown abroad) when young: "He cannot," his sister
had conceded, "be so pleasing as my
fondness makes him"—a coda
to the epistolary cry, "Oh Jane
the last time we were together he
won my affection . . ." What gives one
pause here—otherwise one might not
care, as somehow one does,
for William Wordsworth—
is Dorothy.

"Wednesday. . . . He read me his poem. After dinner
he made a pillow of my shoulder—I read to him
and my Beloved slept."

The upstairs bedroom where the roof leaked
and the chimney smoked, the cool buttery
where water runs, still voluble, under the flagstones;
the room she settled into after his marriage
to Mary Hutchinson, and shared with, as
the family grew, first one, then
two of the children; the newsprint
she papered it with for warmth (the circle
of domestic tranquillity cannot
guard her who sleeps single
from the Cumbrian cold) still legible:
such was the dreamed-of place, so long
too much to hope for. "It was in winter
(at Christmas) when he was last at Forncett,
and every day as soon as we rose from dinner
we used to pace the gravel in the Garden
till six o'clock." And this,
transcribed for Jane alone from
one of William's letters: "Oh, my dear, dear Sister
with what transport shall I again
meet you, with what rapture . . ." The orphan
dream they'd entertained, that she had named
The Day of My Felicity: to live
together under the same roof,
in the same house. Here,
at Dove Cottage.

"A quiet night. The fire flutters, and
the watch ticks. I hear nothing else
save the breathing of my Beloved . . ."

Spring, when it arrived again, would bring
birch foliage filmy as the bridal veil
she'd never wear; birds singing; the sacred stain
of bluebells on the hillsides; fiddleheads
uncoiling in the brakes, inside each coil
a spine of bronze, pristinely hoary;
male, clean-limbed ash trees whiskered
with a foam of pollen; bridelike

above White Moss Common, a lone wild cherry
candle-mirrored in the pewter of the lake.
On March 22nd—a rainy day, with William
very poorly—resolves were made
to settle matters with Annette, in France,
and that he should go to Mary. On the 27th,
after a day fraught with anxiety, a morning
of divine excitement: At breakfast
William wrote part of an ode. It was
the *Intimations.*

The day after, they took the excitement to Coleridge
at Keswick, arriving soaked to the skin. There, after dinner,
she had one of her headaches.

A bad one's ghastly worst, the packed ganglion's
black blood clot: The Day of My Felicity
curled up inside a single sac with its
perfidious twin, the neurasthenic
nineteenth-century housemate
and counterpart of William's incorrigibly
nervous stomach: "I do not know from what
cause it is," he wrote, "but during
the last three years I have never
had a pen in my hand five minutes
before my whole frame becomes a bundle
of uneasiness." To ail, here in this place,
this hollow formed as though to be the vessel
of contentment—of sweet mornings
smelling of jonquils, of tranquillity
at nightfall, of habitual strolls
along the lakeshore, among the bracken
the old, coiled-up agitation
glistening: birds singing, the greening
birches in their wedding veils,
the purple stain of bluebells:

attachment's uncut knot—so rich, so dark,
so dense a node the ache still bleeds,
still binds, but cannot speak.

COLEORTON

Again, at evening, the winter walks
supported on her brother's arm—not,
as at Forncett, snatched, fugitive,
but an entitlement, an earned dependency,
the welding of everything somehow since
lived through: her brother's wedding day,
those vows whose undertow was of such force
it laid her prostrate on an unfamiliar bed:
Mary, her sister now, delivered
of three babies—"all famous," declares
their father, who can be a wag, can
quite well write a letter when he chooses,
"for being exceedingly ill-managed":
sweet, stolid, vengeful Johnny; Dora,
a tireless chatterer; and poor Thomas, in
the midst of teething, who cries and cries:
three safe lyings-in, cut through by one
fearful bereavement: washed ashore
weeks after the *Abergavenny* foundered,
the body of John Wordsworth lies
in Wyke churchyard, on the Dorset coast. No stone
marks it. Two years will soon have passed.
They have not gone there. At Grasmere,
every gale that shudders in the chimneys
is his memorial—made the more poignant
by months, night after night, of worrying
over Coleridge.
            Whom they await here,
while the forebodings thicken: worse,
yes, worse even than their brother's shipwreck
(though that has left her shrunken, pitiful
and old at thirty-five—"They tell me,"
she writes, "I have never looked so well
in my life. This *I* do not believe"), the shock
of Coleridge returned from Malta,
bloated, despondent, sodden. The ruined
landmarks of dependency mere breath,
oneself a leaf, a weak vine lifted, dandled,
dropped: the poet's whimper of "There is
a change, and I am poor": to be deprived
for life of what not even she, whose shoulder
he'd made a pillow of, after the labor,

the lying-in of genius: a genius unstable,
large, of little note, sneered at
by the reviewers: deprived of what
not even she can any longer offer! This it is
that throbs between them like an abscess
as they pace, at evening, below
Coleorton Hall.
                        His altered look:
the gray-eyed luminary of the day,
not quite a decade since he first,
leaping that stream, had been admitted
to the startled core of their attachment,
now sunk in fat: the stillborn squalor
of their late reunion, the meeting he'd
repeatedly eluded, more charged with dread
than the stark loss of John, so wholly
to be depended on, so blameless.
Without blame, only an overweening,
hurt solicitude, they wait for him
to end the maundering requitals, the
evasions of an ending, and quit the ruin
that is his marriage; while the hum
and tremor of a blander tie, the bondage
of a new endearment, is entered on
with Lady Beaumont, whom they're beholden to
for this lent space, these walks at evening,
the unobstructed sunsets of which at Grasmere,
"shut up as we are in our deep valley,
we have but a glimpse. . . . On Wednesday evening,
my Brother and I walked backwards and forwards
under the trees . . . until the sky
was all over gloomy, and two lights
(we supposed from coal-pits) were left to shine . . .
I have kept back from speaking of Coleridge,
for what can I say? . . ."
                        They wait.
The Poem of Her Brother's Life, that portico
to the unbuilt cathedral of his mind—"divine"
had been the word set down by Coleridge himself
that day when, listening high among the tarns,
he'd felt the lintel of it soar, heard an
entire design reverberate—that prelude
to a greater undertaking waits. Turned

landscape architect meanwhile, her brother
charts for his patron a winter garden
"which shall present no image of chillness,
decay or desolation when the face of nature
everywhere is cold, decayed or desolate. . . .
We never" (he continues) "pass in our evening walk
the cluster of holly bushes . . . but we unsettle
a number of small birds which have taken shelter
there. . . . The whole Bush seems aflutter. . . ."
His mind wanders backward into summer, to a time
when what had seemed the idyl of dependency
rushed into blossom: "I never saw so beautiful
a shrub as one tall holly . . . near a house
we occupied" (another house not theirs—
how many since those winter walks at Forncett,
the scene of their resolve to live together
under one roof!) "in Somersetshire:
it was attired with woodbine, and upon
the very tip of the topmost bough
'that looked out at the sky' " (a tremor
here—fallacious pathos of the one
red leaf, last of its clan, that dances
topmost) "was one large honeysuckle flower,
like a star. . . ."
                    They wait. Together,
as the older stars come into bloom
above the coal-pits, they look up
and feel the prospect darken.

RYDAL MOUNT

"Now, I must tell you of our grandeur,"
she'd written. "We are going to have
a *Turkey*!!! carpet in the dining room . . .
You stare . . . 'Are they changed, are they
setting up for fine Folk . . . ?' " Yes,

they were changed. One year had seen
comic, crippled Catharine, aged three,
and Thomas, of whom much had been expected,
both laid in Grasmere churchyard; then
their father, already gray and elderly

at just past forty, set in a position:
Distributor of Stamps for Westmorland,
canvasser for the Lowthers, who all but
owned Penrith ("Sad, sad, sad," radical
John Keats would mutter, passing through).

Soon she'd be caught up with him in all
the brouhaha of a bought election. Yes,
there had been a change: De Quincey, so
lately of their household, so innocently
besotted with Catharine, married now

to opium and the simple girl he'd gotten
a bastard by. "Ruined," D. pronounced. And
paid no more visits. From Dove Cottage—
the talk there, the incandescent silences
beside the fire ("I hear nothing else save

the breathing of my Beloved")—indeed
there was a change. Her brother wrote
now, grandly, of Mutability, of outward
forms (unspecified) that melt away
like hoarfrost. Surprised by joy (he wrote),

he'd turned to share the transport—turned
to whom but Catharine, with a sublimity
he could no more come down from than she,
poor mite, in life could walk upright. Aloft
at such an eminence, he'd grown more craggy;

nobody argued with him; much wifely tact
was spent, a whole household of amanuenses
circled him on tiptoe. Reputation sealed in,
spicule by spicule, the old sore wounds—
grief, ridicule, the worm of conscience:

Annette and Caroline, the larger work undone.
Word came that Coleridge was dead. "A long
sit with knitting on my knee," his sister
noted in her diary. Words for the chill
he felt came more slowly: *power frozen*

at its marvellous source . . . Our haughty
life is crowned with darkness, like London
with its own black wreath. There had been
great alteration: that was the year
his sister—the ruin of her youth beset

by mass defections from within the body,
the firebrand of her old vivacity half-
quenched, a hutch of glowworms—in flight
from grandeur, vicissitude, fine Folk,
took refuge in the nunnery of madness.

Fits of verse, poured out from memory.
Churchwardens mocked. Unseemly noises.
Outbursts. Children and strangers kept away.
Small, shrunken, wild-eyed, she'd command
whoever came into the room to stir the fire.

There would be remissions. "News—news,"
she'd write. "I must seek for news. My
own thoughts are a wilderness . . . The
laburnum with its naked seedpods shivers. . . ."
"Stir the fire!" Her brother, poet laureate

since Southey died, obeys her, sits here
with her, watching: a doddering pair, like
gypsies camping out, the way they'd camped
one night at Tintern, the untended grandeurs
of a time gone dim gone dim behind them.

THE ODESSA STEPS

Old lady with the pince-nez whirling,
there on the steps, to meet the bayonets—
would she, given, in that twinkling of an
eyeglass smashed, the option, have gone home
and shut the door before the trouble started,
preferring ikon and samovar to all those changes,
promises of an upheaval far too heady
to be kept: or would she have declared
that to have died there, where the action was,
inhaling an ozone that only in transit
tastes like splendor, was to have been lucky?

Dark mother of an ailing boy, aghast
as at a long atrocity exhumed, the damp
of catacombs still on it: shade
from the same cleft that opened, halfway
around the world, on an Ohio hillside
where shots were fired—a kneeling,
incredulous dark girl's mouthed O
the Soviet cinema's unconscious ape:
a runaway, picked up two years after
for loitering with intent, her moment of
pure grief, fame's discard, an unhoused ruin.

Wheels of the upended baby carriage
flailing, there on the steps, a visionary
metaphor derailed: where are the wheels
Ezekiel saw ablaze, where are the eyes,
the voice, the noise of many waters?
Who looked for openings, for signs
of a new age beginning, finds instead
a shutdown: these gray lives' torpor,
the labor gangs, the litter on the freeway,
fleered-at shapes of windmills gone rotten,
the Satanic millwheels still grinding.

AN ANATOMY OF MIGRAINE

In memory of Annette Leo

I

Inquire what consciousness is made of
with Galen, with Leonardo, Leeuwenhoek
or Dr. Tulp, and you find two hemispheres,
    a walnut in a bath of humors,

a skullcapped wreath of arteries, a weft
of fibrous thoroughfares along the walls
of Plato's cave, the cave walls of Lascaux:
    those shambling herds, this hollow

populous with fissures, declivities,
arboreal thicketings, with pairings
and degrees, this fist-sized flutter,
    mirror-lake of matter,

seat of dolor and jubilee, the law of Moses
and the giggling underneath the bedclothes,
of Bedlam and the Coronation Anthem—all
    these shut up in a nutshell.

Go back, step past the nadir of whatever
happened to divide our reckoning, a fraction
of an anti-millennium, a millennium and more
    ago, and hear Hippocrates declare

the brain is double. Since then, as to
where, in these paired hemispheres, the self—
with its precarious sense of *I am I,*
    with its extremes of possibility—

resides, we've come no nearer than
Descartes, who thought he'd found it in
the pineal teardrop. (Now no one's sure
    what that gland is for.)

Inquire what consciousness is made of
of Simone Weil, and she answers: Pain.
The drag of gravity. The sledge of time.
    A wretchedness no system

can redeem, extreme affliction that
destroys the *I*; nothing is worse, she
wrote. And knew whereof she wrote, who'd
      drudged, with an ineptitude

only the saints would find becoming,
in a Renault assembly line; had seen
the waste, how small the profit, how
      many suffer and learn nothing, how,

as Kate Croy observed (and chose accordingly),
deprivation made people selfish, left them
robbed of the last rags of character,
      preyed and put upon, enmired in rancor.

She'd seen, was not immune, had been there;
had her own cliffs of fall within the skull:
headache, driven by whose cringing thud
      she'd scrupulously noted

a craven urge within herself to cause
someone, anyone, to suffer likewise.
Is the mind divided, as Hippocrates
      declared the brain is?

Did she invite in what all but unhinged her?
She'd known well-being, however threaded
with crevasses; been witness to the white
      stars' stillness overhead, the white

drift of petals from the apple trees: such
tranquil spanglings of the retina of time,
she could not doubt the universe
      is full, that splendors

of entity, of grace past meeting face
to face, project, each one, its fearful
opposite, its double—as each electron
      in the universe its Manichaean

anti-particle: in every molecule of
every nerve cell, such forces within

forces within forces, the marvel
   is that anyone is ever well,

that consciousness is ever other than
a frazzled buzz, one long sick headache.
My father never gave the name of migraine
   to that locked-in retribution

of the self against—against who knows
what or whom? Fenced brutes, barbed wire
and rawhide, fear of a father's anger,
   mere heredity? His father,

to a grandchild seemingly so mild, so
equable, had labored, I would one day
learn, through that same territory:
   days of headache, nights so worry-

racked he thought his mind would go.
Heredity: finally, in a little memoir
impelled by painful rectitude, he'd
   set down how dread

of what had made him made *his* father
by temper hard: got out of wedlock,
the old conundrum—*Who am I? where did
   I come from?*—twice riddled,

learning whose bastard he was, he'd
manfully assumed that surname. Stirred
or unstirred, the generations' cesspool
   fills; the circle of the wrathful,

ventilated, usurps the crawl space:
all Hell's hand-me-downs hung from
the spindle of Necessity, each sprung-
   from-two, spun-out-of-nothing

being crying from within, *I, I,*
while time that bears the thinking
being toward what it cannot bear
   impales it here.

II

Here is impaled—hinge, mirror-image,
cleft, and crossing-place—the hard
world-knot of entity, the One not one
       at all but contradiction,

Nohow and Contrariwise, chiasmus through
the looking-glass: fraternal inter-
twinings, at the very core a battle;
       so the neurobiological

dilemma of the paired, the hemispheric,
re-ramifies—bright, dark; left, right;
right, wrong—and so euphoria gives way to
       spleen, its obverse, as though

the cosmos repented of itself, of all those
promises, all those placebos: the sun-flooded
square, stone blossoming, each canvas seen as
       a live aperture, a space

to step into; then the usual consequence,
of waking to another migraine: three days
in a darkened room, the drastic easement
       of ergot, derivative of poisoned

rye long known to midwives, proscribed for
her too fragile bloodways. (Lift the hem
of medicine, and you discover torture
       and placebo twinned, still there.)

No cure. This happened, was set down.
I read the manuscript amazed. We hadn't met.
Letters had been exchanged, her driven,
       bannered penmanship an

army out of *Alexander Nevsky*—the whips,
the wolves, the keening steppes, the Russian
mother-lap her history had been torn from.
       One day a parcel came,

impeccably hand-wrapped, inside it an
uncrafted something—three sea-winnowed
sandstones, a wave-buffed driftwood elbow—
  from the beach at Malibu.

I blushed, both flattered and adroitly
remonstrated with: the manuscript (so many
women writing books, their scripts unread,
  still hoping for some recognition!) I'd

said I'd look at not yet opened. I opened
it that day—though not before an ounce
of Maine-coast beach glass had been
  wrapped and sent, transcon-

tinental reciprocity—and read it through.
The migraine on the day she was to fly
to Italy, a frame and a foreshadow
  of that volatile chiaroscuro,

a life repeatedly, strenuously, just barely
put back in order—that migraine (*You too!*)
set her instantly, for me, with an elite
  vised by the same splenic coronet:

Dorothy Wordsworth, George Eliot, Margaret
Fuller, Marx, Freud, Tolstoy, Chopin, Lewis
Carroll, Simone Weil, Virginia Woolf:
  a gathering of shades, of

forebears and best friends who'd all gone
to that hard school. Since Homer peered
at Tartarus, we've looked into a gazetteer-
  authenticated Hell, a place for

meeting with—for hearing yet again the
voices of—the dead. The cosmos, looped with
bigfoot odysseys set down in moon dust, now
  gives it no place but in the hollow

of the skull: that Amazon where no explorer
goes except on hands and knees, the strait
last entrance to the fields of asphodel
  where, say, Simone Weil

and Virginia Woolf might meet and find no distance,
after all, in what they'd finally perceived—
what the latter wrote of as " 'reality' . . . beside
     which nothing matters"; she who'd,

at moments, bridged the mind's crevasse: "Lying
in bed, mad, & seeing the sunlight quivering, like
gold water, on the wall, I've heard the voices of the
     dead here, and felt, through it all, exquisitely

happy." Anny, friend by mail, what I would give
for time to talk of this! We met just once; at ease
at once, walked barefoot on the sands at Malibu,
     the blue air that afternoon, by

some semantic miracle, angelic; picked up stones,
observed the dolphins. A last letter, in that script
her unemphatic beauty stanched without a trace.
     Then, in a hand I did not recognize—

cramped, small, precise—one from the husband
who'd survived her: dead in her sleep. No
warning. But she'd known, had written of, in
     one half-retracted note, a premonition.

I miss her. Though our two lives just touched,
the torn fabric of some not-yet-imagined
prospect hangs there, streamered, splendid,
     vague: well-being rainbowed

over a lagoon of dark: all that I'm even
halfway sure of marked by that interior cleft
(black, white; sweet, sour; adazzle, dim), I
     live with shades of possibility,

with strangers, friends I never spoke to, with
the voices of the dead, the sunlight like gold
water on the wall—electron-charged, precarious—
     all tenuously made of consciousness.

ALICE

For an Oxford don, doomed during term to sit
night after night at the high table,
the pardon of a little girl afloat
on an unstygian Thames. No Sibyl
gloomed or ranted at the rabbithole
she entered by—a time-obsessed fussbudget
of a rabbit her Virgil—into the hell
her elders were so grandly glum about.

Persephone and Beatrice among the shades,
she showed the monstrous region underground
for what he'd always thought it was:
the screeching shams, the burbled pieties,
the flummoxes and trapdoors of the mind:
all Oxford flattened to a pack of cards.

Four Attachments, Links,
Dependencies

LONDON INSIDE AND OUTSIDE

Looked back on happily, the ivy-hung,
back-wall-embowered garden of our
pied-à-terre and domicile in Chelsea
seems oddly like some dream of living
halfway down the well that sheltered
Charles Dodgson's Elsie, Lacie
and Tillie—with those geraniums
in urns, that lily-of-the-valley
bed not quite in bloom, those churring
ringdoves, those thrushes murderously
foraging for earthworms: an exterior
so self-contained, a view so inward
that though at night we'd note
faint window-glimmerings eclipsed by ivy,
we seemed to have no neighbors either
to spy on or be spied on by.

Those strolls at dusk, the sidewalks
puddled underfoot, the streetlamps
an aloof processional (a footfall
once or twice, then silence)
at the hour not of the pulling down
of shades but rather of the drawing
in of curtains on their rods, with
an occasional small, to-be-savored
lapse—the glimpse in solitude
of the young woman meditatively
taking off her coat: or of
the table laid, the TV
in the dining room tuned to the news,
a South-Sea-bubble porthole open
on the mysteries of domicile,
of anchorage, of inside-outside!

The night we took the Underground
to Covent Garden, we found the foyer
at the opera a roofed-in waterfall
of crystal, the staircase we sat on
at the interval to eat our ices
carpet-luscious (even to the shod
sole) as a bed of crimson mosses,
the rose-red lampshades erotic

as hothouse hibiscus. Floated
overhead, a firmament of gilt
and turquoise; as that goes dim,
beneath the royal monogram the bell jar
of illusion lifts, and yet again
we're inside-outside: Norina's
rooftop vista (the duenna
furiously knitting) of a hot-bright
Bay of Naples. In the obscurity
of our neck-craning balcony, we
snuggled undetected. Outside there waited
a shivering, rain-speckled exodus among
dark gardens of the inevitable
umbrellas going up.

BABEL ABOARD THE HELLAS INTERNATIONAL EXPRESS

Border halt, an hour out of Saloniki.
Washrooms already filthy. Corridor
a frisson of peaked caps, red-seaweed
postage-stamp outlandishnesses at a
standoff. *Gastarbeiter* bound for Munich

in a second-class couchette: sad Greek
whose wife is sick (he tells us in
sepulchral German), who can't stop smoking—
a brown, brown-suited man, his runneled
face a map of nicotine. Slaves of caffeine,

we hop down, throng the last-chance café (none
aboard the train, none in Yugoslavia. No
food either. Warned, we've brought aboard
bread, cheese, wine, olives, peaches), stoke
ourselves with swarthy oversweetened coffee

while brown man lays in his own supply
of—what? It's yogurt: five, six, seven
plastic-lidded tublets' curded slime. He
stacks them (and we shudder) on the filthy
floor. We cut cheese. He smokes. He can't

stop smoking. By designation the compartment
is *Nicht Raucher,* Ἀπαγορεύεται τὸ Κάπυισμα.
Useless to complain. We're sorry for him.
And anyhow there's a fourth occupant, a
brown man too, who seems inscrutable (he might

be Greek, or might not be) and who, without
apology, murkily, incessantly *ist auch ein
Raucher*—though mainly in the corridor.
Dusk. We're moving. We've crossed the border.
We halt again. We're sots and thralls

of Babel and demography. New ghouls
have come aboard. We scare each other,
telling of papers gone astray. We're passing
through a gorge. The lockstep trudge brings in
new hues, new snarls of peaked-cap seaweed,

old mores, old anxieties: our pasteboard
vitals handed over, peered into, returned or
not returned, repeatedly. It's dark outside.
Glimpses of halted freight cars. Someone
flourishing a flashlight walks the track, to spy

out what spies? what contraband? It's coffee,
someone says. They opened up somebody's suitcase
back there, found it packed with kilo bagfuls. Took
them all. Detained the passenger. We're pouring
wine. Trudge, trudge. Visa control again:

passports one by one are handed back. Mine
not among them. Why? Where is it? Ghoul
shrugs. Trapdoor opening—fright, indignation,
fury, sputtered futile questions. Gallantry
between us: "I'll stay with you." "No,

no. You go on to Munich. You know
you must." I don't believe a word of this, of
course. I take a Miltown. Reiterated gusts
of asking why, dire glee of strangers. Next,
Skopje. I'm being brave. I'm not being brave, I am

in fact behaving childishly. Washroom
so filthy you can't squat. No drinking
water either. Worse: it now turns out
I'm not a martyr. The latest peaked-cap
wearer fingers my shoulder bag. I look

and squirm: It's there. Who put it back?
No way of knowing. "I do feel such a fool.
You won't tell anyone? I'll never live it down."
"It might have been some trick of theirs,"
you say, still gallant. Maybe. I doubt it.

The Skopje passengers flood in. "Komplett!
Komplett!" Our brown companions fend them off.
We settle onto our couchettes. Wake in Belgrade.
No coffee. Hawkers of pasty, tasteless pastries.
New hordes crowd aboard. It's Sunday morning.

"Komplett! Komplett!" All Yugoslavia is traveling,
won't be kept out. The kerchiefed proletariat
from Istanbul, who got on back at Nis, may
be deterred, but not the middle class.
A couple and their little boy have joined us—

sad, tight-garbed, stodgy-prosperous.
Their little boy is blind. Their burden,
shared, is our affliction. Salamander-pale,
he sways, croons, laughs convulsively,
is told to hush; whimpers, subsides again

to sea-cave solitudes we can't envision.
At Zagreb they leave us. The crowds are worse.
"Komplett! Komplett!" No use. Disconsolate
brown man whose wife is sick climbs back
onto top berth to sleep—the one last solace.

His untouched yogurt has begun to spill. A mess.
The washrooms are by now a costive-making,
hopeless *cauchemar*. The Serbs, Slovenes,
Croatians, Bosnians, Albanians, who knows what
else, who swarm the corridors, are civil,

appeal to reason, persist, at last prevail.
Stout ruddy woman; lean, fair-haired, ruddy man;
two small dark nondescripts; one human barrel,
chalk-stripe-tailored, curly-brilliantined,
Lech Walesa–mustachioed, jovial: with these,

till Munich, we're to share what space there is.
They speak some common dialect, we're not
sure which. A bag of prunes is passed.
We offer olives. The conversation grows
expansive: we listen in on every syllable,

uncomprehending, entranced. A bottle
circulates: I hesitate, see what it is,
and sip. Stupendous. Not to be missed,
this brew. It burns, it blazes. Anecdote
evolves, extends, achieves a high adagio,

grows confidential, ends in guffaws. O
for a muse of slivovitz, that fiery booze,
to celebrate this Babel, this untranslatable
divertimento all the way to Munich,
aboard a filthy train that's four hours late!

SALONIKI

For Ben Sonnenberg

Rust-hulled freighters in
a violet bay; lean cats
that slink, finches
that sing and sing;
sunflowers' exotic
hunchback candlesticks

beside the hovel of an
early Christian church,
later a mosque: Byzantium
profaned shored up again,
Ezekiel bird-caged in prophetic
fire's faint shreds, a relic
of the arson of the Turks.

Apricots, sweet cherries,
hazelnuts—what's not
for sale here? Bird-market
cheepings, the interminable
murmurings of doves and politics;
under the arcades of Odos
Aristotelous, the plastic
of a hundred thousand fakes.

VENICE REVISITED

*While the Frenchmen and Flemings abandoned themselves in a
frenzy of wholesale destruction, the Venetians kept their heads. They
knew beauty when they saw it.*
        JOHN JULIUS NORWICH, *A History of Venice*

I

Guise and disguise, the mirrorings and masquerades.
brocaded wallowings, ascensions, levitations:
glimmering interiors, beaked motley; the hide-
and-seek of Tintoretto and Carpaccio. From within
walled gardens' green enclave, a blackbird's warble—
gypsy non sequitur out of root-cumbered
terra firma, a mainland stepped from
to this shored-up barge, this Bucintoro
of mirage, of artifice. Outside the noon-dim
dining room, the all-these-years-uninterrupted
sloshing of canals; bagged refuse, ungathered
filth; the unfed cats, still waiting.
                                To breathe again
the faint stink of this place I had not thought to
revisit in this life; to catch, through shutters
half-latched for the siesta, the same glimpse
of a young girl's laundry—a glimpse half-
preternatural, like an encounter with some
evidence of resurrection: re-entering, to swim
above the mild tumuli of San Marco,
that last surreal upwelling of Byzantium,
is also to disinter the vertigo
of the homesteader's wife who, numb
in the face of the undisguised
prospect of the place she'd come to, drove
a post into the yard outside the sodhouse
to have something, she said, to look at.

11

The place they'd come to—treeless, its sole prospect
the watery skin-scurf of reedbeds, of mudflats
cowering shivering in the dark or sweltering
at noon, no place to hide from vertigo—was no
less desolate. They lived at first
dispersed, in dens of osier and wattle,
hemmed by no familiar dolomite, no tree-blurred
watershed to lift the eyes to—the lagoon
a wan presentiment of the great basin's
vastness—a place for a homesteader's wife
to drift and drown, or else to settle and
grow stolid as a driven post in.
                             Postpiles driven
into the muck of the lagoon—a million-plus of them,
a thousand-plus times over—would one day undergird
the multiplicity of domes, arcades, façades
of variegated marble, stilts for the stupendous
masquerade of history: the Bucintoro
with the Doge afloat, rowed to the cheering
of lubricious throngs, the whimpering
of lutes: a stage set above the windings
of these onetime sloughs, the hidden
thoroughfares obscure and treacherous
as the dim wagon tracks the homesteaders
would inevitably follow into the disguiseless
grassland, the desolation of
the place they'd come to.

III

Magnificence of guise and disguise, of the given
and the taken: that a body thought to be
that of Saint Mark—Evangelist, witness to
the crime that had then given birth to faith,
subscriber to the possibility of resurrection—
had been brought here from somewhere, is
believed to be historical. Whether the box
they brought it in—the filched cadaver,
the purported-to-be-sacred relic—in fact contained
merely another masquerade, has long since
ceased to matter. Maskers, lovers of shows,
of music, looters who knew beauty when
they saw it, who (while others rampaged,
raped, or merely smashed) made off with
the famous four bronze horses, and much else,
they did know beauty: give them
at least that credit.
                          What stolen relics,
sacred or bogus, what odor of sanctity
or of corruption, would the descendants
of the homesteader's wife who drove
that post to keep herself from going
mad, bring home, to furnish and inform
the likewise unhandsomely acquired
terrain she'd come to? What mainland—
if there is a mainland any more for any
emigré's descendants to return to—
can they claim? What's to be said for
their, for our own faltering empire,
our most unserene republic, other
than that while crusaders of our own
rampaged in Asia, one set foot also
on the maskless, indubitable
wasteland of the moon?

MAN FEEDING PIGEONS

It was the form of the thing, the unmanaged
symmetry of it, of whatever it was
he convoked as he knelt on the sidewalk
and laid out from his unfastened briefcase
a benefaction of breadcrumbs—this band

arriving of the unhoused and opportune
we have always with us, composing
as they fed, heads together, wing tip
and tail edge serrated like chicory
(that heavenly weed, that cerulean

commoner of waste places), but with a
glimmer in it, as though the winged
beings of all the mosaics of Ravenna
had gotten the message somehow and come
flying in to rejoin the living: plump-

contoured as the pomegranates and pears
in a Della Robbia holiday wreath that had
put on the bloom, once again, of the soon
to perish, to begin to decay, to re-enter
that dance of freewheeling dervishes,

the breakdown of order: it was the form
of the thing, if a thing is what it was,
and not the merest wisp of a part of
a process—this unraveling inkling
of the envisioned, of states of being

past alteration, of all that we've
never quite imagined except by way of
the body: the winged proclamations,
the wheelings, the stairways, the
vast, concentric, paradisal rose.

PROGRESS AT BUILDING SITE
WITH (FEWER) PIGEONS

Visitors, a lost last remnant,
to the pilgrim shrine
of something neither we
nor they know what
to make of,
they hang in, homing,
above the pit a swiveling
derrick gangles out of—
at its foot, far down,
a yellow scutterer
of an earth mover

engaged in trading
with a red, caterpillar-
pedestaled steam shovel
at street level,
crawfuls (gouged,
precarious, self-undermining)
of the very precipice
it's perched on—such
large gobblings
and regurgitations
miming a

by now obliterated
memory of being fed,
eons ago, atop
some window ledge,
the ghostly lost
escarpment of an
extinguished other country. See
how the winged vagrants
still hover, haunting
the laddered cage's
gusty interstices

like the question no one
poses, as to what we're,
any of us, doing
here: what is this
elbowed, unsheltering,
obtrusively
concatenated fiefdom
we poor, cliff-dwelling
pseudo-pioneers
have somehow
blundered into?

MIDSUMMER IN
THE BLUEBERRY BARRENS

Away from the shore, the roads dwindle and lose themselves
among the blueberry barrens. The soil is tired;
what little there was of it in these upland
watersheds wore out years ago.

This is a region rich only in lilacs. Vacancy
stares from the half-drawn blind of an
upstairs window; the porch sags; the abandoned van,
its wheels gone, rusts underneath the evergreens.

The children are already too listless, their elders
too much defeated, to think of pomp or high jinks
on midsummer eve; instead of pagan bonfires
there will be some drunkenness, some wives will be beaten.

In *bella Firenze,* on the feast of San Giovanni Battista,
young men of good family, in biretta and doublet, the velvets
of a day more ceremonious, if not necessarily happier
or more just, ride toward the Duomo. *"Lei piace?"*
someone, smiling, inquires of a tourist.

And the tourist, here in the city of Savonarola,
is pleased, if a trifle bewildered. John the Baptist
came crying repentance, to prepare the way for simplicity,
for such as are capable of sorrow. To do so, then as now,
was to be labeled a common scold or a public nuisance.

Along the shore, away from the blueberry barrens,
the larger houses are being aired,
the clay courts are being rolled for the tennis matches,
the pleasure craft, their sails furled neatly,
rock at their moorings.

Life is good, here by the shore; simply to look at the ocean
is tranquillizing, a cure for anxiety. At St. John's
by-the-Sea, where the sacrament of the Lord's Supper
every first Sunday is one of the pleasures,
the name-day of the Baptist is absently remembered.

"Prepare the way," he came crying, but the world
was not ready for him. A princess danced
with his head on a salver. Here by the shore,
away from the blueberry barrens, we are still not ready
for such singleness, for so much sorrow.

266

TIDEWATER WINTER

After the treetop-filtered
tangerine of dawn,
the zenith's frescoed-by-
Tiepolo cerulean,

an afterglow of thinnest
autumn-crocus-tinted
porcelain, looked up into
through seedpod-

skeletal crape myrtles:
the light for days
replayed itself in some such
phased transparencies,

then dimmed one morning
to a daylong monochrome
of snow, and on the next to
ground fog's numb,

windless whiteness,
muting the waterways,
muffling the cypresses'
pendulous residues

of other weathers, the
dried chandeliers
of tulip trees, the sweet gums'
dangled pomanders,

muffling the lumberyards,
pine plantations, warehouses,
the hunched or gangling
shapes of enterprises

either with or without
proclaiming patronyms
(here's Nabisco, here's Lone Star
Cement); the loading platforms,

watertanks and power lines. Along
the borders of the cypress-knee-
filled, thawed or frozen
inlets of the Chickahominy,

the locomotive sways and sings
the long single
song, the brayed, incessant,
searching syllable

of passing through, of
always moving on.
Tidewater left behind, by Richmond
the ground fog's gone.

RUNES, BLURS, SAP RISING

In January, shed twigs of hemlock
leave their runic offprint of an
autograph on thawing snowbanks

whose meltwaters go down loquacious
in torques, in curdlings, cadenzas
by the earful. Today, out walking

among the evergreens—toplofty
taperers, cones, puptents—I've come
upon the guarded quiddity of how a

beech tree signs itself, in punctual
lifts, in skaterly glissandos;
how the alder neatly, minutely

rounds off each period with a
catkin's knob; and just now, in an
embrasure of the understory, this

deciduous tightrope processional,
these leaf-buds like a thing afire:
looked at up close, their quasi-

bronze a finely grooved, a paired
and pointed Asian gesture, self-
effacingly inscrutable. What

will it be? A viburnum, green
wings erupting, then a foaming
torque of bloom? No telling—

other than, come April, all
linear pronouncements will be
awash with leaf-blood's delible,
      blurred, tidal signature.

CONTINENTAL DRIFT

As from a freckling on
the paving to a mottling
to a merging blur, the rain
invents a continent of
inundation: or
as the minute, sharp, shining
leaf buds at each
twig-tip of the
linden in the garden
open from translucent
dappling to an overlapping
gloom of green, of
summer shadow
that will yellow

and unroof, leaf
by down-drifting leaf,
into a fallen continent,
a sediment of leaf mold,
the seethe of entity
undoes what's done,
the sieve unselves,
the drift within
proceeds from dark
to dark, from rift to
rift, from mooring
to castoff
off uncharted
continental shelves

THE WATERFALL

Orb-weaver shivering
among the filaments: how many
fibers generated from within
transect the air?

How many hirsute, sightless
gropings anchor
these redwood trees, suffuse
the flowery traceries

of the oxalis? The veining
in this hand, these
eyeballs, the circuitous
and scintillating

leap within the brain—
the synapse,
the waterfall, the black-
thread mane of fern

beside it—all, all
suspend, here:
everywhere, existences
hang by a hair

A HERMIT THRUSH

Nothing's certain.   Crossing, on this longest day,
the low-tide-uncovered isthmus, scrambling up
the scree-slope of what at high tide
will be again an island,

to where, a decade since well-being staked
the slender, unpremeditated claim that brings us
back, year after year, lugging the
makings of another picnic—

the cucumber sandwiches, the sea-air-sanctified
fig newtons—there's no knowing what the slamming
seas, the gales of yet another winter
may have done. Still there,

the gust-beleaguered single spruce tree,
the ant-thronged, root-snelled moss, grass
and clover tuffet underneath it,
edges frazzled raw

but, like our own prolonged attachment, holding.
Whatever moral lesson might commend itself,
there's no use drawing one,
there's nothing here

to seize on as exemplifying any so-called virtue
(holding on despite adversity, perhaps) or
any no-more-than-human tendency—
stubborn adherence, say,

to a wholly wrongheaded tenet. Though to
hold on in any case means taking less and less
for granted, some few things seem nearly
certain, as that the longest day

will come again, will seem to hold its breath,
the months-long exhalation of diminishment
again begin. Last night you woke me
for a look at Jupiter,

that vast cinder wheeled unblinking
in a bath of galaxies. Watching, we traveled
toward an apprehension all but impossible
to be held onto—

that no point is fixed, that there's no foothold
but roams untethered save by such snells,
such sailor's knots, such stays
and guy wires as are

mainly of our own devising. From such an
empyrean, aloof seraphic mentors urge us
to look down on all attachment,
on any bonding, as

in the end untenable. Base as it is, from
year to year the earth's sore surface
mends and rebinds itself, however
and as best it can, with

thread of cinquefoil, tendril of the magenta
beach pea, trammel of bramble; with easings,
mulchings, fragrances, the gray-green
bayberry's cool poultice—

and what can't finally be mended, the salt air
proceeds to buff and rarefy: the lopped carnage
of the seaward spruce clump weathers
lustrous, to wood-silver.

Little is certain, other than the tide that
circumscribes us, that still sets its term
to every picnic—today we stayed too long
again, and got our feet wet—

and all attachment may prove at best, perhaps,
a broken, a much-mended thing. Watching
the longest day take cover under
a monk's-cowl overcast,

with thunder, rain and wind, then waiting,
we drop everything to listen as a
hermit thrush distills its fragmentary,
hesitant, in the end

unbroken music. From what source (beyond us, or
the wells within?) such links perceived arrive—
diminished sequences so uninsistingly
not even human—there's

hardly a vocabulary left to wonder, uncertain
as we are of so much in this existence, this
botched, cumbersome, much-mended,
not unsatisfactory thing.

WESTWARD

(1990)

TO THE MEMORY OF
MY PARENTS
AND MY GRANDPARENTS

. . . And bade it to the East
Be faithful . . .
EMILY DICKINSON

One   Crossings

JOHN DONNE IN CALIFORNIA

Is the Pacific Sea my home? Or is
Jerusalem? pondered John Donne,
who never stood among these strenuous,
huge, wind-curried hills, their green
gobleted just now with native poppies'
opulent red-gold, where New World lizards run
among strange bells, thistles wear the guise
of lizards, and one shining oak is poison;

or cast an eye on lofted strong-arm
redwoods' fog-fondled silhouette,
their sapling wisps among the ferns in time
more his (perhaps) than our compeer: here at
the round earth's numbly imagined rim,
its ridges drowned in the irradiating vat
of evening, the land ends; the magnesium
glare whose unbridged nakedness is bright

beyond imagining, begins. John Donne,
I think, would have been more at home
than the frail wick of metaphor I've brought
to see by, and cannot, for the conflagration
of this nightfall's utter strangeness.

MEADOWLARK COUNTRY

For Doris Thompson Myers

Speaking of the skylark in a New England classroom—
nonbird, upward-twirler, Old-World hyperbole—
I thought how the likewise ground-nesting
Western meadowlark, rather than soar unsupported
out over the cattle range at daybreak, takes up
its post on a fencepost. I heard them out there,
once, by the hundreds, one after another:
a liquid millennium arising from the still
eastward-looking venue of the dark—

like the still-evolving venue of the young, the faces
eastward-looking, bright with a mute,
estranged, ancestral puzzlement.

NOTES ON THE STATE OF VIRGINIA

Ground fog blurring the dogwood,
black haw, sweet gum, sassafras
and hickory along the waterways,
the branches overhead so full
of warblers on the move toward
destinations, habitats they're

ignorant of any need to find
their way to, to explore,
exploit, alter the face of:
prevailing winds, disheveled
shores, the wet brink's tidal
waverings: the branches overhead

so full of small, unfrightened
quicknesses that if you shook
them they'd simply flutter free
in loosened gusts, ink-straked,
eye-ringed, wing-barred, marked
or cowled with dark, or vivid as

these loosening streams—oxblood,
crimson, flame, clear yellow—
from the already stripped, half
stark, half still gorgeous wood-
lands we glimpse in passing.
Glooming through fog, the cypress,

up to its knees in tidal muck,
will likewise stand bare under
the winter rains. The burnished
tenacity of holly and magnolia, the
scissored undercroft of boxwood,
look like permanence. Ringingly,

the mockingbird—a virtuoso in
and out of season—declares
it lives here, unsubjected
to prevailing winds or tides, to
anything it chooses not to notice:
laws, controls, confederations

don't faze its self-assertive
stances: not the stocks, the
statehouse with the Union Jack atop
it, church every Sunday, monuments,
earthworks, battlefields, the vague
repositories of the dead. Upwards

of forty different tribes . . . having
never submitted themselves to any
laws, any coercive power. . . . Were it
made a question, whether no law
or too much law . . . submits man
to the greatest evil, one who

has seen both conditions of
existence would pronounce it
(thus Jefferson) to be the last.
The mockingbird, an opportunist
ready to expand its range where
there's an opening, lives well,

sings in all weathers, gives no
heed to the accustomary collection
of bones, and deposition of them,
in barrows (since obliterated)
by parties moving through the
country, whose expressions were

construed to be those of sorrow:
ignorant of royal grants, crests,
charters, sea power, mercantile
expansion, the imperative to
find an opening, explore, exploit,
and in so doing begin to alter,

with its straking smudge and smear,
little by little, this opening in
the foliage, wet brink of all our
enterprise: the blur of bays, the
estuarial fog at sunrise, the glooms
and glimmerings, the tidal waters.

KUDZU DORMANT

Ropes, pulleys, shawls,
caparisons, tent curtains
the hue of mildew, strung
above the raw, red-gulleyed
wintering hide of Dixie—

rambunctious eyesore,
entrepreneur (as most are)
from away off somewhere,
like the overdressed though
feral daffodils that prosper

under burnt-out chimneys, in
middens, lethargies, debris
of enterprise that's slipped
into the lap of yet another
annal of the poor: deplore

it dormant or, on principle,
admire it green, a panacea
rampant is what's muscled
in—a charming strangler
setting the usual example.

THE FIELD PANSY

Yesterday, just before the first frost of the season,
I discovered a violet in bloom on the lawn—a white one,
with a mesh of faint purple pencil marks above the hollow
at the throat, where the petals join: an irregular, a waif,
out of sync with the ubiquity of the asters of New England,

or indeed with the johnny-jump-ups I stopped to look at,
last week, in a plot by the sidewalk: weedily prolific
common garden perennial whose lineage goes back to
the bi- or tri-colored native field pansy of Europe:
ancestor of the cloned ocher and aubergine, the cream-white,

the masked motley, the immaculate lilac-blue of the pansies
that thrive in the tended winter plots of tidewater Virginia,
where in spring the cutover fields at the timber's edge,
away from the boxwood and magnolia alleys, are populous
with an indigenous, white, just faintly suffused-with-violet

first cousin: a link with what, among the hollows of the
great dunes of Holland, out of reach of the slide and hurl
of the North Sea breakers, I found growing a summer ago—a
field pansy tinged not violet but pink, sometimes approaching
the hue of the bell of a foxglove: a gathering, a proliferation

on a scale that, for all its unobtrusiveness, seems to be
worldwide, of what I don't know how to read except as an
urge to give pleasure: a scale that may, for all our fazed
dubiety, indeed be universal. I know I'm leaving something out
when I write of this omnipresence of something like eagerness,

this gushing insouciance that appears at the same time capable
of an all but infinite particularity: sedulous, patient, though
in the end (so far as anyone can see) without consequence.
What is consequence? What difference do the minutiae
of that seeming inconsequence that's called beauty

add up to? Life was hard in the hinterland, where spring arrived
with a gush of violets, sky-blue out of the ground of the woodlot,
but where a woman was praised by others of her sex for being
Practical, and by men not at all, other than in a slow reddening
about the neck, a callowly surreptitious wolf-whistle: where the mode

was stoic, and embarrassment stood in the way of affect:
a mother having been alarmingly seen in tears, once only
we brought her a fistful of johnny-jump-ups from the garden,
"because you were crying"—and saw we'd done the wrong thing.

DALLAS–FORT WORTH: REDBUD AND MISTLETOE

Terrain that from above, aboard the hurled
steel spore, appears suffused with vivid
ravelings, the highways' mimic of veinings

underground, the fossil murk we're all
propelled by, for whatever term: as with
magenta freshets of Texas redbud, curled

among dun oaks fed on by yellowing nuggets
of old mistletoe, the sometime passport
to sulphurous Avernus (*the golden leafage*

rustling in light wind), though here we hugely
deafen to the hiss of Nemesis: *so turns
the wheel of change; so turns the world.*

DELETED PASSAGE

In the dead of January, while snow fell
dwindling, a lisp inside a drafty flue,
lying in bed alone I dreamed of furnaces.
At the bland beginning there were conferees
in a hired room, the scrape of folding chairs,
a chartered bus, and then a border crossed,
a meadow in another climate: deep
in that alien grass, I turned and saw
and recognized at once—changed, strange,
unrecognizable—a friend long dead,
instantaneity of dreaming fusing
fluidity and rigor, the once child-hater
become a shepherdess of children—nymphets
with madonna faces, their long hair flowing
as they ran, as they came racing
through the foreign grass
to offer us, with all the pampered charm
of their estate, the keys: we sat with them
in kitchens and at secret tables,
knowing ourselves beguiled.
                              And then a change.
There is something I have forgotten: how or why
we are once more on the move, and who is at the wheel
here in the dark, the thrilling foreign dark.
But what, having veered from the ordinary way,
we are seeing, what we are being shown,
is privileged: there is someone
who does not and who must not know
we have been witnesses of what we are now
witness to: dome after dome
along the secret road, enceinte
with scarlet, licking maws.
                              It is too late.
I have looked, I have seen
the stokers hunkering. It is too late
now to unthink the worst.

SEDER NIGHT

When he lost his way in the Hagodah
    they knew: a year from then
the moonlight traveling the bedclothes
    would find him gone.

Rooftop-occluded, the Passover moonrise
    shrinks to a talisman;
memory's thumbed-over congeries,
    year by year, wears down,

goes bald, loses its smell, its senses
    to the denomination of a coin,
a pair of cufflinks in a drawer,
    a wedding photograph, a son—

an only son, an offshoot of the larger
    process of uprooting
from the shtetl, the movement westward—
    the ritual yearning:

Jerusalem: assimilations, dispersals,
    furnaces: Never again!
The vacated bedclothes, the rising of
    the seasonal moon.

MULCIBER AT WEST EGG

. . . headlong sent
with his industrious crew to build in hell.
MILTON, *Paradise Lost, Book I*

An old man bundled into a long ulster
who'd telegraphed and then taken the day coach
from somewhere in Minnesota, having read
about what happened in the papers—"it was all
in the Chicago papers. I started right away"—

Henry C. Gatz, seduced out of his grief
by the arts of Mulciber, now looked about him
and saw for the first time the light and splendor
of the place, rooms opening into other rooms.
"If he'd of lived, he'd of been another

James J. Hill," the old man told Nick Carraway.
No, he didn't want to take the body West.
"He rose to his position in the East.
If he'd of lived . . ." It isn't Gatsby
but his daddy, the unlegendary Henry C.,

who daunts me: docile, unpresentable, bewildered,
not even a has-been, just a never-was-much
out of the past, the sticks, the shtetl,
clinging to each and every one of us who ever
meanly dazzled an un-up-to-date sure loser

with What's What. "He rose to his position
in the East": built a show place, lived
in splendor, and for all whom fiction
cannot disabuse, his fall—no Hurstwood
on the dole—is as the fall of Lucifer.

AT A REST STOP IN OHIO

Forth from the hand
of God, or, proximately,
the cavern of a westbound

Greyhound, the little
simple soul, at no
great distance still

from its scathed and
shivering first cry,
its gasping first, blind

mouthful, here and now
wallows howling, as
though there were no

elsewhere: What ails it?
The dark night of the
little simple soul, without

so much as the resources
to demand to know
Why was I born? is

dark indeed. Bound though
it may be for the city
of the angels, snow

warnings intervene,
to discommode a mother
ebony of cheekbone

and more than comely
but listless to realign
the warp of history by

more than a snippet, or
forestall, when the wailing
stops, the looming torpor—

except from, just possibly,
inside the fragile
ambush of being funny.

IOLA, KANSAS

Riding all night, the bus half empty, toward the interior,
among refineries, trellised and turreted illusory cities,
the crass, the indispensable wastefulness of oil rigs
offshore, of homunculi swigging at the gut of a continent:

the trailers, the semis, the vans, the bumper stickers,
slogans in day-glo invoking the name of Jesus, who knows
what it means: the air waves, the brand name, the backyard
Barbie-doll barbecue, graffiti in video, the burblings,

the dirges: *heart like a rock, I said Kathy I'm lost,*
the scheme is a mess, we've left Oklahoma, its cattle,
sere groves of pecan trees interspersing the horizonless
belch and glare, the alluvium of the auto junkyards,

we're in Kansas now, we've turned off the freeway,
we're meandering, as again night falls, among farmsteads,
the little towns with the name of a girl on the watertower,
the bandstand in the park at the center, the churches

alight from within, perpendicular banalities of glass
candy-streaked purple-green-yellow (who is this Jesus?),
the strangeness of all there is, whatever it is, growing
stranger, we've come to a rest stop, the name of the girl

on the watertower is Iola: no video, no vending machines,
but Wonder Bread sandwiches, a pie: "It's boysenberry,
I just baked it today," the woman behind the counter
believably says, the innards a purply glue, and I eat it

with something akin to reverence: free refills from
the Silex on the hot plate, then back to our seats,
the loud suction of air brakes like a thing alive, and
the voices, the sleeping assembly raised, as by an agency

out of the mystery of the interior, to a community—
and through some duct in the rock I feel my heart go out,
out here in the middle of nowhere (the scheme is a mess)
to the waste, to the not knowing who or why, and am happy.

ANTIPHONAL

Passed and repassed on the way to Vespers,
a nun-cultivated rose, day-vivid
exemplar of things not seen, concurs

with not only the primordial snuffler
at the root but, also, the apprehension
lodged no one can say precisely where,

of an expanding state of being, tier
on beatific tier, that's entered only
by the strait stairwell of the ear:

the antiphonal, the as-though-single
exhalation of an entire community
informs the hollow, paired, frail,

seashell-like neighbor to the brain's
immured and numerable corridors
with inklings of an omnipresence,

a not-yet-imaginable solstice
past that footstone (O terror)
the unsupported senses cannot cross.

A NOTE FROM LEYDEN

Rain-drenched, Rhine-drained,
cobbled, moated, durable: an all
but innumerable multitude of eardrums
played on by centuries of
chink and clatter, the downpour
from bell tower and flèche
above the flatland: the fragile
polder, each green stanza of
its made earth metrical,
the watery hem, the duneland
pocked, unstable, flowery—
pools at nightfall harbored in
ghost-wineries of evening primrose,
the daylight tremulous,
the North Sea vapors a towering
tumid purple or a slack, ungirdled,
silksack impermanence: nuanced,
cloudbanklike dishevelings
of silver poplar, the undersides
of willows mercurial above
the waterways, a colloquy
with something tugged at
elsewhere, otherwise:
                              Arise, arise
and to your scattered bodies go . . .
Out of the hinterland an already
halfway disembodied circumstance,
out of the fleeing, the reckless
habitat of past sensation: *All*
whom the flood did . . .
                              The flood,
an inkling of it: far from this
moated, painterly estrangement
a night of roaring, the morning
dimly sodden: never had there been
such rain—the creek below the garden
swollen, sheeted, the willow foliage
we'd unimaginably played in the shade of
a muddied den of drowning. *Whom*
the flood did, and fire shall
o'erthrow . . .

Not elsewhere,
not otherwise: in that same
hinterland, one schoolday a sick
lilac haze that came, they said,
from forests burning somewhere
to the north. (How far? I'd never
seen a forest.) On the morrow
a bleared thickening, the whole
world gone yellow. At noon
schoolbuses came to take us home.
Such dark, such howling under
the sun, was Biblical. John Donne
had not considered dust storms. Nor
had, here in Leyden, William Brewster,
with his flock of souls. The Dutch
from their drenched enclave at
the brink of empire could not
have done so. And we? We were,
and did not know we were, the future
no forefather could precisely, could
even flickeringly foresee.

HAVING LUNCH AT BRASENOSE

Possible by now, one would suppose,
to look out, coming down from London,
at the wheatfield poppies, the dogrose
    and elder, the water meadows,

and after the foursquare nightmare
of cooling towers at Didcot, again
at the occluded, sliding signature
    of domes, finials and spires,

with no particular pang or tremor
for what one had been—irretrievably,
it seemed then to a dazed latecomer—
    so long ago undone by:

the burgeoning of stone, the shiver
everywhere—it was spring, with the
English chill, and one was very young—
    of the longstanding:

sequesterer of such carelessness,
such poise, lit up by the dazzling
gaze of him with whom one was, of
    course, at once in love

overwhelmingly, cravenly half aware
even then it was no merely erotic
trap one had fallen into, it was
    centuries of enclosure,

it was the walls, not the riotous
break-in of all that was happening,
mainly, in one's own imagination:
    the fact of brass,

the shapeliness, the perpendicular
heft of the Bodleian, the Radcliffe Camera's
hovering poise, yes, and the hard nose
    of the eponymous

brazen lion one has now the luck
of another look at, decades later—
to uncover, lodged in a bedrock
   older than marble or

the bronze of monuments, this
brazen waif, this changeling—
the intransigeance, the airy
   indignity of being young.

WESTWARD

For Anthony Kemp

Distance is dead. At Gatwick, at Heathrow
the loud spoor, the grinding tremor,
manglings, accelerated trade routes

in reverse: the flyblown exotic place,
the heathen shrine exposed. A generation
saw it happen: the big-eyed, spindling

overleapers of the old slow silk route
shiver in terylene at Euston, grimed
caravansary of dispersal, where a lone

pigeon circles underneath the girders,
trapped in the breaking blur of sound waves—
a woman's sourceless voice interminably

counting off the terminals, a sibyl's
lapful of uncertainties. There's trouble
to the north, the trains are late: from

knotted queues the latest émigrés
of a spent Commonwealth look up: so many,
drawn toward what prospect, from what

point of origin? Bound for Iona in
the Western Isles, doleful, unlulled
by British Rail, lying awake I listen

to the clicking metronome as time
runs out, feeling the old assumptions,
aired, worm-tunneled, crumble,

thinking of the collapse of distance:
Proust's paradise of the unvisited,
of fool's-gold El Dorado. At Glasgow

there's still trouble, but the train
to Oban's running. Rain seeps in;
past the streaked, streaming pane,

a fir-fringed, sodden glimpse, the
verberation of a name: Loch Lomond.
"Really?" The callow traveler opposite

looks up, goes back to reading—yes,
it really is Thucydides: hubris,
brazen entitlements, forepangs of

letting go, all that. At Oban, a wet
trek to the ferry landing, where a
nun, or the daft counterfeit of one

(time runs out, the meek grow jaded,
shibboleths of piety no guarantee):
veil and wimple above dank waterproof,

nun-blue pantsuit protruding—lugs
half a dozen satchels ("tinned things
you can't get up here"), has misplaced

her ticket, is so fecklessly egregious
it can't (or could it, after all?) be
contraband. From Craignure, Isle of Mull,

a bus jolts westward, traversing, and
it's still no picnic, the slow route
Keats slogged through on that wet

walking tour: a backward-looking
homage, not a setting forth, as for
his brother George, into the future:

drowned Lycidas, whether beyond the
stormy . . . And of course it rained,
the way it's doing as I skitter up

the cleated iron of the gangway at
Fionnphort; Iona, an indecipherable
blur, a slosh of boots and oilskins,

once landed on, is even wetter.
Not that it always rains: tomorrow
everything will be diaphanous

as the penumbra of a jellyfish:
I'll ride to Staffa over tourmaline
and amethyst without a wrinkle;

will stand sun-warmed above the bay
where St. Columba made his pious landfall,
the purple, ankle-deep, hung like a mantle

on the starved shoulder of the moor.
Heather! I'd thought, the year I first
set foot, in Maine, among blueberries'

belled, pallid scurf; then—But there's
no heather *here*. Right to begin with:
botanically, they're all one family.

I saw that pallor, then, as an attenuation
in the west: the pioneers, the children's
children of the pioneers, look up from

the interior's plowed-under grassland,
the one homeland they know no homeland
but a taken-over turf: no sanction, no cover

but the raveled sleeve of empire: and yearn
for the pristine, the named, the fabulous,
the holy places. But from this island—

its nibbled turf, sheep trails, rabbit
droppings, harebells, mosses' brass-
starred, sodden firmament, the plink

of plover on that looped, perennial,
vast circumnavigation: at ground level
an incessant whimpering as everything,

however minuscule, joins the resistance
to the omnipresent wind—the prospect
is to the west. Here at the raw edge

of Europe—limpet tenacities, the tidal
combings, purplings of kelp and dulse,
the wrack, the blur, the breakup

of every prospect but turmoil, of
upheaval in the west—the retrospect
is once again toward the interior:

backward-looking, child of the child
of pioneers, forward-slogging with
their hooded caravels, their cattle,

and the fierce covered coal of doctrine
from what beleaguered hearth-fire of
the Name, they could not speculate,

such was the rigor of the Decalogue's
Thou Shalt Not—I now discover that
what looked, still looks, like revelation

was not hell-fire, no air-splintering
phosphorus of injunction, no Power,
no force whatever, but an opening

at the water's edge: a little lake,
world's eye, the mind's counterpart,
an eyeblink of reflection wrung from

the unreflecting seethe and chirr and
whimper of the prairie, the wind-
stirred grass, incognizant incognito

(all flesh being grass) of the mind's
resistance to the omnipresence of what
moves but has no, cannot say its name.

There at the brim of an illumination
that can't be entered, can't be lived in—
you'd either founder, a castaway, or drown—

a well, a source that comprehends, that
supersedes all doctrine: what surety,
what reprieve from drowning, is there,

other than in names? The prairie eyeblink,
stirred, grows murmurous—a murderous,
a monstrous world rimmed by the driftwood

of embarkations, landings, dooms, conquests,
missionary journeys, memorials: Columba
in the skin-covered wicker of that coracle,

lofting these stonily decrepit preaching
posts above the heathen purple; in their
chiseled gnarls, dimmed by the weatherings

of a millennium and more, the braided syntax
of a zeal ignited somewhere to the east,
concealed in hovels, quarreled over,

portaged westward: a basket weave, a
fishing net, a weir to catch, to salvage
some tenet, some common intimation for

all flesh, to hold on somehow till
the last millennium: as though the routes,
the ribbonings and redoublings, the

attenuations, spent supply lines, frayed-
out gradual of the retreat from empire, all
its castaways, might still bear witness.

Two Habitats

GRASSES

Undulant across the slopes
a gloss of purple
day by day arrives to dim
the green, as grasses

I never learned the names of—
numberless, prophetic,
transient—put on a flowering
so multiform, one

scarcely notices: the oats grow tall,
their pendent helmetfuls
of mica-drift, examined stem
by stem, disclose

alloys so various, enamelings
of a vermeil so
craftless, I all but despair of
ever reining in a

metaphor for: even the plebeian
dooryard plantain's
every homely cone-tip earns a
halo, a seraphic

hatband of guarantee that
dying, for
the unstudied, multitudinously,
truly lowly,

has no meaning, is nothing
if not flowering's
swarming reassurances of one
more resurrection.

ALDERS

The roadway's sallow, puddled furrow
uncurls like a root among the alders,
then flops up where the granite surfaces,
a bare outcrop. Alders are hard to stop—
impossible, even, unless you're really serious.

Someone who wasn't, from the look
of it, has done a little hacking at them
along the edges; but to deal with the alder—
the way it's dealt with down by the inlet—
means slash and burn, year by year by year.

It's not only the alders. Nothing's
the way it was. The jack pine's closing in—
a herd of brassy, burgeoning antlers
now bars the opening down to the shore.
Cut off, branch-stung, I find myself in tears

for all sorts of likely and unlikely reasons.
We try another way, between green-creamy
headlamps of mountain ash, wet peat moss
underfoot, dim elegiac voices of white-
throated sparrows above a dwindling trace

we halfway recognize, to a high ledge
where we once picnicked—a tight, finical
medallion that turns out to be a bench mark
setting its seal on the would-be primeval,
while everywhere the alders take the tundra back,

take back the fields and the four cellar holes
left by the settlers who made it their business,
come spring, to clear away the winter's frost-
heaved boulders, and to keep down the alders.
I'd once supposed these acres had no past—

that entity, no virgin, bled with the season,
burgeoned, withered, bloomed and bled again,
uninterfered with, like the pattern of a dance,
not the unarmed uprising of this
landlock, these tough true inhabitants.

BLUEBERRYING IN AUGUST

Sprung from the hummocks
of this island, stemmed,
sea-spray-fed chromosomes
trait-coded, say, for eyes
of that surprising blue
some have, that you have:
they're everywhere, these
mimic apertures the color
of distances, of drowning—

of creekside bluebells
islanded in the lost world
of childhood; of the
illusory indigo that moats
these hillocks when
the air is windless.

Today, though, there is
wind: a slate sag occludes
the afternoon with old,
hound-throated mutterings.
Offshore, the lighthouse
fades to a sheeted,
sightless ghost. August
grows somber. Though the blue-
eyed chromosome gives way,
living even so, minute to
minute, was never better.

THE BEACH PEA

For Susan Rich Sheridan

That first summer, what little
we'd learned of the geography
kept its own counsel—a vaporous
drip and sob, the whistle buoy
lowing offshore, the mittened
treacheries of ledge and tidefall,
mysteries of repose lapped and
delivered in a shawl of breakers.
Blundering through fog, late
one day, along an alder-bordered
track disclosed a meadow, at
its seaward edge a house,
its looming, boarded-up remoteness
big with soliloquy.
                    A decade later
we skirted that same meadow, in
daisy-freckled sunshine, to find her
kerchiefed, statuesque
among the rocks—a collie
her one companion where
the beach pea flourished
untended, garish in the midst of
such concussion and dismemberment,
tide after tide, gale after gale; the house
behind her, its now unshuttered
solitudes delivered into daylight,
and back of that the larger
solitude of alder pockets, snarled
spruce, tamarack, pincushion
plush and calico of heath plants,
rockbottom footholds of the
purple iris, the sphagnum deeps,
small vivid orchids with
their feet in quicksand.
                        Before her,
poised at the edge—the day
was one of bone-white splendor,
a slow surf filleting the blue—
lay a view such as one comes to
be at home with, to rest in,
intimate as with the hollows of
a lover's body: needled diadem

and fractured granite centered,
as in an altarpiece with kneeling
figures, on the inverted pendant
of 'Tit Manan light, its turning
gaze above the driftwood
phased like a moon.
                    No sometime
visitor, by then, she'd come, drawn
by some such perception (she herself
was never so explicit) to live here;
come in fact—though we'd not, from
any hint of hers, have guessed—
to die here.
                    The weight of an
adieu, each summer, overhangs
the solstice—the weightier,
the more immaculate the daylight's
interfusing blue. Some throb
of sorrow, of the apprehended
and consented to, reproved
our quashed tiff (we'd been bickering,
the two of us, for days) the day
we saw her last, that summer,
that serene, last,
perfect afternoon.
                    Word came
in January: she might just possibly
live through the spring. Midsummer,
that year, found us in Northumberland:
white midnights, gray days
of drizzle, the laburnum's
golden dross on all the sidewalks—
kin of broom and gorse, of
the acacia, the beach pea . . .
The beach pea! That, in retrospect,
was the connection: tough,
ubiquitous, perennial, intimate
of granite and driftwood, of all
those ponderous displacements
at the edge: so unaspiring,
so mundane, except—
except for, looked at
up close, those tendrils,
those reaching rings
that now encircle nothing.

HIGH NOON

The poplars gray as a ghost by the creek,
fiddlehead coils still in fuzz, the spruces
tipped fingerling green, tamaracks gauzing
the bog, the aspens translucent, a tremor
      lit from within—oh, and the air

here, the sea air an easterly rinsing
of appletrees so decrepit, so crabbed
at the knuckle, it's a wonder they manage
to keep it up, year after year, though
      the fragrance is ageless:

carmine love-knots unclenching to a rose-
pink pucker that whitens as it breaks open,
admitting the offices of pollen-combing, nectar-
siphoning bees: all these, at the beginning
      of June, one could count on,

could even halfway ignore, as one tends to
ignore the ubiquitous roadside spindrift
of the cinquefoil—spreading, prodigal,
threadily elaborate rehearsal in minuscule
      of the roses to follow:

all this is dependable, companionable even,
in its way, as the weather is—the gales
and the fog, if you're not a fisherman. What
we've tended, cravenly, to shy away from is
      the dolor of the particular:

who's not speaking to whom, who's ailing
and doesn't get out any more, who's still
around and who's not. We've seen Lorna
out weeding her dahlia bed, we've noted
      her tough old tomcat

snoozing as usual at the door of her trailer,
and though she complains that with her back
and all she's not good for much, she seems
cheerful as ever. It's about Amanda
      we keep putting off inquiring

as the days pass, and the poplars are out
of their dim natal down, the shade's
a deckled gallery of ferns, the woodwind
tremolo of the first of June is subsumed
     by the monotone of midsummer,

and while the cinquefoil blooms and blooms
as though time had no meaning, and
the last limp tatters have frayed from
the appletrees, and in the air, here and there,
     the smell of roses is already

voluptuous, one day we meet her, out walking:
still light of foot as a girl, not a thread
of white in the nest under the hairnet, though
it's thirteen years since Ned died, and
     she still wakes up screeching

sometimes in the night, it's so lonesome
there in that childless, scrubbed, painfully
immaculate house; and the sidelong indigo
of her look—what an incorrigible flirt she
     still is!—has closed down now

to a pinpoint, she can't see to piece together
another quilt block, embroider a pillowcase, or
do wildflower watercolors the way she used to; but
she hasn't ceased to keep track of what's opening
     by the roadsides; just yesterday,

she tells us, she went over to the neighbors'
with a bouquet in her hand, announcing,
"What this house needs is pink roses!"
Down by the shore, where we are, there are
     masses of *Rosa rugosa,*

which thanks to some spin of the chromosomes,
instead of the gaudy usual quasi-magenta
come out (with just the slightest
hint of a blush in the bud beforehand)
     moon-white at high noon,

and strange. In a blown-up photograph she
once showed us, it's that time of day, she's
gone down to the beach with a girlfriend,
and there she is, laughing, unmistakably
   ravishing, in that welter

of foliage and thorns and silk uncrumpling,
moon-white at high noon, as though when the sun
leaves the zenith (if it ever does) of that
monochrome, it will utter its frivolous last
   gasp in a smother of roses.

A WHIPPOORWILL IN THE WOODS

Night after night, it was very nearly enough,
they said, to drive you crazy: a whippoorwill
in the woods repeating itself like the stuck groove
of an LP with a defect, and no way possible
      of turning the thing off.

And night after night, they said, in the insomniac
small hours the whipsawing voice of obsession
would have come in closer, the way a sick
thing does when it's done for—or maybe the reason
      was nothing more melodramatic

than a night-flying congregation of moths, lured in
in their turn by house-glow, the strange heat
of it—imagine the nebular dangerousness, if one
were a moth, the dark pockmarked with beaks, the great
      dim shapes, the bright extinction—

if moths are indeed, after all, what a whippoorwill
favors. Who knows? Anyhow, from one point of view
insects are to be seen as an ailment, moths above all:
the filmed-over, innumerable nodes of spun-out tissue
      untidying the trees, the larval

spew of such hairy hordes, one wonders what use
they can be other than as a guarantee no bird
goes hungry. We're like that. The webbiness,
the gregariousness of the many are what we can't abide.
      We single out for notice

above all what's disjunct, the way birds are,
with their unhooked-up, cheekily anarchic
dartings and flashings, their uncalled-for color—
the indelible look of the rose-breasted grosbeak
      an aunt of mine, a noticer

of such things before the noticing had or needed
a name, drew my five-year-old attention up to, in
the green deeps of a maple. She never married,
believed her cat had learned to leave birds alone,
      and for years, node after node,

by lingering degrees she made way within for
what wasn't so much a thing as it was a system,
a webwork of error that throve until it killed her.
What is health? We must all die sometime.
      Whatever it is, out there

in the woods, that begins to seem like
a species of madness, we survive as we can:
the hooked-up, the humdrum, the brief, tragic
wonder of being at all. The whippoorwill out in
      the woods, for me, brought back

as by a relay, from a place at such a distance
no recollection now in place could reach so far,
the memory of a memory she told me of once:
of how her father, my grandfather, by whatever
      now unfathomable happenstance,

carried her (she might have been five) into the breathing night.
"Listen!" she said he'd said. "Did you hear it?
That was a whippoorwill." And she (and I) never forgot.

A WINTER BURIAL

From tall rooms, largesse of peonies,
the porches summercool, the bed upstairs
immaculate in its white counterpane,

to kerosene-lit evenings, the wind
an orphan roaming the silver maples,
sudden widowhood: to meaner comforts,

a trumpetvine above the kitchen door,
then one night her new husband didn't
come in from the milking: to the lot

she bought with what that place went
for, dwindlings in a doll's house: to
the high-rise efficiency condominium,

television on all day, to the cubicle
in the denominational home, to total
unprivacy of bed and bedpan, nurse shoes,

TV with no picture or else coming in waves,
a vertigo: to, one nightfall when the last
weak string gave way that had held whatever

she was, that mystery, together, the bier
that waited—there were no planes coming in,
not many made it to the funeral, the blizzard

had been so bad, the graveyard drifted
so deep, so many severed limbs of trees
thrown down, they couldn't get in to plow

an opening for the hearse, or shovel
the cold white counterpane from that cell
in the hibernal cupboard, till the day after.

PORTOLA VALLEY

A dense ravine, no inch
of which was level until
some architect niched in this
shimmer of partition, fishpond
and flowerbed, these fording-
stones' unwalled steep staircase
down to where (speak softly) you
take off your shoes, step onto
guest-house tatami matting,
learn to be Japanese.

There will be red wine,
artichokes, and California
politics for dinner; a mocking-
bird may whisper, a frog rasp
and go kerplunk, the shifting
inlay of goldfish in the court-
yard floor add to your vertigo;
and deer look in, the velvet
thrust of pansy faces and vast
violet-petal ears, inquiring,
stun you without a blow.

A MINOR TREMOR

Lunch hour in flowery,
eucalypt-boled Berkeley:
a spume off the Pacific
just scathed the easy-going sun
as equilibrium
on surreptitious horseback

bucked, dipped, swung
like a censer. A minor
tremor, said the habitué.
I looked about me
with no alarm.
We had been talking

of Milton, I remember.
The oracles are dumb;
with hollow shriek the steep
(he wrote) *of Delphos leaving.*
Not so. The unbroken broncoes
of Horse Poseidon

are the least of it. Moloch
is back, a still bigger spender.
Frenzy's a drugstore commodity.
The lost sheep feast daily
on the scaly horror
with Perrier and french fries.

SAVANNAH

For Bee Close Lane

Not quite diaphanous, not Spanish,
not a moss, weft after weft
depends from chambered
rafterings of liveoak,
green square leading
to green square, from
opening to opening, as
in a courtship—at whose
discovered center leaps
this rose-leaf
relinquishment,
this falling.
          Yes.
To fall. To ripen
and then wither.
That is all.
          Oh, not all
at all. The bed-curtained,
quickening and ripening
dream of the body,
of fair women, torn
by an obelisk
to the Confederate dead:
the ramparts breached,
the powder magazine's
uproar, the maimed,
sullen giving way,
inform these
mansionings.
          A stillness
out there, past thicketings
of juniper, bullbrier
and yaupon, flailed
thrashings of palmetto,
out past the hiss
of cordgrass:
enveloping
the drop-sleeve
creak of shrimp boats,
a dim, large,
smothering,
incessant
shrug.

AMHERST

May 15, 1987

The oriole, a charred and singing coal,
still burns aloud among the monuments,
its bugle call to singularity the same
unheard (she wrote) as to the crowd,
this graveyard gathering, the audience
        she never had.

Fame has its own dynamic, its smolderings
and ignitions, its necessary distance:
Colonel Higginson, who'd braved the cannon,
admitted his relief not to live near such
breathless, hushed excess (you cannot
        fold a flood,

she wrote, and put it in a drawer), such
stoppered prodigies, compressions and
devastations within the atom—*all this
world contains: his face*—the civil
wars of just one stanza. A universe
        might still applaud,

the red at bases of the trees (she wrote)
like mighty footlights burn, God still
look on, his badge a raised hyperbole—
inspector general of all that carnage,
those gulfs, those fleets and crews
        of solid blood:

the battle fought between the soul and No
One There, no one at all, where cities
ooze away: unbroken prairies of air
without a settlement. On Main Street
the hemlock hedge grows up untrimmed,
        the light that poured

in once like judgment (whether it was noon
at night, or only heaven at noon, she wrote,
she could not tell) cut off, the wistful,
the merely curious, in her hanging dress discern
an ikon; her ambiguities are made a shrine,
        then violated;

we've drunk champagne above her grave, declaimed
the lines of one who dared not live aloud.
I thought of writing her (Dear Emily, though,
seems too intrusive, Dear Miss Dickinson too prim)
to ask, not without irony, what, wherever she
        is now, is made

of all the racket, whether she's of two minds
still; and tell her how on one cleared hillside,
an ample peace that looks toward Norwottuck's
unaltered purple has been shaken since
by bloodshed on Iwo Jima, in Leyte Gulf
        and Belleau Wood.

THE HURRICANE AND
CHARLOTTE MEW

The trees are down all over the south of England—
        the green, tossed
tops of beeches and sycamores in the deer park at Knole,
the Sussex oaks, the clumped pine-tufts in what had been
        left of Ashdown Forest,
upended by the winds of a hurricane hurled in,
improbably, all the way from the Caribbean, on the
        heels of what began
        as an ordinary rain

like the fine gray rain she remembered had been falling
        the day the last
roped bole at the end of Euston Square Gardens, after
a week's work of sawing, dismembering, and carting off,
        gave way and fell,
and what gave way within her, for what was gone, had
a finality that, for her, was apocalyptic, but was also
        no more tangible
        a wisp than the handful

she'd seen the shade-catchers, sister and brother, snatch
        as they ran past.
But that would have been while the great tossed tops at
        the end of the garden
stood, as they were standing all over the south of England
until that night, surprised by some flaw in the flow of the
        Gulf Stream, they fell
by the thousand, the tens of thousands. Ashdown Forest will not
        be the same again.

What persists, what is not to be uprooted or dismembered,
        I would discover,
sauntering there with a girl and a boy with a kite, last year,
        is the vast,
skittish, shade-catching turmoil of more usual English weather—
        the wet, head-high bracken,
the drippingly black-and-gold gorse we sheltered under.
Notwithstanding the great, stunned, fallen stems that lie there,
Charlotte Mew, had she been with us, would have been
        part of the fun.

DEJECTION: A FOOTNOTE

Out of a bow-windowed, mingy, doleful
little room at Keswick—August throngs
moiling wet cobblestones—I fled
offended into worsening weather,

wrapped in a flapping gale's
extravagance, the vestment of an id
that's not at home, that finds no comfort
other than in visions of disaster,

fire, famine, slaughter, shipwreck:
it's there in all of us, as Coleridge knew,
invoking for a surrogate this flailing
at the shores of Derwentwater:

had known since, eight years old,
he fled the prospect of a whipping
he admittedly deserved to some
degree, to hide down by the river,

thinking (half of Ottery St. Mary
out looking for him all night long),
with horrid relish, what misery all
this misery must cause his mother.

Calves stood bawling in the field;
the weather worsened; ponds were dragged;
at dawn he was discovered, rigid, and
borne home. Two decades later,

here in the shadow of the same Skiddaw
(I watch from an unheated loo the vapors
dragged along its glum green velvet
like an udder or a trawl, and hear

that same surrogate, still screaming
worse than a blizzard or a fiend,
as though the date weren't August
but the middle of the winter)

at some recollecting noise, he
found the scene exactly as he'd left it:
the bawling calf, the howling infant,
the self a willful, a total stranger.

EASEDALE TARN

Annuities of peat moss,
sedge, bog cotton, bracken
to be trekked through

halfway up the beck's hung
watershed, today still
unwalled common, where

a sheep, though owned
and earmarked, may
still go astray, may

utter its little cry, or,
suddenly aware of where
it's come to—this crag,

this waterfall, this rosebush
arched and glittering
beside it—freeze,

feel the earth's forward
motion, its hurtling,
harrowing retrograde:

past farmsteads, through
gated openings they,
Dorothy and William,

must also, repeatedly,
have passed through,
bound for the source

of all the babble
down there among the
hollies and the hazels—

the mountain basin
still withheld from
view, though to the

inland-moving gulls
that hang above it
it's in no way secret,

nor is it to these
vaporous tributaries,
nor to the air that's

everywhere the habitat
of rising to just such
occasions as the twain

who once inhaled it, in
this very place, may be
said to have invented—

primeval cisterns'
tremor, the blazing
drumskin of rain.

FIREWEED

A single seedling, camp-follower
of arson—frothing bombed-out
rubble with rose-purple lotfuls

unwittingly as water overbrims,
tarn-dark or sun-ignited, down
churnmilk rockfalls—aspiring

from the foothold of a London
roof-ledge, taken wistful note of
by an uprooted prairie-dweller,

less settled in St. Martin's Lane
(no lane now but a riverbed of
noise) than even the unlikely

blackbird that's to be heard here,
gilding and regilding a matutinal
ancestral scripture, unwitting

of past devastation as of what
remains: spires, finials, lofted
domes, the homiletic caveat

underneath—*Here wee have no
continuing citty*—by the Dean
whose effigy survived one burning.

Three   A Sort of Foothold

VACANT LOT WITH POKEWEED

Tufts, follicles, grubstake
biennial rosettes, a low-
life beach-blond scruff of
couch grass: notwithstanding
the interglinting dregs

of wholesale upheaval and
dismemberment, weeds do not
hesitate, the wheeling
rise of the ailanthus halts
at nothing—and look! here's

a pokeweed, sprung from seed
dropped by some vagrant, that's
seized a foothold: a magenta-
girdered bower, gazebo twirls
of blossom rounding into

raw-buttoned, garnet-rodded
fruit one more wayfarer
perhaps may salvage from
the season's frittering,
the annual wreckage.

THE SUBWAY SINGER

Survivor and unwitting
public figure—a gaunter one
since with her cane, accordion
and cup, I last saw her

tap her hard way along
the hurled col, with its serial
crevasses, of an IRT train,
and heard the cracked bell

of her battered alto rung
again above the grope and jostle,
the knee-jerk compunction
of the herd at the faint signal

it's all but past hearing,
from beyond the ashen
headland, the mist-shrouded
hollows of her lifted

sightlessness—seen waiting
now on the platform, as it were
between appearances, a public figure
shrunken but still recognizable,

she links in one unwitting
community how many who have heard
and re-heard that offering's fall
toward the poorbox of oblivion?

MY COUSIN MURIEL

From Manhattan, a glittering shambles
of enthrallments and futilities, of leapers
in leotards, scissoring vortices blurred,
this spring evening, by the *punto in aria*
of hybrid pear trees in bloom (no troublesome
fruit to follow) my own eyes are drawn to—
childless spinner of metaphor, in touch
by way of switchboard and satellite, for
the last time ever, with my cousin Muriel:

mother of four, worn down by arthritis,
her kidneys wasting, alone in a hospital
somewhere in California: in that worn voice,
the redhead's sassy timbre eroded from it,
while the unspeakable stirs like a stone,
a strange half-absence and a tone of weakness
(Wordsworth's discharged soldier comes to mind)
as she inquires, fatigued past irony, "How's
your work going?" As for what was hers—

nursing-home steam-table clamor, scummed
soup fat, scrubbed tubers, bones, knives,
viscera, cooking odors lived with till
they live with you, a settlement in the
olfactory tissue—well, it's my function
to imagine scenes, try for connections
as I'm trying now: a grope for words,
the numb, all but immobilized trajectory
to where my cousin, whom I've seen just once

since she went there to live, lies dying:
part of the long-drawn larger movement
that lured the Reverend Charles Wadsworth
to San Francisco, followed in imagination
from the cupola of the shuttered homestead
in Amherst where a childless recluse,
on a spring evening a century ago, A.D.
(so to speak) 1886, would cease to breathe
the air of rural Protestant New England—

an atmosphere and a condition which
by stages, wagon trains, tent meetings,
the Revival, infused the hinterland
my cousin Muriel and I both hailed from:
a farmhouse childhood, kerosene-lit,
tatting-and-mahogany genteel. "You
were the smart one," she'd later say.
Arrant I no doubt was; as for imagining
scenes, it must be she'd forgotten

the melodramas she once improvised above
the dolls' tea-table: "For the pity's sake!
How could you get us all in such a fix?
Well, I s'pose we'll just have to make
the best of it"—the whole trajectory of
being female, while I played the dullard,
presaged. She bloomed, knew how to flirt,
acquired admirers. I didn't. In what I now
recall as a last teen-age heart-to-heart,

I'm saying I don't plan on getting married.
"Not ever?" "Not ever"—then, craven, "Oh,
I'd like to be *engaged*." Which is what she
would have been, by then, to Dorwin Voss,
whom I'd been sweet on in fifth grade (last
painless crush before the crash of puberty)—
blue-eyed, black-haired, good-looking Dorwin,
who'd later walk out on her and their kids,
moving on again, part of the larger exodus

from the evangel-haunted prairie hinterland.
Some stayed; the more intemperate of us
headed east—a Village basement, uptown
lunch hours, vertiginous delusions of
autonomy, the bar crowd; waiting for
some well-heeled dullard of a male to
deign to phone, or for a stumbling-
drunk, two-timing spouse's key to turn
the small-hour dark into another fracas—

others for California: the lettuce fields,
Knott's Berry Farm, the studios; palms,
slums, sprinklers, canyon landslides,
fuchsia hedges hung with hummingbirds,
the condominium's kempt squalor: whatever
Charles Wadsworth, out there, foresaw
as consolation for anyone at all—attached,
estranged, or merely marking time—little
is left, these days, these times, to say

when the unspeakable stirs like a stone.
Pulled threads, the shared fabric of a
summer memory: the state fair campground,
pump water, morning light through tent flaps,
the promenade among the booths: blue-ribbon
zinnias and baby beeves, the cooled marvel
of a cow, life size, carved out of butter;
a gypsy congeries without a shadow on it
but the domed torpor of the capitol

ballooning, ill at ease, egregious
souvenir of pomp among the cornfields;
kewpie-doll lowlife along the midway,
the bleachers after dark where, sick
with mirth, under the wanton stars,
for the ineptitude of clowns, we soared
in arabesques of phosphorus, and saw—
O dread and wonder, O initiating taste
of ecstasy—a man shot from a cannon.

Too young then to know how much we knew
already of experience, how little of
its wider paradigm, enthralled by that
punto in aria of sheer excitement, we who
are neither leaf nor bole—O hybrid
pear tree, cloned fruitless blossomer!—
suspend, uprooted from the hinterland,
this last gray filament across a continent
where the unspeakable stirs like a stone.

A HEDGE OF RUBBER TREES

The West Village by then was changing; before long
the rundown brownstones at its farthest edge
would have slipped into trendier hands. She lived,
impervious to trends, behind a potted hedge of
rubber trees, with three cats, a canary—refuse
from whose cage kept sifting down and then
germinating, a yearning seedling choir, around
the saucers on the windowsill—and an inexorable
cohort of roaches she was too nearsighted to deal
with, though she knew they were there, and would
speak of them, ruefully, as of an affliction that
    might once, long ago, have been prevented.

Unclassifiable castoffs, misfits, marginal cases:
when you're one yourself, or close to it, there's
a reassurance in proving you haven't quite gone
under by taking up with somebody odder than you are.
Or trying to. "They're my *friends*," she'd say of
her cats—Mollie, Mitzi and Caroline, their names were,
and she was forever taking one or another in a cab
to the vet—as though she had no others. The roommate
who'd become a nun, the one who was Jewish, the couple
she'd met on a foliage tour, one fall, were all people
she no longer saw. She worked for a law firm, said all
    the judges were alcoholic, had never voted.

But would sometimes have me to dinner—breaded veal,
white wine, strawberry Bavarian—and sometimes, from
what she didn't know she was saying, I'd snatch a shred
or two of her threadbare history. Baltic cold. Being
sent home in a troika when her feet went numb. In
summer, carriage rides. A swarm of gypsy children
driven off with whips. An octogenarian father, bishop
of a dying schismatic sect. A very young mother
who didn't want her. A half-brother she met just once.
Cousins in Wisconsin, one of whom phoned her from a candy
store, out of the blue, while she was living in Chicago.
    What had brought her there, or when, remained unclear.

As did much else. We'd met in church. I noticed first
a big, soaring soprano with a wobble in it, then
the thickly wreathed and braided crimp in the mouse-
gold coiffure. Old? Young? She was of no age.
Through rimless lenses she looked out of a child's,
or a doll's, globular blue. Wore Keds the year round,
tended otherwise to overdress. Owned a mandolin. Once
I got her to take it down from the mantel and plink out,
through a warm fuddle of sauterne, a lot of giddy Italian
airs from a songbook whose pages had started to crumble.
The canary fluffed and quivered, and the cats, amazed,
    came out from under the couch and stared.

What could the offspring of schismatic age and a
reluctant child bride expect from life? Not much.
Less and less. A dream she'd had kept coming back,
years after. She'd taken a job in Washington with
some right-wing lobby, and lived in one of those
bow-windowed mansions that turn into roominghouses,
and her room there had a full-length mirror: oval,
with a molding, is the way I picture it. In her dream
something woke her, she got up to look, and there
in the glass she saw she had no face, or whatever
face she'd had was covered over—she gave it
    a wondering emphasis—with gray veils.

The West Village was changing. I was changing. The last
time I asked her to dinner, she didn't show. Hours—
or was it days?—later, she phoned to explain: she hadn't
been able to find my block; a patrolman had steered her home.
I spent my evenings canvassing for Gene McCarthy. Passing,
I'd see her shades drawn, no light behind the rubber trees.
She wasn't out, she didn't own a TV. She was in there,
getting gently blotto. What came next, I wasn't brave
enough to want to know. Only one day, passing, I saw
new shades, quick-chic matchstick bamboo, going up where
the waterstained old ones had been, and where the seedlings—
    O gray veils, gray veils—had risen and gone down.

THE HALLOWEEN PARADE

Rollicking into Bleecker Street
with the maskers, the sashaying
effigies jointed like mantises
or a cornfield come to town, a rube's
    Birnam-to-Dunsinane,

had been more than fun, had been
akin to a levitation, such as
Isabel Archer of Albany, say, may be
said to have traveled to Rome for—
    or anyhow a speeded-up

latterday travesty of it: to be
swept away, caught up in a spate
of appearances, gorgeous, gorgonish,
déraciné—O saturnalian
    anonymity of cities!

Let it be said: though our grandeurs
were tacky, at least we were honest:
what we looked for was no more
than a license to be silly
    about what matters,

or did once, or was supposed to:
all those tessellated acres
under the dome, the soaring
interior spaces Isabel still
    found it possible

to imagine a meaning for, far
from what, in the hinterland,
would already have been happening:
statehouse domes going up like
    a crop of mushrooms,

gilt and marble for schoolchildren
to be herded under, heel plates
skittering; a hireling amplitude,
its meaning gone: what's there
    to admire but speed,

what's left to look up to but a
rocket-thrust, a sitcom celebrity?
This being what all the rush
of westward-the-course-of-empire
        finally comes down to:

to be free, as Isabel Archer pig-
headedly put it, to meet one's fate,
to take one's chances, try on
disguises, the Dies Irae synco-
        pating to Bye, Bye

Blackbird, How Dry I Am—
to meet the Day of Doom
on roller skates, as every
other masker, that year,
        seemed to be doing:

and I wonder now—having heard
piecemeal what became of him,
as I learned how he'd slipped
and fractured an elbow, roller-
        skating—was he there

too, rollicking into Bleecker Street,
having more than fun, upborne
among the effigies—O prodigious
anonymities of Manhattan!—his manner
        more than ever outré,

as the dwindling of the very memory
of manners tends on occasion to
beget a great deal of Manner—
who was to linger in the oxygen
        tent of his fate

for weeks before it claimed him,
one of many and therefore exemplary?
O reedbed Dunsinane of the undone,
of chances taken! To be free to
        throw one's life away

as Isabel Archer, alone in the
dimmed drawing room of her fate,
would know she had done: O how many
have sat like this: a window ledge
    above the lava flow,

the ice floe, the interminable
howling off the Hudson! There was
the student from some other country
who one night slipped out of her room
    to mail a letter

and was not seen again until,
months later, miles upriver, tidal
currents washed whatever had been
left of her ashore. Otherwise,
    only rumors. That was all

a long, long time ago: out of the
rivering anonymity of cities,
the tidal froth of choices
made, the flotsam of All
    Hallows, washed ashore.

NOTHING STAYS PUT

In memory of Father Flye, 1884–1985

The strange and wonderful are too much with us.
The protea of the antipodes—a great,
globed, blazing honeybee of a bloom—
for sale in the supermarket! We are in
our decadence, we are not entitled.
What have we done to deserve
all the produce of the tropics—
this fiery trove, the largesse of it
heaped up like cannonballs, these pineapples, bossed
and crested, standing like troops at attention,
these tiers, these balconies of green, festoons
grown sumptuous with stoop labor?

The exotic is everywhere, it comes to us
before there is a yen or a need for it. The green-
grocers, uptown and down, are from South Korea.
Orchids, opulence by the pailful, just slightly
fatigued by the plane trip from Hawaii, are
disposed on the sidewalks; alstroemerias, freesias
fattened a bit in translation from overseas; gladioli
likewise estranged from their piercing ancestral crimson;
as well as, less altered from the original blue cornflower
of the roadsides and railway embankments of Europe, these
bachelor's buttons. But it isn't the railway embankments
their featherweight wheels of cobalt remind me of, it's

a row of them among prim colonnades of cosmos,
snapdragon, nasturtium, bloodsilk red poppies,
in my grandmother's garden: a prairie childhood,
the grassland shorn, overlaid with a grid,
unsealed, furrowed, harrowed and sown with immigrant grasses,
their massive corduroy, their wavering feltings embroidered
here and there by the scarlet shoulder patch of cannas
on a courthouse lawn, by a love knot, a cross stitch
of living matter, sown and tended by women,
nurturers everywhere of the strange and wonderful,
beneath whose hands what had been alien begins,
as it alters, to grow as though it were indigenous.

But at this remove what I think of as
strange and wonderful, strolling the side streets of Manhattan
on an April afternoon, seeing hybrid pear trees in blossom,
a tossing, vertiginous colonnade of foam, up above—
is the white petalfall, the warm snowdrift
of the indigenous wild plum of my childhood.
Nothing stays put. The world is a wheel.
All that we know, that we're
made of, is motion.

Four   The Prairie

THE PRAIRIE

. . . her praises celebrated by no one, she is needed by no one, and amid her joyous accents you detect the melancholy call for "A bard! a bard!"
ANTON CHEKHOV, *The Steppe*

*. . . that everything in this life is, in a sense, but a pattern in a carpet.
Trodden underfoot.* JOSEPH BRODSKY, *Flying from Byzantium*

I

The wind whines in the elevator shaft. The houseless
squinny at us, mumbling. We walk attuned
to the colubrine rustle of a proletariat

that owes nobody anything, through a Manhattan
otherwise (George Eliot's phrase) well wadded
in stupidity—a warren of unruth, a propped

vacuity: our every pittance under lock and key
a party to the general malfeasance. Saurian,
steam-wreathed rancors crowd the manholes,

as though somebody grappled with the city's
entrails: Laocoön, doomsayer, by a god
or gods undone. Whom nobody believed, of course.

No, better, as the muse of what's become
of us, invoke Chekhov's imagined Jew who put—
out of demented principle—the rubles he'd

inherited into the stove. Money-burning:
however jaded you may think you are, now there's
a scandal for you. Six thousand rubles,

and he burns them: shows no respect, fears
no one, is a man possessed, the evil sprite
out of a nightmare: thus Chekhov, scandal-

mongering. Grandson of a serf, son of a
storekeeper, brought up to the chink of kopecks
at Taganrog: spring mud and summer dust,

burdocks, beatings, piety. Money and profits:
the mainspring for all of us, except that brother
of a tavernkeeping Jew, who mocks us,

boasting he put his money in the stove.
So Chekhov tells us—who, half a nomad,
consorted with the nomads of Sakhalin—yurt-

dwellers who never washed, who planted nothing,
saw the plow as a transgression; whose numbers
were already in decline; who smelled, up close,

as all unbathed and houseless wanderers do,
of sweat, soil, urine: living nit-encrusted,
matted, shivering. One forgets, here in

half-stupefied Manhattan, how much of everything
that happens happens (Simone Weil's relentless
phrase) far from hot baths. The wind howls

from across the Hudson: lost, lost. Marx
and Engels, Lenin, Red October: since Chekhov
(no ideologue) wrote of the general malfeasance

"We do not care, it does not interest us,"
however much has changed, still nothing changes.
Demagoguery. Boundaries. Forced marches.

Monoculture on the heels of slash and burn.
Land reform. Drought. Insects. Drainage.
Long-term notes. Collectives. Tractor lugs.

Names: brunizem and chernozem; culm,
rhizome and stolon. A fibrous, root-fattened
hinterland of grass. The steppe. The prairie.

A chance fact leaps into place: that Anton Chekhov
came howling (as only the stillborn can
fail to do) into existence at Taganrog

the year my father's father, no doubt howling
too, endured the shock of entry. Add the link
of early memory: the prairie, the steppe—

a shimmering caul of namelessness, of voices,
unauthenticated, multitudinous, in wait
for (so Chekhov wrote) a muse, a scribe, a bard.

II

The year is 1860. February. Still hard winter.
A cabin of hewn logs, on sixty acres
of raw grassland, prairie yet unturned.

One bed. Snow sifts through roof chinks.
Some nights the kettle freezes on the stove.
My great-grandfather gets what rest he can

on a quilt-covered pile of straw. A settler
from Indiana, his mind scarred by whippings;
a smattering of schooling, an appetite for land.

A hinterland of grass: tough, fertile,
root-nurtured chernozem ("black earth"
in Russian), nameless hitherto: lush midriff

of an empire Napoleon, having retaken it
from Spain (who didn't exactly own it) was now
hard pressed to trade for cash: bought in a hurry,

unlooked-at, for four cents an acre, by envoys
who'd exceeded their instructions, but who knew
what was imperative: land so rich, the more-

than-man-high panicles so dense, the nomad
aborigines for centuries had shunned it. Treaties
and forced marches brought them to it—treaties

made by chiefs who knew no better. Boundaries
were drawn; section by quarter section
platted, parceled, sold, speculated on,

built on; torn open, for the first time ever,
by plowshares—shouldering a dimming memory
of what had been, would never be again, aside.

A dimming memory of campsites: skin cones
smoke-stained, the base aglow, the moving shadow
of the life within revealed: two half circles

ranged about the sacred tree-bole, gift of
Wakonda, shining summoner of thunderbirds from
their imagined corners. A dimming memory of how,

toward the ending of the Moon When Nothing Happens,
spring thunder and the early-morning trilling
of meadowlarks returned, among the sloughs

the whooping cranes moved in again to dance
before they coupled—carmine-faced up close,
like painted women—and on higher ground

big-wattled prairie chickens thudded, courting.
All long gone. My father's father, as a boy
prone to anxieties, night terrors, straying

sometimes at dusk in unfenced spaces where
bell-clappered cattle roamed, had seen them—grand,
pagan, dreadful as the tree-bole of Ashtoreth.

The white man does not understand America,
a red man wrote: *the roots of the tree of his life
have yet to grasp it.* A dwindling memory

among the Omaha, a woodland people once,
whose remnant, up close, smell of the usual
sweat, soil, urine, vomit: a way of living lost.

Hard work. The settlers put a beleaguered foot down
against the shiftless, as their forebears had
concerning maypoles and the sanctus bell. Hard

work. Drainage ditches. Fences to keep in
the cattle. Now and then a grown man, entoiled
by evangelical dismay, would cry, "Lost! Lost!"

III

A nerve storm, a lapse or lesion, a blizzard
in the brain: at sixteen, grown up bookish,
hesitant, susceptible, my father's father

would blurt—his little sister looking up aghast,
the half-cleared supper table a bleak witness—
something about being done for, damned to hell—

something like that; to find, almost before his mother,
always the quicker one, could speak, the revulsion
gone; elation following, an astonished lightness.

What did it mean? He was never sure. A brimstone
rhetoric imbibed? A flareup—something in the glands,
like acne? He'd put it, at all events, behind him.

At twenty, wary of certitude, he shared questions,
and a bed, with one best friend. Nights, they
read Emerson together; after the swimming wick

went under, they'd go on talking. What was it
kept him so often wakeful, awed, while
the friend slept—what plank in reason, laid

unbroken, precarious, across the slough
of namelessness, its chucklings, its slitherings,
its shrieks, its spearheaded leaps and lunges?

Egorooshka, Chekhov's child-deputy, cocooned
among the wool bales, crossing the steppe,
heard the uneasy buzz and stir, the turmoil

when the wind rose. *An inlet into the deeps
of Reason,* Emerson had written: *out of
unhandseled savage nature, out of the terrible*

*Druids and Berserkirs . . . We have listened too long
to the courtly muses. In self-trust all the virtues
are comprehended. . . .* Self-trust. Man Thinking.

When—my father's father might have wondered—
was Man Thinking, self-reliant, other than
alone in the vast stammer of the inarticulate?

An absence. Creeks and timber. Wild plum, crabapple,
sumac along the fencerows. Tilled acres. Section lines.
Farmsteads that clot the vacancy, that cannot fill it—

the sense of exile, of something wrong: a dim
compunction finds Man Thinking anxious, as
all animals are anxious. In heath, duneland,

savanna, all treeless spaces, the immersing
sense of waiting, the unfathomable lassitude,
the purling, the quick tenuity of things.

The dead, wrote Emerson, aged twenty-two, *sleep
in their moonless night. All history is an epitaph.
A few days more, and idle eyes will run*

over your obituary, the world forget you.
The tenuity of being: Chekhov, who'd later
become a doctor, down with a fever, crossing

the steppe, tended by that innkeeping Jew.
My father's father ill with typhoid in a
Dakota roominghouse, a jolting two-day train ride

away from home. In that region of wind he'd bought,
with borrowed money, a treeless piece of land.
Back here, he'd met a girl—small, sprightly, husky-

voiced—who promised, when he headed north again,
to write. He found the homesteaders burning hay
for fuel. The season was wet and cold, the wind unending.

By midsummer he'd turned, with team and plow,
the sod of eighty hitherto uncultivated acres.
He took his bride there on their honeymoon.

IV

We have listened too long to the courtly muses.
Perhaps. My father's father, from the spring
he turned the sod out there, preserved a sonnet:

There crowd my mind (he wrote) *vague fancies*
of Aeolian harpings, twined with weird oaks'
murmurings. In those wind-scathed solitudes,

impelled by absence so immense it all but
unpropped Man Thinking, he'd reached for that
old lore for reassurance—as one day a grandchild,

likewise impelled, would travel eastward,
backward to the precincts of grass-overrun,
mere, actual Dodona. A venture he'd

have been bemused by. I feel a halfway need
to justify, to whisper, Please don't disapprove,
don't think me frivolous. Can the courtly muses

of Europe, those bedizened crones, survive
the manholes, the vaunt and skitter of Manhattan, or
consort with the dug-in, the hunkering guardians

of the Dakotas? The Louisiana Purchase
passing (as it were) from hand to hand,
my father's father, having staked a claim

by planting trees there, rented out the eighty,
trekked back with his bride, a homing pair,
to set up as a storekeeper's son-in-law.

The year is 1885. Next spring will see a son
delivered yelling into the rooms above the store.
Still nobody is settled. The railroad

has made people restless. Chekhov too: in 1887,
bound from Moscow to Taganrog, he'd cross
the steppe again, this time by rail; would see

the wheelbarrows, the dugouts where the work crews
lived, mounded under the moon. By spring
of that same year, a railborne exodus

to California, the latest Land of Promise,
of figs and pomegranates, had begun. Whole
neighborhoods were going. In September

my grandparents-to-be would be among them.
From an uncushioned sleeping car, the first
arid glimpse of Colorado. The Spanish Peaks.

A washout in New Mexico. Immoderate heat
and chill. The desert's rigors and mirages.
Then Pasadena. Date palms. Dust. Ramshackle

houses. Gamblers. The bare arroyo. The mountain
wall. Pregnant again, my father's mother
had been trainsick all the way. Pasadena:

the name a borrowing from the Chippewa, who'd
never lived there. Of those who did, what history
there is is an erasure. Called—after the mission

that came to save them, that brought in measles
and the common cold—the Gabrielinos, they sickened
as the mission prospered, came to own the valley,

carved it up and sold it off, rancho by rancho.
Irrigated, planted to vines, walnuts, oranges,
with prairie-dwellers hurrying in, the ranchos

yet again were subdivided and sold off: a pandemic
frenzy of land changing hands. *The country's mind,
aimed low, grows thick and fat:* thus Emerson,

who looked for such as ravished from the East to rise,
to blaze forth in the West. A West that proved—as
one, musing, would later write—to be, essentially . . .

V

Essentially a customer: thus the exile, musing
of empire's westward course, of intertwinings:
everything is, in a sense (he wrote), *a pattern*

in a carpet. Trodden underfoot. The West
(in short) *was offering nothing.* Whatever
it might choose to take, it took: zeal, doctrine,

manpower: all trodden underfoot. No new thing
usage cannot foul. Who was San Gabriel? Who
thinks of archangels, of angels in Los Angeles?

That winter, while blizzards caromed screaming
over Dakota, Chekhov in Moscow, out of who knows
what stored-up fervor and revulsion, for

the money-fond, obliging Jew who'd tended him,
brought forth a disturbed, disturbing, money-
loathing brother, with his strange smile, so

complex, expressive of such feeling, in which
what predominated was an unfeigned scorn.
February, the tale written and sent off, would see

my father's father with a surveyor's transit,
plotting a tract of greasewood and sagebrush—
desert really. The wells there would soon go dry.

The year is 1888; the place, North Raymond Avenue
in Pasadena. Here, where many still lived under
canvas, in a shake-roofed, newsprint-papered

shack, long since demolished, on the sixth of April—
no doubt yelling as we've all done—my father
entered on a scene of which he'd have no memory.

They'd stay, all told, not quite two years.
How can a descendant, pondering this, not
pause, bemused by the fortuity of things?

The fever runs its course. Less land
changes hands; more wells fail. Jobs dry up.
Hired by a grocer, for six months my father's

father handled accounts, while sick headaches
made his life hell. Eyestrain, he surmised
it was. What was he good for but what

he'd been brought up as, a dirt farmer?
Unless you counted such a thing as friendship.
The best friend, best he'd ever have, would

stay on out there; would, unracked by misgivings,
prosper. The in-laws would likewise trade,
seduced, a banshee-ridden interior winter

for living at the edge, with earthquakes.
Living at the edge, or near it, the Pacific
twenty miles away: in all that time they'd

never seen it. Driving, one day, a hired team
to Long Beach, where the descendants of ten
thousand settlers these days throng, they found

a boardwalk, a cliff above the moiling surf,
the sands. What did it mean, that roaring?
Existences, as they listen and then turn away,

tremble: fate, memory, seaweed-clotted
poluphloisboio thalassēs pouring in immense,
immersing all and every road not taken:

the pagan muse, unwizened, living out there
at the edge, with earthquakes, not to be
counted on. They listen, turn away, head east

toward an interior without a rim, an absence
that can, and does, unsettle—my father's
mother motion-sick, again, much of the way.

VI

Years later, even so, they'd go again: the journey
through snowdrifts ending in a blaze of oranges,
the bridged arroyo in winter spate, the in-laws

waiting. With the best friend, said now to be
all business, no time for folks, proving how
a mover and shaker could still remember, talk

deep into the night, as always; passing mention
of unease, something the matter with a kidney;
a last wave from the platform. He'd be dead

within a year. Decades after, my father's father
would ponder that luminous implicit thing,
that bonding. Of how it was, what happened,

the language he groped for is all that's left.
The language, the occasional rhyme and meter:
There crowd my mind . . . His letters, her replies,

that spring he'd turned the sod, off in Dakota,
would one day, as so much foolishness, go
up in smoke. Love letters, another medium

of exchange, burned like the rubles. Chekhov
in 1890 trekked eastward, toward the squalors
of Sakhalin; far from hot baths, item by nit-

encrusted, shivering item, he'd spell out
the exiles' situation. My father's father,
meanwhile, spelled out his own: the eighty

they now lived on, the Dakota tree claim, debts
totaling eight hundred; a wife, two boys, a new-
born daughter. The headaches miserably persisted.

Chekhov would come back spitting blood, with
fourteen years to live. My father's father,
prospering, would acquire more land; eventually

he'd own half a section, put up a house, surround
it with shade trees, an orchard. (My earliest memories
are of that place—an eden of wonder, as though

its secret coves had always been.) He'd be named
county surveyor: chain and compass, plumb bob,
witness trees; lost corners, cemeteries,

culverts, highways. The Louisiana Purchase
pieced and platted, all of it owned. Land-
ownership: the sense of it: he found he liked it.

The headaches did not abate. Behind
the gradual increment of ease, a lurking
hint of something wrong. A twitching

about the neck: What? What? Something was wrong.
A tic, a turning or nodding, an assent or
a denial. As a child, trapped in the doldrums

of Sunday morning, an exile from the modern times
I fervently believed in, I'd observe among
the old ones, the settlers and their shriveling

wives, how many were likewise afflicted.
What did it mean? A giving in to what
could not but be? A judgment? Unwilled

adherence to the devil's party? A sclerosis,
he was told, a hardening about the brain stem.
Mortality stared from within. No, he was told:

the tic was functional, a thing that could
be lived with. He did, for forty years.
Lived anxious, as all animals are anxious:

The stasis between fight and flight. The burrow.
The interminable trilling. Unthinkable,
unthinking space. The distances. The stars.

VII

The mysteries of what lived out there, the hunter
and the hunted intertwined; the species that
persisted and that vanished, trodden underfoot:

the linked, perishable, humming webs that only
an unformulating mind could follow, trodden
under: the pattern in the carpet, arabesques

of namelessness, of dreamings; the overlaid
procedure, forethought, accumulation. Assets.
Title deeds. Hot baths. Across the globe,

the neat and fearful grid of settlement. What
stays outside dismissed. Consider the puccoon,
the pasqueflower, the compass plant, the vervain,

as no quasi-monoculture will. Consider the
trout lily, the bluebell and bloodroot my father's
mother brought in from the creekside. A domesticator

born, she made her flowerbeds, her houseplants,
her quilt blocks, her tidy, sunny house the norm:
diffident, adorable, quick to throw up her hands at

what didn't match: "Oh, for the land's sake!"
(What in the world, one wonders now, did that mean?) —
wary of phrases, her love letters expendable:

confront her with what won't come in, won't accept
the settlement: the strange smile of the Jew who
burned the rubles: what then? Imagination

turns, still irresponsible, to Henry James,
a landless, exquisite sort of nomad, who found
no comfort for the dolors of Man Thinking

but in hesitations, velleities, the secret coves
of a surprise the landed, pacing their stiff saraband,
could not have known they harbored: a region

unauthenticated hitherto, awaiting, as
the steppe still did, a muse, a scribe, a bard.
Oh, one can guess what he'd have made of

that strange smile: had he not deemed
Oscar Wilde—who'd die shunned, a rococo
affront to landed propriety—unspeakable?

Chekhov (who wrote plays—that's one connection)
also would die abroad: four years after wild
Oscar; six months after *The Cherry Orchard* opened.

Everything connects, you see: the pattern
in the carpet, trodden underfoot, of Property:
Lopakhin out there hacking at treetrunks:

"Mine! The cherry orchard's mine!" He'd
subdivide it, put up cottages where his fore-
bears, serfs, had felt the knout, where he'd gone

barefoot in winter. . . . No slaves on the prairie, it
may be said. Quite true. A war my great-grandfather
served in saw to that. No chattel slavery—

merely treaties and forced marches. Better the rifle,
some would conclude. Black Hawk's War, the massacre
at Spirit Lake. The losers, what's left of them,

nowadays live on the reservation. That's
what it's called, except by those who live there.
French traders, ransacking their hunting grounds,

called them, from their totem, Renard. They knew
themselves as the Mesquakie. Shunted west to Kansas,
sick, bemused by the black riverbottom land

they'd left, cannily they aped the white man's
game, raised cash, made their bid; signed
papers; moved in; took up the settled life.

VIII

The settled life: no landed estates, no manors,
no eminences grander than the county courthouse
with its spiked cannon, its humdrum pigeonholes.

Woodlots knot the horizon, pull one in.
The gossip. The scathing whisper. Party lines.
Consensus. Stratifyings: oh yes, even in

a place so nearly level, someone to look
down on—renters; hired men and their unwashed
progeny; the drifter from nowhere; the sinner

found out out of wedlock. Fear of mortgages
foreclosed. Dreams of escape: out of the settled life's
fencerow patrols, into their licensed overthrow:

excess, androgyny, the left wing; anonymity-
celebrity: escape achieved that's no escape,
the waiting misstep, the glassy fjord-leap.

Living anxious. The wind a suicidal howling
in the elevator shaft. The manholes' stinking,
steaming entrails. Dreams, now and again,

lopsided fantasies of going back, weak-kneed,
through the underbrush, and getting even.
One comes to terms, in the long-drawn-out

shadow-war against the old ones: comes
to terms, if one lives long enough, with places
that go strange, that vanish into something else:

is ready to go back, at last, to gravesites, headstones,
the fenced grassland where so many forebears' bones
are boxed and labeled, my grandparents' among them,

my father's and my mother's ashes too. A tranquil
place, unfrightening, now that they rest there:
one comes to terms there, almost, even with dread.

To be landless, half a nomad, nowhere wholly
at home, is to discover, now, an epic theme
in going back. The rootless urge that took

my father's father to Dakota, to California,
impels me there. A settled continent: what
does it mean? I think of nights, half wakeful,

under the roof of their last house, the haven
I knew it as long gone, whoever lives there,
its streetlit solitudes, the clock's tock,

the wooing snuffle of a freight train traveling
along a right of way whose dislodged sleepers now
lie scattered like the bones of mastodons.

I think of Dakota, the wind-raked shelterbelts,
the silos' hived anxiety, the trembling
B-52s. I think of Pasadena: date palms,

hibiscus, pepper trees, the feckless charm
found mainly in the habitat of earthquakes:
half-kempt, aging bungalows gone bridal

under a flowery surfeiting of vines: the desert
fanned, sprinkled, seductive from its bath
of purloined rainbows. North Raymond

not quite a slum; a niggling tenderness
for the outmoded thrives on the scandal
of ways lost, of names gone under. No one

I know or ever heard of lives there now.
On Summit, from some long-obliterated
snapshot, I thought I recognized the house

a great-aunt lived in once: the number
not quite right, the tenant an old
deaf Mexican who did not understand.

A
SILENCE
OPENS

(1994)

O the great stars.
The rising and the going down. How still.
As though I were not. Am I part of it?
RAINER MARIA RILKE

The Outer—from the Inner
Derives its Magnitude—
EMILY DICKINSON

. . . un antiguo silencio esperando ser oido.
CECILIA VICUÑA

I

SYRINX

Like the foghorn that's all lung,
the wind chime that's all percussion,
like the wind itself, that's merely air
in a terrible fret, without so much
as a finger to articulate
what ails it, the aeolian
syrinx, that reed
in the throat of a bird,
when it comes to the shaping of
what we call consonants, is
too imprecise for consensus
about what it even seems to
be saying: is it *o-ka-lee*
or *con-ka-ree,* is it really *jug jug,*
is it *cuckoo* for that matter? —
much less whether a bird's call
means anything in
particular, or at all.

Syntax comes last, there can be
no doubt of it: came last,
can be thought of (is
thought of by some) as a
higher form of expression:
is, in extremity, first to
be jettisoned: as the diva
onstage, all soaring
pectoral breathwork,
takes off, pure vowel
breaking free of the dry,
the merely fricative
husk of the particular, rises
past saying anything, any
more than the wind in
the trees, waves breaking,
or Homer's gibbering
Thespesiae iachē:

those last-chance vestiges
above the threshold, the all-
but dispossessed of breath.

DISCOVERY

For Katherine Jackson

The week the latest rocket went
up, a pod (if that's the word)
of manatees, come upriver
to Blue Spring where it's
always warm, could be seen
lolling, jacketed, elephantine,
on the weedy borderline
between drowsing and waking,
breathing and drowning.
As they came up for air,

one by one, they seemed numb,
torpid, quite incurious. No
imagining these sirenians
dangerously singing. Or
gazing up yearningly. (So much
for the Little Mermaid.) True,
the long-lashed little ones
might have been trademarked
Cute by the likes of Walt Disney.
His world's over that way,

suitably for a peninsula where
the cozy mythologies we've
swindled ourselves with, on
taking things easy, might even
come true: sun-kissed nakedness
on the beach, year-round, guilt-free
hibiscus and oranges, fountains
welling up through the limestone,
the rumor of Ponce de León, having
found the one he was looking for,

living at ease in, some say
Boca Raton, others Cádiz. A last
bedtime placebo? Still, we keep
looking up. That clear morning,
just warm enough for a liftoff,
the fabulous itself could be seen
unwieldily, jacket by jacket,

in the act of shedding, as
a snake does its husk, or
a celebrant his vestments:

the fiery, the arrowy tip of it,
of the actual going invisible,
trailing its vaporous, ribboning
frond as from a kelp bed,
the umbilical roar of it
stumbling behind, while up in
the belly of it, out of their
element, jacketed, lolling
and treading, the discoverers
soar, clumsy in space suits.

What are we anyhow, we warmth-
hungry, breast-seeking animals?
At Blue Spring, a day or so later,
one of the manatees, edging
toward discovery, nudged a canoe,
and from across the wet, warm,
dimly imaginable tightrope,
let itself be touched.

HISPANIOLA

Note how the bear
though armed and dangerous
caring not at all for
dignity, undaintily
snacks on fat white things
paws strawberry meadows
lunges swinging smeared
through blackberry canebrakes
maps a constellated
dream of bee trees
snoring galaxies
the primum mobile
twanging the gulfs
of slumber   beatific
on the tongue
the kiss of honey :
or so we imagine
a hulking innocence
child's-play bedfellow
to the sapient
omnivorous
prehensile
raptor   world-class
bully : the rumor
brought to Alexander
of, in India, a reed
that brought forth honey
sans the help of bees
began it   a topography
of monoculture
blackening the Indus
Tigris-Euphrates
westward-spreading
molasses stain
island plantations
off the coast of
Africa leapfrogging
the Atlantic
Hispaniola
Spanish Mexico
Peru   Paraguay
along the Amazon

the Portuguese
the Dutch   the British
Barbados Antigua Montserrat
Jamaica   huger and huger
deforestations
making way for
raising cane   to be
holed   planted   cut
crushed   boiled
fermented or
reduced to crystalline
appeasement of mammalian
cravings   slave ships
whip-wielding
overseers   world-class
indignity   the bubbling
hellhole of molasses pits
the bear's
(or if not his, whose?)
nightmare

PAUMANOK

The humped, half-subterranean
   potato barns, the tubers
like grown stones, wet meat
   from underground a bused-in,
moved-on proletariat once
   stooped for, where Paumanok's
outwash plain, debris of glaciers,
   frays to a fishtail,

now give place to grapevines,
   their tendency to ramble
and run on, to run to foliage
   curbed, pruned, trained
into another monoculture—row
   after profitable row
on acre after acre, whole landscapes
   strung like a zither

where juniper and honeysuckle,
   bayberry, Virginia creeper,
goldenrod and poison ivy would
   have rioted, the wetlands
glistening at the margin, the reed-
   bed plumes, the groundsel's
tideline windrows a patina of
   perpetual motion

washed by the prevailing airs,
   where driven human
diligence alone could, now or ever,
   undo the uninstructed
thicketing of what keeps happening
   for no human reason,
one comes upon this leeward, mowed
   and tended pocket,

last resting place of slaves, each
   grave marked by a boulder
hardly more than a potato's size,
   unnamed but as dependents of
Seth Tuthill and his wife Maria,
   who chose finally to lie here
   with their sometime chattels,
   and whose memory too is now
     worn down to stone.

Banks, what little there ever was
to remember long overgrown: the dunes'
expanse, the largesse of it
    past the unsullied

line of breakers, overrun
with grapevines, sassafras,
the massive green of cedars;
    the white birds, startled,

flying up; an unclad, hospitable
people bringing dressed skins,
the shimmer of a glut of pearls.
    Named Virginia,

a place without detriment or
sleight of language. Households.
Marriages. A girl-child
    named Virginia.

Five years later, footprints.
Ruined walls. A half-carved word.
What happened? By whose fault?
    Silence at Werewo-

comoco, seat of Powhatan,
who—as Captain Smith, his match
in guile, did not forbear to say—
    had his own majesty.

Silence at Henrico, the lands upriver,
and at Varina, where John Rolfe
planted the golden weed that one day
    would amount to money—

Varina, where after many inner
wrestlings, after consultations,
mumblings and catechizings,
    he'd bring his bride,

not as Matoaka or, any longer,
Pocahuntus but, renamed in Christ,
Rebecca. What she called herself
    by then is not recorded.

MATOAKA

Christian names, surnames, place names:
Brafferton, called after a manor-
house in Yorkshire, whose rents had been
    bequeathed by Robert Boyle,

a man of learning and great piety,
to bring the infidels of Virginia,
across the water, out of their
    dark and miserable

ignorance to true religion:
Brafferton, a monument
to words we, or some of us,
    once listened to

in fear and trembling: divinity,
hell fire, the Fiend, Redemption,
Eternal Judgment: Brafferton,
    monument at last to

policy, tergiversation and
neglect. What happened? Whose
fault was it few gave credence to
    the awesome news

of Love personified, Who, having
undergone the worst, might still
prove to outlast undoing? Awe,
    in all the stories

we tell ourselves, is finally
what's durable, no matter how
we mollify it, no matter how our
    pieties keep changing.

What happened in the mind of John
Smith's nonpareil, a pagan
without a peer, grown nubile,
    then the shining

jewel of imperial endeavor,
now the mere sullied pawn
of statecraft and testosterone,
    who dares imagine?

After what dazzlements, what
threats, what stirred, fearful
increment of passion, as Mistress
    Rolfe, she crossed

that threshold, who can guess?
Concerning what she thought, miasmas,
quagmires, white birds flying up,
    the Holy Ghost,

deter us. Who's the more lost?
She had, at any rate, her uses.
Newly installed as convert, nursing
    mother and great lady

up the river named for his
increasingly unseemly majesty,
see her embark, chief showpiece
    of colonial bravado.

Now records of a sort begin:
of presentations, masques, levees,
of portrait sittings, wearing
    wig, ruff, mantle

of brocaded velvet; no less,
for a season, than the rage
of foul, fashionable London
    with its spiteful

stares and whispers, its catarrhs,
its bruited rifts and ruinings,
the whole interminable,
    fatiguing catalog

of latest things, the gartered
glitterings, the breathing
propinquity of faces: through
    a pomandered fog

of rooms and posturings arises,
stunningly vivid still yet
dim with distance, a figure
         long gone from Jamestown,

an ocean's retching, heaving
vertigo removed, and more: from
girlhood's remembered grapevines,
         strawberries, sun-

warm mulberries, leapfrog,
cartwheels, the sound of streams,
of names, of languages: Pamunkey,
         Chickahominy . . .

She'd thought him dead. She'd never
been so tired. There in London
a silence opens: Captain Smith,
         repenting to have writ she

could speak English, is witness
of how she turned away—she who,
out of a distance grown by now
         intolerable, had seen

the world, so called: brought face
to face with majesty, with empire, by
that silence she took their measure.
         Amicably, then,

she acknowledged him, and Jamestown;
as for his countrymen (in what tone
and with what gesture?), they were a people
         that often lied.

Details are few. At Gravesend, readying
for the crossing, aged twenty-one,
she seemingly abruptly
         sickened and died.

III

The chancel of St. George's, Gravesend,
gave her Christian burial. That she
would have chosen this we are less certain,
        given our own

tergiversations, the worn-down
pieties we stumble over,
that trip us up—gnarled rootstocks
        of the once counted on,

knobbed, knotted stubs, newer-
than-kudzu cure-alls, defunct
cultures—silk and indigo,
        the golden weed

King James once railed against
(correctly, it latterly appears)
as noxious, till persuaded there was
        money to be made:

tobacco money, sometime mainstay
of a college given royal grant
and charter to propagate a faith
        the courtier Raleigh,

having staked a last flirtatious
toss, and lost it, in
the shadowy predatory tentshow
        we know as history,

declared for: from beyond this earth,
this grave, this dust (he wrote)
the Lord would raise him up. Such was
        his trust. Less certain,

ourselves, of anything except
the omniprevalence of error,
here on the claimed soil of (in
        the words of Drayton,

who never saw it) earth's
only paradise, to stroll
beyond the commemorated
  names of Brafferton,

Blair, Wythe, Ewell, past
Crim Dell, down to where
mere water, rippling, preserves
  the name of one—

her true, her secret name perhaps,
but that's surmise—the world has heard of,
of whom we know so little: to stroll thus
  is to move nearer,

in imagination, to the nub,
the pulse, the ember of what she was—
no stranger, finally, to the mystery
  of what we are.

BROUGHT FROM BEYOND

The magpie and the bowerbird, its odd
predilection unheard of by Marco Polo
when he came upon, high in Badakhshan,
    that blue stone's

embedded glint of pyrites, like the dance
of light on water, or of angels
(the surface tension of the Absolute)
    on nothing,

turned, by processes already ancient,
into pigment: ultramarine, brought from
beyond the water it's the seeming
    color of,

and of the berries, blooms and pebbles
finickingly garnishing an avian
shrine or bower with the rarest hue
    in nature,

whatever nature is: the magpie's eye for
glitter from the clenched fist of
the Mesozoic folding: the creek sands,
    the mine shaft,

the siftings and burnishings, the ingot,
the pagan artifact: to propagate
the faith, to find the metal, unearth it,
    hoard it up,

to, by the gilding of basilicas,
transmute it: O magpie, O bowerbird,
O Marco Polo and Coronado, where do
    these things, these

fabrications, come from—the holy places,
ark and altarpiece, the aureoles,
the seraphim—and underneath it all
    the howling?

THE UNDERWORLD OF DANTE:

CANTO IX

Seeing me stand there green with fear, my guide,
returning, the more quickly bottled up
the look that told me he was newly worried.

He halted, listening; for through that murk,
that black air's vaporous density, the eye
could hardly venture. "Surely in the end

we must win out," he said. "If not . . ."
A pause. "Assurances were given. But so
much time, and still no sign of anyone!"

I heard too vividly how he dissembled,
overlaying what he had begun
to say with words that differed so,

I grew more fearful still—more than,
perhaps, his hesitation warranted,
inferring from it worse than what he'd meant.

"Does anyone," I asked him then, "go deep
as this, into this godforsaken hollow,
from that level where the sole penalty

is hope cut off?" "Rarely," he answered,
"does any of us from that first circle
follow the downward track we travel now—

though I myself once did so, conjured by
the witch Erichtho, whose power it was
to mingle shade with corpse again. My own

remains were not long nude of me before
she summoned me to pass within that wall
and fetch a shade from the abode of Judas—

a circle farther down and darker, more
remote from all that's good, than any other.
Oh, I know the way, you may be certain.

This marsh from which so huge a stench goes up
girdles the doleful metropolis.
Rage will confront us here before we enter."

What he said next I now forget, my sight
being drawn by then to what appeared
lit up by the infernal glare within

those towers: three hellish things that had
in form and attitude the look of women,
blood-smeared, greenly garlanded at waist

and temple by a clutch of water snakes,
wildly writhing, serpentine-haired,
viperish: such were the Furies.

He who well knew these minions from the household
of her who rules where groaning never ends,
named for me one by one the foul Erinyes:

"That is Megaera to the left; the one
who ravens on the right, Alecto; and
between the two, Tisiphone." He halted,

as each clawed or stuck with open palm
at her own person, shrieking so fiendishly
I shuddered, and moved closer to the poet.

"Call for Medusa: she'll turn him to rock,"
regarding us below, they howled as one.
"What Theseus tried here is not yet paid back."

"Turn round, and keep your eyes closed. Were
the Gorgon to appear, and you to look,
all chance of our return would be foregone."

These were the master's words, as his own hands,
not to rely on any act of mine,
closed in an outer band about my forehead.

You who are sound of understanding, note,
I say, what trove of doctrine is concealed
beneath the seeming strangeness of this passage.

There came now from about the turbid moat
an uproar such as caused its shores to rumble—
a fracas of confused alarm, as when

a holocaust of torrid gusts, igniting
without check, engulfs a wilderness,
whose snapped limbs' scorched and crackling litter,

pulverized, grown irresistible,
drives the animals and those who herd them,
gasping and terrified, alike before it.

Uncovering my eyes, my guide said, "Look
now across that antiquated scum,
to just where the fumes are deadliest."

As frogs, when the predatory snake
pursues them, vanish, plunging headlong
into the muck, and squat there, hiding,

ruined souls, more than a thousand of them,
I saw in flight from one who, moving dry
of foot above the Styx, passed swiftly over.

Repeatedly his left hand fanned away
the rank air from before him—the one
sign he gave at all of being vexed.

Well aware of where this being came from,
it was my guide I turned to now, and at
a sign from him, I offered mute obeisance.

Ah, how terrible in indignation
that one appeared! He held a little rod.
I saw the gate give way, without resistance.

I saw him stand there on the horrid threshold.
"O you despised and outcast ones," he cried,
"why do you harbor such excessive rage?

Why such recalcitrance toward that Will
whose purposes endure unmoved forever,
whom to resist adds to your suffering?

What use to butt against what is ordained?
Your watchdog Cerberus still bears those scars
about the neck that are the proof of this."

To the foul thoroughfare he now returned
without a word for us, but with the look
of one who's spurred on by a care beyond

what human thought could possibly encompass.
We moved our steps to pass within, secure
now the angelic words had been pronounced,

and entered without raising any outcry.
Then I, desiring eagerly to learn
the state of those confined in that grim fortress,

cast wondering eyes about me. What I saw
was a vast, open desert place, the haunt
of ire and the most dreadful torment.

As where, at Arles, the Rhone goes stagnant, or
in the low-lying precincts of Quarnaro,
past the Italian boundary at Pola,

the burial mounds that crowd those graveyards make,
on every side, a rough terrain: thus was
it here, but far more grievously:

among the mounds the soil was all afire,
so fervently, each tomb appeared to glare
hotter than any smelter's craft has need for.

Each lid was up, and from below it came
the groans of one within, whose misery,
thus heard, seemed hardly bearable.

"Master," I said then, "what people lie
casketed within those sepulchers,
lamenting without end the end they've come to?"

And he: "Here lie the greatest heretics
of every sect, with all their followers.
More of them than you would suppose are thus

interred, like next to like, in monuments
of varying degrees of burning." Turning
to the right, we passed between those torments
and the high walls that encircled them.

II

SHOREBIRD-WATCHING

To more than give names
to these random arrivals—
teeterings and dawdlings
of dunlin and turnstone,
black-bellied or golden
plover, all bound for

what may be construed as
a kind of avian Althing
out on the Thingstead,
the unroofed synagogue
of the tundra—is already
to have begun to go wrong.

What calculus, what
tuning, what unparsed
telemetry within the
retina, what overdrive
of hunger for the nightlong
daylight of the arctic,

are we voyeurs of? Our
bearings gone, we fumble
a welter of appearance,
of seasonal plumages
that go dim in winter:
these bright backs'

tweeded saffron, dark
underparts the relic
of what sibylline
descents, what harrowings?
Idiot savants, we've
brought into focus

such constellations,
such gamuts of
errantry, the very
terms we're condemned
to try to think in
turn into a trespass.

But Adam, drawn toward
that dark underside,
its mesmerizing
circumstantial thumbprint,
would already have
been aware of this.

WHITE

over the great inland
riverbeds   the greater
lakebeds   a runneled
skitter   by dusk a blur

swarms   interspersing glooms
of conifers the far
side of the pass with
mazily hexagonal

lopsided falling things
or substances   or stuffs
bear paw   ear flap   rabbit
scut   the mirror-haunch of

pronghorn   whiteness of whale
of glacial octopus
such thunderous accu-
mulations' drip and roar

snowmelt   sunbreaks   advances
and retreats   the polar
threatener   tossing to
cherry trees by parking

lots unseasonable
nosegays   leaving on wind-
shields these wet billets-doux
the snow is general

GREEN

These coastal bogs, before they settle
          down to the annual
business of being green, show an
          ambivalence, an overtone

halfway autumnal, half membranous
          sheen of birth: what is
that cresset shivering all by itself
          above the moss, the fallen duff—

a rowan? What is that gathering blush
          of russet the underbrush
admits to—shadblow, its foliage
          come of ungreen age?

The woods are full of this, the red
          of an anticipated
afterglow that's (as it were) begun
          in gore, green that no more than

briefly intervenes. More brief
          still is the whiff,
the rime, the dulcet powdering, just now,
          of bloom that for a week or two

will turn the sullen boglands airy—
          a look illusory
of orchards, but a reminder also
          and no less of falling snow.

Petals fall, leaves hang on all
          summer; chlorophyll,
growth, industry, are what they hang
          on for. The relinquishing

of doing things, of being occupied
          at all, comes hard:
the drifting, then the lying still.

THINKING RED

Swamp maples' unmasked sugars'
underhue, intense as madder,
alizarin or cochineal (a dyestuff

steamed from heaped corpses of an insect
native to Mexico: such the odd lore
of commerce in the exotic a bemused

E. Dickinson took note of): to
grub it out, the sense of it, down
to the madder's fraying final foothold,

the capillaries' threadily
untidy two-way form of discourse;
T. Hardy's ruddleman trundling

his dyeload of ocher; or
the bog-dwelling sanguinary
pitcher plant whose drowning dens

decoct a summer soup of insects
whose mainstay in turn is gore:
the clotted winter melancholy

of the sumac; hawthorn encrimsoned,
dogwood beaded the adorning
pigment of survival; the eyeball's globed,

dendritic riddle: to unencode
the hematite, the iron in the granite,
the carmine in the carapace, one has

to try to think in wavelengths. Light
has, we're told—I have it from G.
Wald—certain properties of waves

but also of particles. That's very
strange: G. Wald again.
Mind stuff, he tells us: physical

reality is mind stuff. In creatures
that puzzle over what it is, he says,
the universe begins to know itself.

Is this good news? I hope so. It's
that holdout, put-upon, reluctant
red (I think) that raises half a doubt.

NONDESCRIPT

There comes, in certain latitudes, a season
      no one would call the fall,
when the year-old foliage of live oaks,
green once but now a nondescript
dun or ocher, goes innumerably twiddling
      and twirling down

in the midst of a mist, a gold dust
      of pollen and petals no one,
so far as I know, has yet written of
as amounting to spring in the middle
of fall, or vice versa: the very notion
      of spring being mainly

defined, come to think of it, by the English,
      at least since Chaucer put it
in the month of April, ignoring all of this
in-betweenness, this process that's less
an advent than it is a wandering vaguely
      nel mezzo del cammin:

not to speak of an April brown down under, or
      a perennial tropical zone,
in Italy also not only the live oaks' non-
descript but the camphor trees' untimely
crimson keeps on coming down, coming down
      in the midst of the green.

THE HORNED RAMPION

Daily, out of that unfamiliar,
entrancingly perpendicular
terrain, some new
and, on minute
inspection, marvelous
thing would be opening—

yet another savory-
flowery permutation
of selene or salvia,
of scabious, of rockrose,
of evening primrose, of
bellflower such as the one

I'd never before laid eyes
on the like of: spurred,
spirily airy, a sort of
stemborne baldachin,
a lone, poised,
hovering rarity, hued

midway between the clear
azure of the rosemary
and the aquilegia's
somberer purple,
that turned out to be
named the horned rampion.

Next day it was no longer
singular but several;
the day after, many.
Within a week it was
everywhere, had become
the mere horned rampion,

had grown so familiar
I forgot it, had not
thought of it since,
it seems, until the moment
a volume of the Encyclopedia
Britannica, pulled down

for some purpose, fell open
at random, and there was
the horned rampion, named
and depicted, astonishing
in memory as old love
reopened, still quivering.

BAYOU AFTERNOON

For Joy Scantlebury

Out of the imprecise, the murk
of bright and dark, the wavering
at the bayou's edge, such

specificity: the egret's samite,
filamented, barbed and folded,
hourly preened and realigned,

just so: the unmistakably,
topheavily crested and cravatted
kingfisher: just so, the wading

ungainly fantasy, paintbox-
tinged pink and green, that's
called the spoonbill, back from

a rim known as extinction: just
so, that afternoon, the colonies,
along the streambank, of lilies,

each perishable hieroglyph
filamented, in a flourish, with
a stroke of purple. Meanwhile,

out on the Gulf, the airs and
vapors had grown monumental,
their huge purple a flickering

testament to, at the rim we
necessarily inhabit, a happenstance
still brimming, still uncodified.

III

IN UMBRIA: A SNAPSHOT

The coldest, wettest spring within living memory
is the way they describe it. At Assisi
there have been six straight weeks of rain.
They blame it on the Gulf War, of which Melina
happily, for the time being, knows nothing.
A vehement "*Good*ness!" is her fiercest expletive.

Little runaway, forget-me-not-eyed, ringlet-
aureoled refugee from a fresco by Lorenzetti—
all those gold-leaf rigors, the theological
murk underneath—whom nobody can begin to
keep up with, or anyhow nobody human. *Her*
peers are the brown-faced saint's familiars:

he of the caninely grinning lope, they of
the barnyard strut and chuckle, the noon-hour
flurry, by the recycled temple of Minerva, of
brakings and hoverings, structure and function
of wingbeats she'd been gleefully part of
minutes before going romping off into a dark

she knows nothing about—or is one, at a year
and eight months, already prey to nightmares?—
that goes back to before the Gulf War. "*La bimba!*"—
the reverberation accused us along the catacomb
she stood crying in, consoled by who knows, by now,
how many strangers: Kodachromed all over Umbria

beaming, the crowd scene in the café or the square
perceived as benediction, one unendingly
extended family: or come to a halt, as now,
halfway up an impossible hill, aware of being
small and alone: incipience a spinning globe
(look! the sun's out), all its great spaces opening.

BIRDHAM

Hemmed by loud seas,
by fractured granite, by island
treescapes each spined like a hedgehog,
as well as wild roses' formidable
coppices, on beholding
an up-late-in-daylight
porcupine, its thicketed
shambling perpendicular a stupor
of armament, I thought

of Birdham, all meek horizontals,
blurred margins, sea meeting land
among lanes and hedgerows:
of mild, tall, approachable
roses and delphiniums, a robin
scavenging the tablecloth at
teatime: of exclaiming, one evening,
"Barbara, there's a hedgehog
out in the garden!"

"Oh," my friend complacently
said then, "that's Henry."
Far-off, long-settled
Birdham is like that.

AT EASTERLY

Fog all day, skim
milk to gruel
and back without
a stirring, a
single needle-
leaf's displacement:
pine trees' idi-
osyncrasy
of layering
and stance, seen from
out there, no freak
but rather as
though graven and
ordained to be
so: expressive
of (it comes to
seem) some patience,
comprehending
instabilities
of wind and
tidefall, under-
writing the running-
through-the-fingers
expenditure
of moonlight on
water, lending
ballast against
vertigo as
tent-pole spruce boles
queasily, at
day's end, begin
to weave and sway:
containing the
far-out reef-slam
of a turmoil
whose rumor stirs,
in these joists and
rafters, tremors
boding of no
more than the least
pointillist tip-
toe expanding

to just such a
downpour as
Grattan Condon
(who's dead now, but
whose intent goes
on without him)
put the roof up
that we're under
to listen for.

HANDED DOWN

Raymond Hodgkins, his dragger last seen
in heavy seas off Schoodic, night falling
and still no word of him; and before him

Buddy Closson, Herb Damon, Ben Day,
Clyde Haskell, Larry Robbins senior,
Alan Thompson: the roll of the names

goes on and on, goes back thirty years
to Ray Dunbar, the day the *Lillian Mae*
broke up between the bar islands: back

to that scene, the men gathering, the women
waiting above the inlet, the skirts they still
wore in those days blowing out behind them

(a painterly embellishment handed down
by Grattan Condon) as one, unanimous
the way gulls are, heading into the wind.

Divers went searching, but found no body;
one of them tripped, fouled in a kelp bed,
came close to drowning. Days passed; nothing.

Then Vin Young—it was Vin, not Vic, his twin,
the way they remember—no more than thirteen,
but old enough to go out hauling, dreamed

one night, and woke up still afraid, of
finding Ray. He told only Vic, the two of them
dawdled and puttered until their father

said, "You kids better get out there
if you aim to earn your keep." So
they went out, and that day, sure enough

(the way they tell it), saw something floating,
a body, and it was Ray Dunbar. It's the names,
the roll call handed on and let down

in heavy seas, the visibility near zero,
the solitude total, night falling—it's the names
of the dead, kept alive, they still hold on to.

MANHATTAN

GRACE CHURCH

A day of gusts and puddles, the vivid
litter of a season no better ordered
than the debris we carry with us, each,

of hurt and counter-hurt, attachments
wrenched from or slowly shed, engulfs
the maudlin fretwork, the pieced glass.

Like kids, unwilling, sent back to school,
we learn how our own history has its exits
and its entrances, its waning phase.

Once, even the wry sendoff to Reno
seemed expansive; the mists and gustings
of champagne, the shipboard trysts,

slip now into the backward and abysm
with the mortgage burnings, tinkling
martini pitchers on the beach at Gilgo;

Southold with its steamer clams, beer
and garrulity; the boozeless week at
Flynn's—Fire Island beach fires,

sunsets on Great South Bay; birthday
bashes, welcomes home, milestone
observances assembling yet again

the loose, patched, decades-frayed,
half-accidental, half-willed Old Crowd.
Habitual molecules have their gatherings

and dispersals: we learn how our,
how every history comes down to
this, the encounter with the starved

handclasp from the wheelchair: to share
the bed of this, seeing it distend,
begin to ooze like an edema: death,

that blear-eyed, feathery noise. He'd
kept a careful regimen—no alcohol,
a daily six-mile run—had coaxed

a rooftop lotus into bloom, thrown
memorable parties. An *Augenblick*
through tokay lampshade-glades,

trompe-l'oeil and calfskin: fey connoisseur
of the unlooked-for (the diagnosis:
cancer of the liver) sharing tête-à-tête

a glimpse he'd noted as he ran: in
Central Park, through early-morning
mist, a surreptitious crew of women,

unmistakably Chinese, with raised
poles harvesting the dun produce
of a stand of ginkgo trees. An

eyeblink of the hand-to-hand, the
elfin bubble of the incorporeal
settles, shivering, as the mind is stilled.

CHARLES STREET

Transplanted from the Carolinas, from
Pittsfield and Sewickley, the raw demes
of Appalachia and Iowa, from the arterio-

sclerotic clot across the Hudson, among
the walkups, the ginkgo-shaded side streets
of Greenwich Village, to claim the privilege

of ignoring one's next-door neighbors, of
getting drunk in bars, of being sick in
hallways, of fornications in strange beds,

solipsist terrors of the mad, the marginal,
the merely totally confused—we'd come
to listen for the West Side Highway's

nightlong silken seethe, for foghorns
mourning the tenor of the day before it
opened, for subliminal harmonic tremors

as the old *Queen Mary* cleared her larynx;
to spy out trivial marvels in mundane
bazaars: I think of the Fourteenth Street

refreshment stand whose reamers gushed,
one balefully faceless fall, with juices
not of crushed citrus or papaya, but

of crammed red-parchment pomegranates'
casefuls of rubies, each with its nucleus
of possibility encysted at the center,

translucent hemoglobin of exotic groves
adrift among dead-end chicaneries, bins
of cut-rate merchandise, all-weather

scavengers of trashcans, the misfit
solitaries, dislocated extended families
from Puerto Rico, the dwindling remnant

of the native Irish. From symbiotic
venoms of achieve or be undone, the candor
of whatever community distilled its own

scarce nostrum finds a remembered center
in gatherings, the back garden lantern-
strung, on Charles Street, where from

occasion to occasion a mazy entity affirmed
itself in loose sendoff talk of ashrams,
of reunions so exotic, the sheer prospect

so like a gem I'd wear it home
and watch it turn into the dawn, an opal's
packed circumference: nowhere to stash it

but in the scuffed insomniac luggage
of a future lately overpast. The scions
of a new uprooting gather now, or wake alone

and scared, on Charles Street; the ginkgos'
bare, bud-nubbed brooms purvey the wizened
gemstones of a dun, unasked-for fruit.

THE STATEN ISLAND FERRY

December, and again an exit, the slow
aftershock of months-old news (inoperable
cancer of the pancreas). At Grace Church

the day after the equinox, we'd seen him
wheeled in starving, the awful door
blown to. Today, a half-involuntary

particle in the shifting habitual
concourse that floods the gangway
as the slung barrier recedes, to board

the shunted, hooting, double-snub-
nosed tub he was as much at home in as
an owned house (he'd been a seaman,

had the lover of precision's ear
for discord; for him, unjaded by
familiarity, it was as though the harbor

could do no wrong), is to feel the stale
hour lose its nerve, grow listless, slip,
marked only, if at all, by some braced

gull's half-obliterated outcry, toward
the solstice: toward the annual foreboding of
a swerve, this year, through outer cold

no longer to be bridged. Hart Crane's
great cabled lyre corrodes: a frayed
strand one day broke, dangled, struck

and killed between the boroughs' apoplectic
upthrust and wrecking claw, the stunned
queue, the gusted, elbowing guffaws,

True Believers in the sanctity of Wear
and Tear, the quaint ordeal of Trickle-Down,
a continent, a people, a consensus unmoored

from any history at all—the whole mythic
mishegass that used him up. Asked why
he shrugged—he shrugged a lot, drank

still more, grew more and more low-
key—he would have murmured, "Is there
a better system, then?" The fossil carbon

of whatever outrage still smoldered in the
wreckage, that fall day, we turned away from.
Beside the stripped carapace of Ellis Island,

gowned Liberty in effigy lofts her
Promethean fable on the decades-sodden
pilings, bile and verdigris—crass icon

of the possible, the yet-, the never-to-be-
ventured-on. From the railing he'd drink in
this daily brew of hubris and sea air

as from a stein. The random particles
disbanding, the estuarial currents merge:
the mind gropes toward its own recessional.

THE WAR MEMORIAL

The rain-god Tlaloc, hungering for blood,
the war-god, hummingbird-gartered
Huitzilopochtli, the drugged booty

of a huger, cleverer hunger, stir
in a museum hall of nightmare, where
Asshur the bellicose and Marduk, who

rode forth to set the world in order,
are neighbors, where the drifts and dunes
of long-immobilized cuneiform begin

to move again, a bas-relief of dread
like the long scar, the black cicatrice
of memory not yet embalmed but raw,

those drifts of origami at its foot:
to trace whose length is to reopen
what George Fox, compelled at Lichfield

to take off his shoes, walked barefoot
in—the channel of the blood of those
who fell. For what? Can someone tell us?

'EIGHTY-NINE

In memory of Andrew Myers

Season of contaminated mists,
    of premises abandoned, the heartland
curdling in a spate of messages—
    the sequined smirk, the flicker
of apocalypse only the young, whose
    prospects who cares to imagine,
        can stand to dance to:
    season of scavengers: how is it,
in the evening light above the landfill
the gulls, massed, hovering, diaphanous,
    take on the look of angels?

John Keats at Winchester, fair-weather
    scavenger of what pleases the eye,
was for the nonce persuaded by just
    such appearances: the stubblefields
suffused, the season's lineaments
    discerned as halfway human. Time
        equivocates: though no epiphany
    outstays the wholly dividual rupture,
above the water meadows' jewelweed and
fennel the midge-swarm hangs, its scrim
    untorn, as without interruption.

Continuity of the winged, the windborne,
    the rooted: reassurance of the made,
the handed down, the durable: glyph
    and vesper bell, trodden cloister and
walled playing field: it was as though,
    that evening, the young athletes
        in their perfect whites, the bat's
    pock, the patter of applause—as though
pure sport had turned the key against
fever and shivering, nausea, hemorrhage,
    the entire obscenity of dying young.

O, or of dying at any age, by degrees
    or by accident: to be alive at all
is no more than an ambuscade, eluding
    the presence of angels, since it is
in the nature of angels to be terrible:
    thralled to the heavings of a visceral
        mass peepholed with ganglia,
    while somewhere in there the big-eyed rabbit
of delirium, cowering, scared witless, waits:
O dense as spiders' spinning trajectories
    at summer's end are these inklings

of undoing; or as the seasonal downpour
    distends to a cording of thongs and sinews,
a knout of wet one gives oneself up to,
    soaked through, having made one's peace with
whatever the elements can do. Or almost.
    For beyond that peace is the shape of
        calamity nobody is ever
    ready for: on a day at the end of summer,
a car going off the road, a mangling
incendiary gasp, and for four young athletes,
    without harbinger all is over.

He was twenty, the one I knew: T-shirted,
    dripping from the shower is the way
I remember him, just passing through. Such
    images console somehow. When the note came,
with the clipping, I saw the capacity for grief
    sit there, in the face of such cautery, inert
        with refusal. But the mother
    had already entered (as she'd later put it)
a place where the things people do for one
have no names: such an inrush, she lived floating
    in a deep lake of it, of that charity.

Mourning her own unborn, uncosseted
    grandchildren, she'd have gone over and over
the lack of evidence of design in the event,
    having met with the messengers, having
found them (and even the archangels are,
    after all, only messengers) inscrutable.
        O how intricate a patterning
in the bracken's yellowing diminishment,
the hornet's fallen factories; in the squirrel's
uncalculated leap a smoke-ring wavelength's
    theorem still fluttering.

What, then, notwithstanding the evidence
    of dance at the heart of the matter,
whatever matter may be, of all the arson
    and concussion, of that blister they call
the Sea of Tranquillity? What of the atom,
    its core no dance hall but a regardless
        demos, disaster's hotbed?
    For all our jargon of knowing and managing,
for all our summoning of the forces of order,
in a season of sour rain, how happily
    we looked at anarchy in bloom.

Strange, what a year it was altogether
    for anniversaries—all the might-have-
beens of human nature seemingly reborn;
    of, even, that November weekend—
the all-night bus ride, the carried candles,
    an exuberance of rage over being lied to,
        and the out-of-season rose
    that turned into an epiphany: in
that uprush of forces, of faces, the anarchic
sweetness of it (it was twenty years
    ago) I had my youth again.

Youth, in Tiananmen Square, arriving just
   ahead of the great anniversary: was it
evidence of design in the weft of things,
   that legion of messengers, headband-
wearers at once lighthearted and terrible,
   as all angels are? O insomniac
     loveliness of arrival, of
   exposure to the downpours of summer,
to the far, forgetful stars, those envoys
of long-undergone concussions, O insouciance
   in the face of the forces of order.

Candlelight on the cobblestones of Leipzig;
   in Prague a complicit candor, as night
after night we were drawn to the tube
   (O brute honey, there in the dark,
though the smirk of mendacity contain it)
   by the flowering, out in the snow, of so
     many faces: now that season's over.
   But that freshet of anarchy,
while it lasted, halfway persuaded us
the archangels, whoever they are,
   at moments are also human.

IV

AT MUKER, UPPER SWALEDALE

To be wet was to be captive, idle and poor. To be dry was to be free,
industrious and comfortable. This was the lesson of the drowning cell.
SIMON SCHAMA, *The Embarrassment of Riches*

The farmer with his milk pail
pausing, a fine rain falling,
burnishing with wet the wind-
nipped roof slates, fingering
the chimney-clumps of dwellings

following no plan or pattern
but that of having sat down,
one by one, as sheep would,
in the moor's high, wall-
ribbed, uncomfortable lee:

so it appears to one come as,
though country bred, a stranger,
to trudge the solitude of footpaths,
then early bed and, out of rural
sleep, dreams that are frantic

as Muker Beck aswirl, hurtling
to enter the River Swale: peat-
dark in spate, hour by hour
engorged with braidings, with
sheeted seethings of rainfall

fallen yet again: the trickle
of the damp's wrung increment
down limestone's fluted hollows
(buttertubs is what the locals
call them) that pock the pass

along the road to Askrigg—
slow, muted, single droplets
like bird notes after dark,
filterings ringleted with
brunet-stemmed spleenwort,

ageless as the lamb's cry,
the bees' noise, the lisp
of aeons. Strange, the lone
lapwing, the streamside fox-
glove, the harebell by the

roadside, the pale-eyed piebald
Swaledale breed, met up with
in one knockdown gathering,
the herdsman's yell (*Git in,
git in, git in, ye buggers*),

the neat small sheepdog doing
what it's bred for, all strange—
even the farmer's quasi-gentlemanly
tweed and Wellingtons: it's only
the milk pail takes me back to

the matriarchal smell of it,
warm from the udder; to manure-
pile, barnyard and stanchion,
green reek of silage, green
scum on the horse-trough,

year-round wall-sweat of old
farmhouses; to pump, sink,
cistern, slop pail for pigs,
the human slop jar, the gray
interminable hank of mildew.

Well, that's changing. Indoor
shivers give way (even here,
now that the heating's central)
to plush, florid wall-to-wall,
rippling fake fire, the daylong

warbling of the telly; to a
comfort wishfully aspired
toward, become no more than
the way we all—or if not all,
then most, or if not most,

the icons of our surrogate
existence—live now. Think,
though, of that roamer in the
rainy deserts of this shire,
the never-to-be-comfortable

George Fox, sworn enemy of
easy livings, of the steeple-
house's dry doldrums—who,
acquainted with the stink of
anybody in a state of nature,

a prisoner wading ankle-deep
in excrement, envisioning
beyond these elements a
heavenly rain descending,
aspired toward pure fire.

HOMELAND

Now and then the smell of apples
wrinkling in the dark wells up
from the earth-walled storm cellar

whose cold floor I last set foot on
so long ago, the wizened resins
of remembering turn into plunder.

To be homesick at all for what
we called the Cave: is it not rather
that we always had been strangers

to a habitat whose surface,
so recently still rippling
like a running weasel,

tree-darkened only in its stream-damp
secret parts, we'd bobbed, hairpinned
and pompadoured with farmsteads?

Windbreak and shelterbelt, the orchard
on its slope out past the feedlot:
against the weather's harnessless,

massive caprice, a corridor
of spruces to fend the blurred
thrust of it when, the last

Wolf River windfall gone to rot
in matted grass, the ciderpress
shut down, the crickets silent,

a shrieking solitude laid down
its curfew: to wring well-being
from indifference, to muster

shade and shelter from a realm
so bare of either: to put in
apple trees, to see them first

roseate, then whitening, then
bowed down with maroon, temptation's
emblem mellowing in the bin:

this was, one would have thought, the way
one came at last to feel at home.
One would have thought—were not

the Cave a witness, like the rod that,
climbing the siding, crowned the rooftree
with its finial, a glassblower's apple,

to unmitigated terror. We'd
been told that Jesus loved us,
but out there the old gods

slithered and swam uncaught,
and though we knew that no one
knew when one of them might next

flatten a crop or set a barn afire,
or worse, the bagged winds' black
archangel, even, had no proper name.

Had our forebears not put all but
plain talk behind them? Such
extravaganzas of suspense—

the brassy calm, the vapors' upthrust,
the lurid porches of foreboding
we lived among, they could be thought of

as a kind of homeland: the unease,
the dim notion of a down-to-earth
transcendence that brought us in,

that raises from the apple bin
long-dormant resonances
of an oncoming winter.

SED DE CORRER

Caught on the move—no knowing what year it was—
through the leaves of the ash tree outside the schoolroom,
the stumbling drone, the ineradicable blush, the botch
of being young: O how can I breathe, the eyes
are all mouths, they are drinking me—that glimpse:
a small bird, some part of it, among streakings
and shadings, the fluttering fan of it, afire
(a Blackburnian warbler? I ask myself now:
a redstart?) uncaught by the impeding
rigors of the vascular, the cambium's moist secrets
locked between xylem and phloem, the great, growing
trunk of it hardening, the mass, the circumference,
the unhurried, implacably already
there, that's to be escaped from:

escape, the urge to disjoin, the hunger
to have gone, to be going: *sed de correr:*
Vallejo in Paris writing (*me alejo todo*)
of fleeing, of running away from what made one,
from everything: Lorca, a stranger to
Morningside Heights, looking out from
that ridge above Harlem: the mire and fireflies,
the lit grid's apertures past counting,
the bleared eyeholes of jails: the tiered rictus
at Creedmore and Brentwood, where the mad
are warehoused, who do not look out of,
who burrow, denying the need for,
the nature and function, the very existence
of windows: holed up torpid, hibernal,
one day possibly (or possibly never),
fluttering, desiccated, frail,
to emerge from that hebetude:

the runaway halt, no opening other than
the starry apertures of paperwhite narcissus
forced in a bowl, cool, onion-rooted,
a sweetness I drank at as though entity
might depend from it: exploring
chlorinated caves of sensation (wet hair,
wool-steam, the pipes knocking), away from
the blare, out there, of certitude,
the glare of injunction: meaning

dwindling to a risen chain of bubbles
in the saucepan on the hotplate: the hurrying
fin far out, the lighthouse,
its pulsing aperture engulfed,
the waves breaking.

Virginia Woolf, having written her note of farewell,
going down to the river, the largest stone
she could manage shoved into her pocket: the body
of Lorca crumpling, shot down at the edge of
a pit on the outskirts of Granada: Vallejo
in Paris, in extremis, crying out on Good Friday
A.D. 1938, "I'm going to Spain!"—pulled up,
cut off from his own roots' torment,
the certitudes, the incursions, the plunder:
having written of the condition of cities,
of being alone among people: the windows looked out of,
the mute telephone, the dementia: Kafka
devising a passage up through the windowless
warren of calculation, contingency, foresight
there's no way out of, metamorphosing
escape in the form—O no, not of a bird,
not he who so fled the open, but of an insect
gravitating unerringly toward the dark:
those feelers, that lustrous, chitinous
lodging among interstices, among systems
we've lost track of the workings of,
and to whose advantage, outwitting
the gathering impasse of language, the screech
of its decibels, the mumble of its circumlocutions,
the mutter, all over Europe, of what sooner and sooner
was bound, was about to happen.

Refugees were arriving. Cut off, adrift, at large
in the fathomless afternoon of arrival,
alone—suppose that to be seen by no one
would be in fact to vanish?—I looked out from
a window ledge on Morningside Heights,
that ridge overlooking the eyesore
of real estate that is Harlem, too scared
to begin to grapple with, to think in
the inexorable terms of, the leverages
of excuse that maintained it: impervious

to the ideologue's whereases and necessarilys,
the thunderous because, the sad, lingering
cadenza of notwithstanding, I was not deaf to
the screech of what had somehow knowably—
how?—been closing in, closing down
ever since I'd begun to remember. Refugees:
it was with a refugee I'd venture,
just once, into Harlem: Jan Muller, who'd later,
vividly, paint his way through an insomniac
excess while he died of it, like Kafka. Refugees:
from the songless amputated tree
Lorca wrote of: leaves fallen, adrift,
the great trunk lost sight of, the stasis
of such scattering, such dispersals.

Adrift among hallways, stairwells, airshafts,
the asphalt of rooftops, among old-law walkups,
the rusting entablatures, fire escapes'
catfoot walkways, upended avenues of thievery,
of escape that is no escape: trailing the shuddering
jointed lurch alongside the platform, elevated
or submerged, the serial unseeing faces
within, the windows traveling, a delirium of them,
of arrivals, escapes that are no escape: cheap
plane tickets from Puerto Rico—to what? Rooftop
rainwater weeping in, the aerials, the hutches
put up by breeders of pigeons: the wild rock dove's
cosmopolitan offspring, their homing swerve
more nearly adapted than these refugees
from the canefields' corridored, murderous green,
caught up in the wingborne roar, the breaking
wave of displacement—so many injunctions
in need of translation—translated here, to
the crass miracle of whatever it is that put up
the South Bronx, street number after street number,
the mailbox pried open, recipient unknown,
moved on, shot down—and has made of it
this byword, this burnt-out, roofless, windowless
testimonial to systems gone rotten.
This arson.

There is much too much to be done: so Vallejo,
a wistful sometime disciple of Lenin,

declared: but who heard him? Not I,
shades drawn against being seen, against systems,
from bohemia's sempiternal cocoon, the hallways
smelling of cat piss and mildew. Who will hear?
Rilke wondered, imagining the rush from out there,
the vast presences, harsh with transcendence,
whose nature it is to ignore one. Not those great wings.
I was too much afraid. By a window
onto an airshaft one night I stood awed
at the sight of two men making love. I'd not
known how it was done. Through thin walls,
year after year, I could not stop up my ears to
the spats, the crudities, the climaxes
faked or unfaked, to (once) the squalled outcry
while others came to the rescue. What
my ears awaited, out past the suicidal refuge
of a fire escape on West Twelfth Street,
was the all-but-inaudible, the lisped *tsip,*
in a back-garden catalpa, the fluttering fan
of a warbler on the move: spring or fall,
that glimpsed inkling of things
beyond systems, windborne, oblivious.

Sed de correr: above Tijuana, where the language,
its streams and islets, begins to change color,
the moiling crawl along the freeway—
la cucaracha, the refuge of Gregor Samsa
writ large, written everywhere—a teenage
entrepreneur selling roses, bull's-blood-
red velvet of a piece with all the matador
kitsch across the border, threading the labyrinth
of the need to flee, to be at once on the go
and in hiding, that's what we've become.
The moving vehicle. The estrangement.
On West Twelfth Street, the tree is dying:
the rough, green-napped, huge heart shapes,
the cigar shapes, the striations at the throat
of the ruffled corolla, year by year, are
expiring by inches. The axe is laid
at the root of the ash tree. The leaves of dispersal,
the runaway pages, surround us. Who
will hear? Who will gather
them in? Who will read them?

A CADENZA

Puccini in hog-butchering time:
blood on the snow   the clockfaced
fearful valentine   DOCTOR IS IN
PLEASE BE SEATED   scarlatina
whooping cough   contagion
in the school gymnasium

Che gelida manina: "Your tiny
hand is frozen," the printed leaflet
idiotically rendered it. Everything
cultural somehow made people squirm.
Puck-seeny? It sounded like
some kind of figleaf: enough

to launch the ninth grade's darling
and her chum (who was plain), that evening,
onto high seas of silliness: "Your tiny . . ."
An aisle away, admiring and desolate,
I saw her as one whom privilege had bound for
the half-world of taffeta and gardenias,

Evening in Paris out of stoppered cobalt,
an apotheosis of merchandise,
la vie de bohème in a garret
become a commodity, along with,
as the houselights go down, malnutrition
and hypothermia, kept, needless to say,

at a tactfully discreet distance
away from the cold, the carcasses, blood
on the snow, the heartbeat thundering
inside the valentine—and the rampant
infection they had no name for. It
struck that same week, a peripeteia

leaving expectation moot. To hear of it,
whose blood did not run cold?
Mine does, still, at that giggling cadenza,
that conclusion dredged up from,
it must be, all of
six decades ago.

SEED

The way it came spinning onto the lawn—
the elm trees' chaffy currency, each piece
with a spot of seed at the center; the katydid-
colored, breeze-littering spindles let fall
by the maples; the squirm of catkins
fattening on the schoolyard poplars;
the way it annually left its smudge
like a bloodletting under the mulberry
in the first weeks of summer:

spring after spring, the same spangling,
smirching rain of it, making way
for yet other excesses—dewed,
swelling, softening to vegetable rot;
the fanged, maculate, pollen-triggering
tigerlily; the bearded rasp and
ripple of the barley; in field after
field, tasseled, seminal, knife-edged,
the green blades' rustle.

Nobody to hear the screams, if there
were any: . . . *found her* (a quasi-
prurient horror as the word went round) *down
in the cornfield. Strangled. And that ain't
all he . . .* Folks those days had trouble
saying it out loud. Some drifter. Never
caught. Whoever first set up the lingam
and called it Shiva—whatever minion of
some gross, overweening stud . . .

But wait. Remember, there was also Krishna,
flute-player, playboy, holding hands with
all the girls: the warm days glistening
with the feckless pollen of him, the nights
alive with yearning, the music of him,
the moist promises. And after? Doing
the reluctant decent thing. In haste,
stood up with by strangers. The neighbors
counting off the months.

Or that other, worse history, unhinted at
so long, appallingly unburdened one night
over a sepia portrait: *The one who died,*
the prettiest of them: what really happened—
even in those days, in that family:
you knew? Or the living issue, the tie
still unacknowledged: *God was cruel*—thus
Mrs. Transome to Denner, servant and
confidant—*when he made us women.*

And Denner: *I shouldn't like to be a man—*
to cough so loud, and stand straddling about. . . .
No matter. The moist, channeling silk awaits
the hanging tassel: *And in multiplying I*
will multiply thy seed as the stars of heaven,
and as the sand which is upon the sea shore. Or
as the storm of stuff the cottonwood squanders
in windrows on the sidewalk—even though
for a man to spend it thus

is, it is written, an abomination: as it is for
a woman to abort. See how the last mystery
rises to a travesty. Golf-cart sitcom.
The lingam huge, no joke. Steel-nippled
gorgon madonna of the primal scene.
I will make a song full of weapons, with
menacing points, and behind the weapons,
countless dissatisfied faces: thus
turbulent, fleshy, sensual,

eating and drinking and breeding Walt Whitman
(whom Emily Dickinson did not read, having
been told he was disgraceful),
celebrating the procreative urge, being himself
without issue: *of wombs and of the father-stuff,*
of sexes and lusts, voices veiled (he wrote),
and I remove the veil—which Edith Wharton
on the dreadful eve (she was twenty-three)
begged to have lifted

("You've looked at statues in museums, haven't you?"
her mother said, and coldly closed the subject):
who, childless, long schooled in discretion,
remembered sitting on the terrace at The Mount
late into the evening, hearing Henry James intone
the *Leaves of Grass,* extolling the father-stuff
above the lake, while fireflies signaled
the unending seedfall, the glinting
feculence of summer.

MATRIX   *(Villa Serbelloni, Lake Como)*

For Karen Chase

Perched for the nonce among such verticals,
such strata (And did the Principessa
have any friends down there?—O no,

she was *nobilità*), where history
is one long redoubt, where underlings
daily feed into the mangle, fold

on fold, the vellum-and-magnolia-petal
linens we sleep between—our dreams
burrow toward bedrock, down to the matrix,

as though the flinging open of so many
windows, such excess of light and air,
of attitude, the ease of bearing

up from the crypt, encysted, lapidary,
such indignities—the plucked eyeball
of Saint Lucy, Saint Roch's leprous thigh,

Sebastian, his lovely nakedness a grove,
a garden of undoing; the gouging
and the piercing, the vials held

by winged minions frantic lest a drop,
a berry from the tree of earthly horror
go unaccounted for; the ooze of blood,

O hideous, O precious—could not
but be requited by some warden of
the long-repressed, exhuming this

wrapped corpse: holy and dreadful,
the undisposed-of body of the mother.
Whose? The nightmare is not being sure.

Down by the lake we note, strolling a dense
memorial clutter, the dead baby, starkly
photographed; wreathed and embedded,

la moglie in mourning overhung
by the carved smirk of an upstart
lord and master; faceless in their nook

outside the walls, the name and birthplace
of the Englishman who drowned, whose fate
now furnishes the stony living-room

we who still live inhabit: outcrop and under-
croft, retaining wall where lizards hide,
the red valerian hangs, and busy daisies

here called *margheritas* burgeon in
a sun the cool spleenwort shrinks from;
precipice in whose still deeper shade

the violets of spring live on, as though
they'd undermine the summer; stone,
nurturer of Europe, the bereaved

exile's lost mother—otherwise
why this going back, these hankerings
after a relinquished privilege,

why her indentured hold on what we are
or could have been, why this unearned
nostalgia for the culture of the vine,

the pruning of the olive? Observing
how a laborer with a scythe, his
immemorial bending curve repeated

all afternoon, turned what had been a meadow
stippled first with buttercups, then the
beginning red of poppies, into a hayfield,

I thought (don't laugh) of Virgil
brooding on unrest in the metropolis,
knowing the countryside to be no idyl—

one's neighbors sly and fickle, played on
by superstitious rant. Some things
hardly change. There came an evening

toward the end of May, the cherries
reddening on the slope, when a small
procession, mainly of women, moved

up through the hayfield to a chapel
built in honor of My, Our, Their
Lady of the Montserrato, as every year

it had for, in this instance, precisely
the last four hundred. Some of us
came down (ah, feudal perquisites)

from dinner to look on. The Lady,
it appears, was Spanish to begin with,
named for a place denoting merely

a serrated peak. And so, above
her altar the Holy Child is shown
with, in his little hand, a little saw.

What *is* all this? Vigil candles
were fluttering; rosary-fingerers,
swaying as they sang, were singing

over and over, "Ave Maria, Madre di
Dio, tu sei la madre della Chiesa"—and
if, swaying with them, the pagan thrill

I felt had in it something wistful,
the thing I hankered after was no
rite but a foundation, the bedrock

that survives, the banded strata,
hurled reliquary of the drowned,
remnant of uncountable transformings:

precipice, gray limestone I've looked up
into the face of until the looking up
amounted to an attitude of worship:

stone that rings underfoot, whose surfaces
grow populous within doors as a tuned
instrument, eloquent of what lived once,

is now the stuff of cliffs, of crypts,
of hideaways. This morning, following
a track down to the lake, I came upon

a hollow in the cliff wall where,
drip-eroded, rosary-hung, dead flowers
littering the cave floor, there she was:

prayed to and put upon, another idol
of the universal mother. What *is*
all this? The infant in us still

won't let her go—lugubrious poppet,
nurturer, devourer: down below,
well-being's amniotic nightmare

still rocking to its own small music,
cradling the precipice—the clear,
uneasy, treacherous green water.

A SILENCE

past parentage or gender
beyond sung vocables
the slipped-between
the so infinitesimal
fault line
a limitless
interiority

beyond the woven
unicorn   the maiden
(man-carved   worm-eaten)
God at her hip
incipient
the untransfigured
cottontail
bluebell and primrose
growing wild   a strawberry
chagrin   night terrors
past the earthlit
unearthly masquerade

(we shall be changed)

a silence opens

§

the larval feeder
naked   hairy   ravenous
inventing from within
itself its own
raw stuffs'
hooked silk-hung
relinquishment

behind the mask
the milkfat   shivering
sinew   isinglass
uncrumpling   transient
greed to reinvest

§

names have been
given   (revelation
kif   nirvana
syncope)   for
whatever gift
unasked
gives birth to

torrents
fixities
reincarnations of
the angels
Joseph Smith
enduring
martyrdom

a cavernous
compunction driving
founder-charlatans
who saw in it
the infinite
love of God
and had
(George Fox
was one)
great openings

NOTES

THE KINGFISHER

THE OUTER BAR (page 9)   An expedition to a bar island off the coast of Maine, as recalled in midwinter, is the occasion and the subject here. Of the particular island Louise Dickinson Rich wrote in *The Peninsula* (Chatham-Viking, 1958, 1971, p. 153): "When there's an unusually low run of tide it's possible to get over there by walking across the exposed sand bar to Inner Bar Island and then scrambling ankle-deep along a rocky reef to Outer Bar. But you can't stay very long. The minute the tide turns you have to start back. If you wait too long you're going to be stuck out there for twelve hours, or until the next low tide; that is, unless you can attract the attention of a passing lobsterman who will take you off." Natural processes have lately made getting there a little easier, but not very much.

"... fall, gall and gash the daylight": this phrase for the breaking surf derives, of course, from "The Windhover" by Gerard Manley Hopkins.

SEA MOUSE (page 10)   At the time of my sole encounter with the sea mouse—a glimpse of a swimming creature in a rock pool at low tide—I had no idea what in the world it could be. It was quickly identified by means of a pocket guide to seashore life. According to the *Columbia Encyclopedia,* it is a "marine worm of the genus *Aphrodite* with a short, broad, segmented body, found in moderately deep water. . . . The entire dorsal surface . . . is covered by long, feltlike threads called setae, which produce a brilliant iridescence. . . . Sea mice commonly reach 6 to 8 inches in length and 2 inches in width. They are classified in the phylum Annelida, class Polychaeta, family Aphroditidae."

THE SUN UNDERFOOT AMONG THE SUNDEWS (page 15)   SUNDEW. Any of several insectivorous plants of the genus *Drosera,* growing in wet ground and having leaves covered with sticky hairs.

—American Heritage Dictionary

BOTANICAL NOMENCLATURE (page 16)   Louise Rich on the seaside *Mertensia* (op. cit., p. 133): "For a long time nobody could tell me the name of what I consider the most beautiful wild flower I have ever seen anywhere. . . . Here it is known colloquially as 'that blue and pink flower that grows along the shore.' Everything about it is beautiful: the large, oval, silvery-green-gray leaves; the trumpet-shaped flowers which are pink when they open but turn to clear, pure blue within hours; and especially the habit of growth. The stems lie along the ground, radiating from a central taproot so symmetrically

435

that the plant is a perfect disk, sometimes as much as four feet in diameter. The stems bear leaves along their entire lengths and the blossoms grow in clusters at the tips." Year by year, the plant has become increasingly rare in the places where I first encountered it.

A PROCESSION AT CANDLEMAS (page 21)   Fernand Braudel, *The Mediterranean and the Mediterranean World in the Age of Philip II,* vol. I, translated by Siân Reynolds (Harper & Row, 1972, pp. 87, 88): "Transhumance . . . is simply one form of the Mediterranean pastoral way of life, alternating between the grazing lands of the plains and the mountain pastures. . . . Nomadism, on the contrary, involves the whole community and moves it long distances. . . . Today nomadism . . . consists of the knot of about ten people who might be seen round a fire at nightfall in one of the outer suburbs of Beirut; or at harvest time in Algeria, a few camels, sheep and donkeys, two or three horses, some women dressed in red, and a few black goat-skin tents amidst the stubble . . ."

Candlemas, celebrated on February 2, is the Christian feast of the Purification of the Virgin and the Presentation of the Infant Jesus in the Temple.

Peter Levi, text of *The Greek World,* photographs by Eliot Porter (Dutton, 1980, p. 77): "Archaeologists have pieced together in some detail the progress of the building on the Acropolis and have identified more than seventy-five different hands on the carving of the sculptures that made up the frieze of the Parthenon. Beginning in the southwest corner of the temple, it represented one of the city's greatest ceremonies, the Panathenaic procession that every four years brought a new sacred robe, the peplos, to Athena. Altogether the carvings showed more than four hundred human figures and more than two hundred animals. Undoubtedly that procession did, in real life, wind past the Parthenon. But the priest and priestess who stand among the gods are the servants of the ancient, doll-like wooden image of Athena, whose sanctuary had always been on the spot where the Erechtheum now stands. And it was to that wooden image—rather than to the monumental figure of Athena, made of marble, gold, and ivory, that was the central feature of the completed Parthenon—that the new robe was offered." Similar wooden images were central to the worship of Artemis at Brauron, and of Hera at Argos and Samos.

THE DAKOTA (page 26)   The most telling lines of this elegy ("all / the lonely people . . . Pick up / the wedding rice, take out / the face left over from / the funeral nobody came to") are lifted almost bodily from "Eleanor Rigby," recorded by the Beatles in 1966.

The Dakota is the apartment house where John Lennon lived, and in whose entryway he was murdered on December 8, 1980.

TIMES SQUARE WATER MUSIC (page 27)   The Times Square subway station in New York City is, among other things, a transfer point between the Interborough Rapid Transit and the Brooklyn-Manhattan Transit lines—hence IR and BM T. The initials N, RR, and QB, on the other hand, refer to particular routes on the BMT line; so far as I know, they mean nothing in particular.

Spleenwort is a kind of fern, and ouzels and pipits are small birds, all associated with water.

THE KINGFISHER (page 42)   The design here might be thought of as an illuminated manuscript in which all the handwork happens to be verbal, or (perhaps more precisely) as a novel trying to work itself into a piece of cloisonné. Its subject is an episodic love affair that begins in England and is taken up again in New York City. Dylan Thomas died there, at St. Vincent's Hospital, in November 1953.

The kingfisher described in the final stanza is the European species, *Alcedo atthis,* which is conspicuous for its iridescent blue-green plumage. It is associated with the story of Alcyone and Ceyx, whom, in Ovid's *Metamorphoses,* Zeus turned into a pair of birds, and with the idea of "halcyon days"—a period of calm seas, and of general peace and serenity.

THE SMALLER ORCHID (page 44)   The flower referred to is one identified as fragrant ladies'-tresses, *Spiranthes cernua var. odorata.* It is notable, according to *Summer & Fall Wildflowers of New England,* by Marilyn J. Dwelley, for having "a strong vanilla fragrance."

From Marcel Proust, *Remembrance of Things Past,* translated by C. K. Scott Moncrieff (Random House, 1934, vol. I, p. 169): "She found something 'quaint' . . . in her orchids, the cattleyas especially (these being, with the chrysanthemums, her favourite flowers). . . ."

BEETHOVEN, OPUS 111 (page 50)   Beethoven's piano sonata no. 32, Opus 111 (the arabic numbers tend to be misread and even, unfortunately, misprinted as a Roman numeral III, which would make it an early rather than a late composition) is his last work in that form, dating to the early 1820s. It figures in Thomas Mann's *Dr. Faustus* (Knopf, 1948; Vintage Books edition pp. 53–56), in E. M. Forster's *A Room with a View* (Knopf, 1932, p. 54), and in Milan Kundera's *The Book of Laughter and Forgetting* (Knopf, 1981, p. 161). I was first exposed to it, so far as I know, at a recital by Norman Carey, to whom the poem is dedicated. The notes by Eric Blom to the recording by Artur Schnabel on the Seraphim label have added much to my own understanding of the music.

Putti: the stylized infant cherubs that appear to soar, plunge, or hover in some Italian and Spanish paintings on Christian themes.

"Beethoven might declare the air / his domicile, the winds kin": in a letter to Count Brunswick dated February 13, 1814, Beethoven wrote: "As regards me, great heavens! my dominion is in the air; the tones whirl like the wind, and often there is a whirl in my soul." Quoted in *Beethoven: The Man and the Artist, as Revealed in His Own Words,* edited by Frederick Kersh and H. E. Krehbiel (Dover, 1964).

THE QUARRY (page 55)   From *Iowa: A Guide to the Hawkeye State* (Hastings House, 1938): "In the limestone quarries at LeGrand, Marshall County, finely preserved starfishes and crinoids (stone lilies) can be found. The abundance of these fossils and their state of preservation have made the limestones of the Mississippian age here of international importance. . . . The collection of B. H. Beane, of LeGrand, is on display at the State Historical Building in Des Moines." The Iowa Guide is also the source of the story of Lyman Dillon and his hundred-mile furrow. The capitol building described here is the one at Des Moines. An earlier building, the Old Capitol at Iowa City, was built of native limestone, not imported marble.

THE WOODLOT (page 57)   Again according to the Iowa Guide, the anonymous inventor of barbed wire was an Iowa farmer.

IMAGO (page 59)   IMAGO. 1. An insect in its sexually mature adult stage after metamorphosis. 2. *Psychoanalysis.* An often idealized image of a person, usually a parent, formed in childhood and persisting into adulthood.
—American Heritage Dictionary

". . . the lit pavilions / that seduced her, their tailed child . . .": the reference is to Hans Christian Andersen's tale of the Little Mermaid, whose yearning to leave the water and become a human biped was fulfilled, but at a price. For reasons I can only guess at, this story affected me more powerfully than anything else I read as a child. Recently I have connected it—however fancifully—with the seas that in past eons covered the region where I grew up. From *Basin and Range,* by John McPhee (Farrar, Straus & Giroux, 1981): "Ohio, Indiana, Illinois, and so forth, the whole of what used to be called the Middle West, is shield rock covered with a sedimentary veneer that has never been metamorphosed, never been ground into tectonic hash—sandstones, siltstones, limestones, dolomites, flatter than the ground above them, the silent floors of departed oceans, of epicratonic seas. Iowa. Nebraska."

PHEROMONES: From Lewis Thomas, *Lives of a Cell* (Viking, 1974, pp. 17–18): "Most of the known pheromones are small, simple molecules, active in extremely small concentrations. . . . The messages are urgent, but they may arrive, for all we know, in a fragrance of ambiguity. 'At home, 4 p.m. today,' says the female moth, and releases a brief explosion of bombykol, a single molecule of which will tremble the hairs of any male within miles and send him driving upwind in a confusion of ardor."

THE LOCAL GENIUS (page 62)   From Glenway Wescott, *Goodbye Wisconsin* (Harper & Row, 1928, p. 38): " 'Ah yes, yes. That was the young man who didn't know where he was born. I thought it very curious.' 'Now what made you think that, father? He was born in the Middle West.' 'But that's just it! I asked him, and that is precisely what he said—all he could tell me.' "

The Iowa Guide, yet again, supplied the name of William Voss, inventor of the washing machine.

PALM SUNDAY (page 67)   "Sing, my tongue, the glorious battle" is from a processional hymn, the *Pange Lingua,* for which the sixth-century priest Venantius Fortunatus (later canonized) supplied the opening lines; it is still sung at church services on Palm Sunday.

438

GOOD FRIDAY (page 68)   George B. Schaller, *Serengeti: A Kingdom of Predators* (Knopf, 1972, p. ix): "Though by inheritance a vegetarian primate, man has been a predator, a killer of animals, for at least two million years. . . . It is no coincidence that visitors to the African parks watch not the impala and zebra, but the lion and leopard. Even in sleep these big cats convey a feeling of barely contained strength, an ever-present threat of death, which man the hunter finds satisfying, though the danger is vicarious from the safety of a car. Our dual past still haunts us. We hear a lion roar and the primate in us shivers; we see huge herds of game and the predator in us is delighted, as if our existence still depended on their presence."

This dual past is the recurring nightmare of Christendom—a theology of the meek somehow trapped into giving its sanction to warfare. Yet the theology remains persuasive because it takes suffering seriously. And so, for all its impassivity, does the Darwinian theory of natural selection, which for many nowadays has acquired an almost theological authority. My own uneasiness gave rise to this meditation on the subject.

Charles Darwin married Emma Wedgwood, of the noted pottery manufacturing family. Three of their ten children died at an early age.

Olduvai Gorge, at the edge of the Serengeti Plain, is the site of the discovery by Louis and Mary Leakey of many prehistoric tools as well as of the fossil remains of proto-human beings.

EASTER MORNING (page 70)   "A stone at dawn": the reference is to the New Testament, as in Mark 16:2–4: "And very early in the morning of the first day of the week, they came unto the sepulchre at the rising of the sun. And they said among themselves, Who shall roll us away the stone from the door of the sepulchre? And when they looked, they saw that the stone was rolled away: for it was very great."

MARGINAL EMPLOYMENT (page 73)   The treasures of the Duc de Berry are described in some detail by Barbara Tuchman in *A Distant Mirror* (Ballantine Books, 1978, pp. 427–28).

Several phrases straight out of the two "Byzantium" poems of William Butler Yeats will be noted.

TEPOZTLÁN (page 74)   From the *New Larousse Encyclopedia of Mythology* (Prometheus Press, 1959): "Huitzilopochtli ('hummingbird of the South,' or 'He of the South'), the god of war, was worshipped in the temple of Tenochtitlán where numerous human sacrifices were made to him."

". . . unaware that in some quarters / the place was famous": it had been made so, in anthropological circles, by Robert Redfield in *Tepoztlán, A Mexican Village: A Study of Folk Life* (University of Chicago, 1930), and later by Oscar Lewis in *Life in a Mexican Village: Tepoztlán Restudied* (University of Illinois Press, 1951).

". . . or, in their / musical Nahuatl, of *Huehuetzintzin*, / the Old Ones": Nahuatl is one of the languages spoken in Mexico before the Spanish conquest. Of the Old Ones, Gilbert Murray wrote in *Five Stages of Greek Religion*

(Doubleday Anchor Books, 1955, p. 35): "You go to the Chthonian folk for guidance because they are themselves the Oldest of the Old Ones, and they know the real custom."

REMEMBERING GREECE (page 76)   From *Face of North America*, by Peter Farb (Harper & Row, 1963, pp. 20–21): "The myriad offshore islands on the Maine coast are the summits of hills drowned by the advance of the ocean upon the land. . . . In preglacial times some of the islands that now loom out of the ocean, such as Monhegan, must have been mountains that soared above the plain. . . . One obvious cause of the submergence of the shoreline is the melt of the glaciers. . . . But the immense weight of the glaciers themselves probably accounted for the major part of the submergence. . . . The land has since rebounded somewhat, but it is still about 1200 feet lower than at the beginning of the glacial age."

Aeschylus, *Agamemnon,* translated by Richmond Lattimore (*Complete Greek Tragedies,* vol. 1, Modern Library, p. 70):

> . . . My maidens there!
> Why this delay? Your task has been appointed you,
> to strew the ground before his feet with tapestries.
> Let there spring up into this house he never hoped
> to see, where Justice leads him in, a crimson path.

TRASIMENE (page 78)   From Baedeker's Touring Guide to Italy, 1962: "Situated near the constantly varying watershed between the Arno and the Tiber, in the marshy Chiana depression, the turquoise-blue Lake Trasimene represents the last untapped survivor of the sub-Apennine basin-lakes. . . . It is now fed by rainwater only, and is expected to dry up in the not distant future."

RAIN AT BELLAGIO (page 79)   The scheme may be clearer if this poem is thought of as a meditation in the form of a travelogue: the narrator, just arrived in Italy, is met at Naples by a friend who has been living with her father at a villa on Lake Como, and who is about to join an order of contemplative nuns in England.

Fernand Braudel, *The Mediterranean and the Mediterranean World in the Age of Philip II,* vol. I, translated by Siân Reynolds (Harper & Row, 1972, pp. 74, 76): "Rice growing in Lombardy meant the enslavement under terrible conditions of workers who were unable to voice any effective protest since they were not organized. Rice fields do not require labour all the year round, but large numbers of casual workers for a few weeks, at the times of sowing, transplanting, and harvest. This kind of agriculture depends entirely on seasonal migration. It hardly requires the landowner to be present except for paying wages and overseeing the gangs at work. . . .

"The vast low-lying plain of the Sienese Maremma, a real fever trap, is, like its neighbour the Tuscan Maremma, dotted with noblemen's castles. . . . Most of the year the masters live in Siena, in the huge town houses still standing today, palaces into which Bandello's lovers find their way, with the ritual complicity of the servants. . . . [The] dénouement would take place in secret in the old castle in the Maremma, far from the town gossip and family control. Isolated from the world by fever and the sultry heat, what better place could there be for putting to death, according to the custom of Italy and the century, of an unfaithful wife—or one suspected of being so?"

OR CONSIDER PROMETHEUS (page 89)   It was Daniel Gabriel, in a poetry workshop at The New School, who led me to Charles Olson's *Call Me Ishmael* (City Lights Books, 1947), as a book no American poet should fail to read. For this advice, along with much else, I here acknowledge my indebtedness.

"The smuggled gem / inside the weed stem": Prometheus is said to have carried fire down from Olympus inside the stalk of a giant fennel.

Whales, dolphins, and porpoises are all air-breathing mammals; even though they spend their entire lives in the water, they must rise to the surface periodically to replenish their supply of oxygen. It is presumed that they evolved from a land-dwelling ancestor, whose ancestor in turn was an ocean-dwelling fish. What prompted this return to a life in the oceans is a matter of speculation—and although volition has no place in any theory of evolution, strictly speaking, the notion of a Road Not Taken becomes almost irresistible when the habits of the ocean-dwelling mammals and those of the tree-dwelling, prehensile, visually oriented monkeys (whose habits our own so much resemble) are compared.

THE DAHLIA GARDENS (page 96)   An account of the self-immolation of a thirty-two-year-old Quaker, Norman Morrison, in front of the Pentagon in Washington appeared in *The New York Times* on November 3, 1965. Although his name has since been forgotten in the United States, in 1978 it was (according to an American visitor whose report I happened to hear) still remembered in Vietnam.

"Midway between Wilmington and Philadelphia": the refineries of Marcus Hook, Pennsylvania, with their perpetual gas flares, will be familiar to anyone who has traveled through the region via Amtrak.

Charles Olson's observation that the first oil well had been drilled as recently as 1859 was what dramatized for me the transitoriness of an entire culture founded on the use of petroleum: people to whom I report this fact are almost invariably startled, as though it could not possibly be true.

THE BURNING CHILD (page 101)   The account from which the epigraph is taken appears at the beginning of Chapter VII of *The Interpretation of Dreams*, "The Psychology of the Dream-Processes," and is quoted here from the translation by James Strachey (Avon, 1965, pp. 547–48).

WHAT THE LIGHT WAS LIKE

THE AUGUST DARKS (page 108)   "Herring prefer to come inshore on the dark of the moon," according to a report published in the *Ellsworth* [Maine] *American* for August 5, 1982, and headlined "The August Darks."

From *Middlemarch,* by George Eliot, Book II, Chapter 20: "If we had a keen vision and feeling of all ordinary human life, it would be like hearing the grass grow and the squirrel's heart beat, and we should die of that roar which lies on the other side of silence. As it is, the quickest of us walk about well wadded with stupidity."

LOW TIDE AT SCHOODIC (page 109)   From *The Geology of Acadia National Park* by Carlton A. Chapman (Chatham Press, 1970): "An outstanding feature of Schoodic Point is the abundance of dark-colored basaltic dikes, which range up to many yards in width and run through the granite ledges. . . . About 450 million years ago . . . the sea covered a large part of New England and widespread layers of sand, silt, and mud were accumulating upon its floor. . . . After these . . . had accumulated to a total thickness of hundreds and perhaps even thousands of feet, the southeastern portion of Maine became an unstable region and crustal movement (diastrophism) set in. . . . Hot fluid, similar to the black lava of Hawaii's volcanoes, was squeezed upward and sought the easiest means of access to the stratified rocks above. Zones of weakness, such as large fractures in the crustal rocks, permitted rapid influx of the magma. . . ."

From *The Audubon Society Field Guide to North American Seashore Creatures* by Norman A. Meinkoth (Alfred A. Knopf, 1981): "The white barnacles seen at low tide covering rocks and pilings on the seacoast are sedentary crustaceans. They secrete limy shells composed of many interlocking plates, often with a trapdoor opening at the top that can be closed for protection."

CLOUDBERRY SUMMER (page 112)   On barnacles, from *A Field Guide to the Atlantic Seashore* by Kenneth L. Gosner (Houghton Mifflin, Boston, 1978): "The adult animal has been described as shrimplike and glued down by the top of its head. When covered with water, the barnacle rhythmically opens and closes its trapdoors to extend the six pairs of feathery *cirri* like a small hand, grasping blindly for any planktonic or detrital morsels adrift in the water."

On lemmings, from *The Hunting Animal* by Franklin Russell (Harper & Row, New York, 1983, p. 209): "Family after identical family came out of the earth, one new generation every thirteen or fourteen days. A little more than one hundred days of breeding spewed out seven hundred and fifty descendants from one family. Children were breeding, and grandchildren, and very soon, great-grandchildren approached each other to mate. . . . After the plowing, the lemmings polluted. What they did not eat down to the roots, which was almost everything, they despoiled with their sewage, changing the flowering earth into a wasteland. This sent them into hasty movement, urgent mini-migrations. But horde met horde. Finally, when all was eaten out for miles, the hordes combined and began mass movements, anywhere, everywhere, nowhere. It was not true that they committed suicide by jumping into the sea. They had to leave the land because they had eaten it bare."

A CURFEW (page 130)   On Alfred Russel Wallace, from *Darwin and the Mysterious Mr. X* by Loren Eiseley (E. P. Dutton, New York, 1979, pp. 25–26), "During the early months of 1858 Wallace was living at Ternate in the Molucca Islands off the western tip of New Guinea. He was suffering severely from intermittent fever, and during one of these attacks, while he lay weak but lucid on his bed, his mind began to revolve upon the 'species problem' which had fascinated him. . . . 'Something,' he says, 'brought to my recollection Malthus's *Principle of Population* which I had read about twelve years before.' In a lightning flash of insight, it occurred to the feverish naturalist that Malthus's checks to human increase—accident, disease, war, and famine— must, in similar or analogous ways, operate in the natural world as well. 'Vaguely thinking over the enormous and constant destruction which this implied, it occurred to me,' he tells us, 'to ask the question, "Why do some die and some live?" ' The answer, Wallace felt, was clear: the best fitted live. 'From the effects of disease the most healthy escaped; from the enemies the strongest, the swiftest, or the most cunning; from famine, the best hunters. . . . Considering the amount of individual variation that my experience as a collector had shown me to exist, then it followed that all the changes necessary for the adaptation of the species to the changing conditions would be brought about; and as great changes in the environment are always slow, there would be ample time for the change to be effected by the survival of the best fitted in every generation.' "

On Democritus, from *The Worlds of the Early Greek Philosophers* by J. B. Wilbur and H. J. Allen (Prometheus Books, Buffalo, New York, 1979, pp. 183, 187): "Democritus was called the Laughing Philosopher by Cicero and Horace, presumably because of his reaction to human folly. . . . For Leucippus and Democritus, . . . everything must be explained in terms of movements in a void of material atoms governed by necessity. . . . "

On Heraclitus, from the same source, pp. 66, 67: "Fundamental to Heraclitus' ontology is his notion of the pervasiveness of change. . . . The theme of the flowing river epitomizes Heraclitus' approach to change—so much so that he has been called 'the river philosopher.' (Frg. 91, 1st part) 'It is not possible to step twice into the same river. . . .' "

URN-BURIAL AND THE BUTTERFLY MIGRATION (page 132)   From *Hydriotaphia,* by Sir Thomas Browne, Chapter 1: "Time hath endless rarities, and shows of all varieties; which reveals old things in heaven, makes new discoveries in earth, and even earth it self a discovery. That great antiquity *America* lay buried for thousands of years; and a large part of the earth is still in the Urne unto us. . . . Many have taken voluminous pains to determine the state of the soul upon disunion; but men have been most phantasticall in the singular contrivances of their corporall dissolution: whilest the sobrest Nations have rested in two wayes, of simple inhumation and burning. . . . Some being of the opinion of *Thales,* that water was the originall of all things, thought it most equall to submit unto the principle of putrefaction, and conclude in a moist relentment. Others conceived it most natural to end in fire, as due unto the master principle in the composition, according to the doctrine of Heraclitus. . . . the old Heroes in *Homer* dreaded nothing more than water or drowning; probably upon the old opinion of the fiery substance of the soul. . . . " From Chapter 3 of the same work: "How the bulk of a man should sink into so few pounds of bones and ashes, may seem strange unto any who considers not its constitution, and how slender a masse will remain upon an open and urging fire of the carnall composition. Even bones themselves reduced into ashes, do abate a notable proportion. And consisting much of a volatile salt, when that is fired out, make a light kind of cinders. Although their bulk be disproportionable to their weight, when the heavy principle of Salt is fired out and the Earth almost only remaineth. . . . "

MONARCH. . . . 4. a species of large, migrating butterfly of North America, having reddish-brown, black-edged wings: the larvae feed on milkweed.
—*Webster's New Universal Unabridged Dictionary*

VOYAGES: A HOMAGE TO JOHN KEATS (page 141)   In the summer and early fall of 1816, John Keats spent two months at the seaside resort of Margate, on the English Channel. It was here that he saw the ocean for the first time. He was not quite twenty-one, and had only recently begun to think of himself as a poet. Not long after his return to London he stayed up all one night reading aloud with a friend from George Chapman's translation of the *Odyssey,* and wrote his now famous sonnet, "On First Looking into Chapman's Homer." In the spring of the following year he was back at Margate, reading Shakespeare and working on a long poem of his own. On May 10, 1817, he wrote to his friend B. R. Haydon, "I have been in such a state of Mind as to read over my Lines and hate them. I am 'one that gathers Samphire dreadful trade' the cliff of Poesy towers above me. . . ."—a reference to Act IV, Scene 6 of *King Lear:*

> Come, sir; here is the place: stand still. How fearful
> And dizzy 'tis to cast one's eyes so low!
> The crows and choughs that wing the midway air
> Show scarce so gross as beetles; half way down
> Hangs one that gathers samphire, dreadful trade!

(Samphire or glasswort is a fleshy seaside herb that is at least better to eat than nothing.) In that scene Gloucester, who has been blinded for remaining loyal to King Lear, is being led through the countryside near Dover, which is not many miles down the coast from Margate itself—a circumstance that must have added to its effect on Keats's own imagination. The powerful way in which literature can become a link with times and places, and with minds, otherwise remote, suggested itself to me as I read W. Jackson Bate's biogra-

phy, *John Keats* (Harvard University Press, 1963). It was here that I came
upon the account by a contemporary, Joseph Severn, of how Keats would
pause during a walk across Hampstead Heath to watch the passage of the
wind over a field of grain: "The sea, or thought-compelling images of the sea,
always seemed to restore him to a happy calm." The idea of John Keats paus-
ing to take in a sight that had been familiar to me since childhood connected
itself in turn with images of the ocean in the work of Whitman and Hart
Crane. For connecting Keats with Osip Mandelstam, there is at any rate the
authority of Nadezhda Mandelstam's observation (in *Mozart and Salieri,* p.
23): "Akhmatova used to say that Keats almost physiologically reminded her
of Mandelstam." And that Wallace Stevens might also be intimately linked
with Keats was suggested to me by an essay of Helen Vendler, "Stevens and
Keats' 'To Autumn' " (in *Part of Nature, Part of Us,* Harvard University Press,
1980), for which I wish here to acknowledge my enormous indebtedness.

The lines quoted in the epigraph are from an untitled octet, as translated
by David McDuff in *Selected Poems of Osip Mandelstam* (Farrar, Straus and
Giroux, 1975; p. 129). Other poems paraphrased or alluded to in the conclud-
ing poem of the sequence may be found on pp. 11, 37, 111, 123, and 163 of the
same volume.

In the final poem of the sequence, the third and fourth stanzas draw upon
"Porphyro in Akron" from *The Complete Poems and Selected Letters and Prose of
Hart Crane,* edited by Brom Weber (Anchor Books, New York, 1966, pp.
144–46), which concludes:

> But look up, Porphyro,—your toes
> Are ridiculously tapping
> The spindles at the foot of the bed.
>
> The stars are drowned in a slow rain,
> And a hash of noises is slung up from the street.
> You ought, really, to try to sleep,
> Even though, in this town, poetry's a
> Bedroom occupation.

THE REEDBEDS OF THE HACKENSACK (page 165)   REED, n. . . . 1. any of var-
ious tall, broad-leaved, related grasses with jointed, hollow stems which grow
along the banks of streams . . . especially *Phragmites communis,* the common
reed. This is the largest of all the grasses of northern climates, and one of the
most universally diffused. It is used for thatching, for protecting embank-
ments, for roofing, etc. 2. a mass of these, growing or dried. 3. a rustic musi-
cal instrument made from a hollow stem or stalk and played by blowing
through it: used as the symbol of pastoral poetry.
                    —*Webster's New Universal Unabridged Dictionary*
From *Return to the Marshes: Life with the Marsh Arabs of Iraq* by Gavin
Young (Collins, London, 1977, pp. 16, 34): ". . . often, out of some appar-
ently deserted reed-jungle, a full-throated human voice soared into the
silence—a young Marsh Arab singing a love-song as he harvested the

rushes. . . . In that great solitude, where the men of Ur once poled their canoes and where 'in the beginning,' according to Sumerian legend, Marduk, the great God, built a reed platform on the surface of the waters and thus created the world, the effect is one of unquenchable and universal yearning. . . . The numerous Sumerian city-states . . . were large and sophisticated settlements consisting of suburbs, satellite towns, gardens and orchards. . . . In the cities on the fringe of the giant reed-beds, writing was born (about 3000 B.C.) and developed, at first in the form of pictographs, simple drawings scratched on clay with reed stalks. . . ."

Allusions to and/or borrowings from the poems of William Carlos Williams, Dante, Milton, Keats, and Shakespeare will be noted in this poem, which may be regarded as a last-ditch effort to associate the landscape familiarly known as the Jersey Meadows with the tradition of elegiac poetry.

REAL ESTATE (page 169) "Urban Relocation (Not A / Governmental Agency)": A private firm retained by the owners of tenement buildings intended for demolition but still inhabited, Urban Relocation had chosen a name of such bureaucratic portentousness that it was obliged to distinguish itself in this fashion.

HOMER, A.D. 1982 (page 177) The descriptive epithet πολυφλοίσβοιο-θαλάσσης (variously translated as "loud-roaring," "heavy-thundering," or simply "murmuring" and pronounced *poluphloísboio-thalássēs*) recurs throughout the *Iliad;* its first appearance is in line 34 of the first book, in which the reader sees "the spurned priest of Apollo shrink along the shore." The surprising eloquence of Odysseus is described in lines 216–23 of the third book, and the scene in which the infant Astyanax is frightened by the sight of his father Hector in the horsehair-plumed war helmet he wore as he said goodbye to his family occurs in Book 6, lines 466–70.

LOSING TRACK OF LANGUAGE (page 182) The Canzone of Petrarch referred to in the second stanza is the one beginning, "Chiare, fresche e dolci aque." The poem of Sappho referred to in the concluding stanza is Number 20 in *Sappho: A New Translation* by Mary Barnard (University of California Press, Berkeley and Los Angeles, 1958).

A CURE AT PORLOCK (page 185) "In the summer of the year 1797, the Author, then in ill health, had retired to a lonely farm-house between Porlock and Linton, on the Exmoor confines of Somerset and Devonshire. In consequence of a slight indisposition, an anodyne had been prescribed, from the effect of which he fell asleep in his chair. . . . The Author continued for about three hours in a profound sleep, at least of the external senses, during which time he has the most vivid confidence that he could not have composed less than from two to three hundred lines. . . . On waking he appeared to himself to have a distinct recollection of the whole, and taking his pen, ink, and paper, instantly and eagerly wrote down the lines that are here preserved. At this moment he was unfortunately called out by a person on business from

Porlock, and detained by him above an hour, and on his return to his room, found . . . that . . . with the exception of some eight or ten scattered lines and images, all the rest had been passed away like the images on the surface of a stream into which a stone had been cast. . . . " This is Samuel Taylor Coleridge's account, written some years later, of the composition of "Kubla Khan." The anodyne he mentions was presumably a form of opium, to which he was addicted for much of his adult life. The ravages of such addiction, as embodied in the character of John Jasper, form a major theme of Dickens's unfinished last novel, *The Mystery of Edwin Drood*.

ARCHAIC FIGURE

ARCHAIC FIGURE (page 197)   From E. Homann-Wedeking, *The Art of Archaic Greece*, translated by J. R. Foster (Greystone Press, 1968, pp. 96–97, 98): "There [on the island of Samos], about 560 B.C., a donor erected in the sanctuary of Hera a long base on which six marble statues stood side by side. . . . All the figures had names inscribed on them. The artist, Geneleos by name, also inscribed his own name. . . . The execution of each individual figure is unsurpassable. The statue of Ornithe can serve as an example. The special delicacy of the surface texture lies in the quite shallow modelling and the tender, tranquil play of the folds of drapery. . . . The garment is brought to life by the quiet gesture of the right hand lightly catching up the material. Statues like that of Ornithe were the prototypes which inspired the sculptors of the other regions of Greece to produce similar works. The clothing alone would show that Ionia was the source of these figures. There the oldest of them are dressed in the chiton, a tunic-like garment made of thin, delicate material. . . ."

From Fernand Braudel, *The Mediterranean* (Harper & Row, 1975, vol. 1, p. 241): "The truth is that the Mediterranean has struggled against a fundamental poverty, aggravated but not entirely accounted for by circumstances. It affords a precarious living, in spite of its apparent or real advantages. It is easy to be deceived by its famous charm and beauty. Even as experienced a geographer as Philippson was dazzled, like all visitors from the North, by the sun, the colours, the warmth, the winter roses, the early fruits. Goethe at Vicenza was captivated by the popular street life with its open stalls and dreamed of taking back home with him a little of the magic air of the South. Even when one is aware of the reality it is difficult to associate these scenes of brilliance and gaiety with images of misery and physical hardship."

ANO PRINIOS (page 200)   The title is the name of a mountain village in Greece.

TEMPE IN THE RAIN (page 202)   From *The New Larousse Encyclopedia of Mythology* (Prometheus Press, 1968, pp. 95–96): "The mariner who sailed into the gulf of Therme (today the gulf of Salonica) would feel himself filled with religious awe when he perceived against the hard blue line of sky the lofty profile of Mount Olympus. Everything concurred to reveal to him the fearful majesty of the gods. In the first place he had no doubt that Olympus was the highest mountain in the world. Then he would remember that the narrow Vale of Tempe, which separates Olympus from Ossa and cradles under its willows and plane-trees the peaceful stream of Peneus, had been hollowed out by Zeus during his struggle with the Titans."

OLYMPIA (page 204)   From *Hope Against Hope,* by Nadezhda Mandelstam (Atheneum, 1970, p. 120): "In the summer of 1935 M. was granted the favor of receiving an identity paper valid for three months, accompanied by a residence permit for the same period. This made our lives much easier. . . . People who live in countries without identity papers will never know what joys can be extracted from these magic little documents. In the days when M.'s were still a precious novelty, the gift of a benevolent fate, Yakhontov came to Voronezh on tour. In Moscow M. and he had amused themselves by reading from the ration books which were used in the excellent store open only to writers. M. refers to this in his poem 'The Apartment': 'I read ration books and listen to hempen speeches.' Now Yakhontov and M. did the same thing with their identity papers, and it must be said that the effect was even more depressing. In the ration book they read off the coupons solo and in chorus: 'Milk, milk, milk . . . cheese, meat. . . .' When Yakhontov read from the identity papers, he managed to put ominous and menacing inflections in his voice: 'Basis on which issued . . . issued . . . by whom issued . . . special entries . . . permit to reside, permit to reside, permit to reside. . . .'"

THERMOPYLAE (page 205)   From Book Seven of the *Histories* of Herodotus, translated by Aubrey de Selincourt (Penguin Books, 1954, p. 493): "There was a bitter struggle over the body of Leonidas; four times the Greeks drove the enemy off, and at last by their valour succeeded in dragging it away. So it went on, until the fresh troops with Ephialtes were close at hand; and then, when the Greeks knew that they had come, the character of the fighting changed. They withdrew again into the narrow neck of the pass, behind the walls, and took up a position in a single compact body—all except the Thebans—on the little hill at the entrance to the pass, where the stone lion in memory of Leonidas stands to-day. Here they resisted to the last, with their swords, if they had them, and, if not, with their hands and teeth, until the Persians, coming on from the front over the ruins of the wall and closing in from behind, finally overwhelmed them."

LEAVING YÁNNINA (page 206)   Yánnina: a lakeside town in northern Greece. *Volta:* the evening promenade that is a custom in Mediterranean countries.

DODONA: ASKED OF THE ORACLE (page 207)   From *The New Larousse Encyclopedia of Mythology,* p. 98: "The most famous sanctuary of Zeus was that of

Dodona, in Epirus. It was also the oldest, dating back to the Pelasgians. People came there from all parts of Greece to consult the oracle of a sacred oak whose rustling and murmurs were regarded as the words of Zeus himself. On the origin of this oracle Herodotus, who claims to have heard it from the lips of the priestesses of Dodona, says: 'Two black doves flew from Thebes in Egypt, one to Libya and the other to Dodona. The latter, alighting in an oak tree, began to speak in a human voice and to ask that an oracle of Zeus should be founded in this place. The people of Dodona believed that they had received an order coming from the gods, and on the dove's advice founded the oracle.' . . . The goddess Dione . . . was venerated at Dodona at the side of Zeus, here taking over the role of Hera."

MEDUSA (page 211)   On the Gorgons, from *A Handbook of Greek Mythology*, by H. J. Rose (Dutton, 1959, pp. 29–30): "With regard to the Gorgons, it has been rightly pointed out, for instance by Miss Harrison, that we hear of the head of the Gorgon before anything is told us of the Gorgon herself. The kernel of the myth is, that there existed sometime and somewhere a creature of aspect so terrible that those who saw her turned at once into stone. . . . Once started on its way, this idea would naturally blend with the widespread superstition, common in both ancient and modern Greece, of the evil eye. . . . The older Greek art . . . shows a horrible, grinning head, with flat nose, lolling tongue, and staring eyes, sometimes adding a striding, winged body. With this the descriptions of poets later than Homer correspond. In particular several passages give the Gorgons serpents in their hair or girdles, with other monstrous features. . . . As a result of the Greek hatred of ugliness, or possibly to avoid representing Poseidon as being in love with anything so misshapen as the traditional Gorgon, later art shows Medusa as a beautiful woman, from about 300 B.C. on with a look of terror or pain about the eyes."

HIPPOCRENE (page 215)   From *The Diary of Virginia Woolf*, edited by Anne Olivier Bell (Harcourt Brace Jovanovich, 1980, vol. 3, p. 113): "Thursday 30 September. I wished to add some remarks to this, on the mystical side of this solitude; how it is not oneself but something in the universe that one's left with. It is this that is frightening & exciting in the midst of my profound gloom, depression, boredom, whatever it is: One sees a fin passing far out. What image can I reach to convey what I mean? Really there is none I think. The interesting thing is that in all my feeling & thinking I have never come up against this before. Life is, soberly & accurately, the oddest affair; has in it the essence of reality. I used to feel this as a child—couldn't step across a puddle once I remember, for thinking, how strange—what am I? &c. But by writing I dont reach anything. All I mean to make is a note of a curious state of mind. I hazard the guess that it may be the impulse behind another book. . . ."

ATHENA (page 216)   **ae´gis, e´gis,** n. [L. from Gr. *aigis,* a goatskin, from *aix, aigos,* a goat.]
　1. in Greek mythology, a shield or breastplate; originally applied to the shield worn by Jupiter. In later times, a part of the armor of Pallas Athena,

appearing as a kind of breastplate covered with metal scales and the head of the Gorgon Medusa, and fringed with serpents.

—Webster's Unabridged Dictionary

THE NEREIDS OF SERIPHOS (page 217) James Theodore Bent's classic travel book, *The Cyclades: Or Life Among the Insular Greeks,* was published by Longmans, Green and Company, London, in 1885.

A. M. Mulford's account of the tornado he witnessed appears in the *History of Hardin County, Iowa,* published in 1883.

SERIPHOS UNVISITED (page 220) What little Lawrence Durrell has to say of Seriphos is to be found on p. 254 of his *The Greek Islands* (Viking-Penguin, 1978).

ATLAS IMMOBILIZED (page 222) The story of how, after refusing hospitality to Perseus, the giant Atlas was transformed into a mountain, is told in the *Metamorphoses* of Ovid, Book IV.

MEDUSA AT BROADSTAIRS (page 227) *Selections from George Eliot's Letters,* edited by Gordon S. Haight (Yale University Press, 1985, pp. 100–102), contains the texts of two letters from Marian Evans to Herbert Spencer dating to July 1852. In the first she wrote of her state of mind at Broadstairs, "I think of retiring from the world, like old Weller, if my good landlady will accept me as a tenant all the year round. I fancy I should soon be on an equality, in point of sensibility, with the star-fish and sea-egg—perhaps you will wickedly say, I certainly want little of being a *Medusa*. . . ."

From *Adam Bede* (Everyman Edition, reprinted 1973, p. 369): "It was the same rounded, pouting, childish prettiness, but with all love and belief in love departed from it—the sadder for its beauty, like that wondrous Medusa-face, with the passionate, passionless lips."

HIGHGATE CEMETERY (page 229) In a letter to Robert Bridges dated 28 October 1886, Gerard Manley Hopkins wrote: "How admirable are Blackmore and Hardy! Their merits are much eclipsed by the overdone reputation of the Evans-Eliot-Cross woman (poor creature! one ought not to speak slightingly, I know), half real power, half imposition. . . ." (*Selected Prose,* edited by Gerald Roberts, Oxford University Press, 1980, p. 148.)

MARGARET FULLER, 1847 (page 231) From *Memoirs of Margaret Fuller Ossoli,* quoted by Paula Blanchard in *Margaret Fuller: From Transcendentalism to Revolution* (Delta/Seymour Lawrence, 1979, p. 167): "Once I was almost all intellect; now I am almost all feeling. Nature vindicates her rights, and I feel all Italy glowing beneath the Saxon crust. This cannot last long; I shall burn to ashes if all this smoulders here much longer. I must die if I do not burst forth in genius or heroism."

GRASMERE (page 234) Whatever may be conjectured about the attachment between Dorothy Wordsworth and her brother William—and there has been much conjecture, most recently by Robert Gittings and Jo Manton in *Dorothy Wordsworth* (Oxford, 1985)—the undisputed circumstances are that they were born a year apart, were separated at the age of seven and eight respectively and saw little of one another until they were in their teens; that once re-united, they lived together, with brief separations, from 1794 until William's death in 1850 (Dorothy, although for many years incapacitated, survived him by five years); that during a stay in France, William fell in love with Annette Vallon, by whom in 1792 he had a daughter, Caroline; and that in 1802 William married Dorothy's longtime friend Mary Hutchinson, by whom he had five more children—John, Dorothy, Thomas, Catharine, and William, Jr. From December 1799 until the spring of 1808, the Wordsworths made their home at Grasmere, in what is now known as Dove Cottage; here, at various times, Samuel Taylor Coleridge, and later Thomas De Quincey, were part of the household. In 1813, after living briefly at two other houses in Grasmere itself, the family moved to Rydal Mount, where Dorothy, William, and Mary would all reside for the rest of their lives.

COLEORTON (page 237)   "Wordsworth . . . has been described," wrote Douglas Bush in *Mythology and the Romantic Tradition in English Poetry* (Harvard University Press, 1969, p. 51), "as Coleridge's greatest work, and, like all his other works, left unfinished."

From the letters of Dorothy Wordsworth, as quoted in Gittings and Manton, pp. 155ff.: "We are crammed in our little nest edge full as you will suppose. . . . Every bed lodges two persons at present." (January 1806) "Our continuing here during another winter would be attended with so many serious inconveniences, especially to my Brother, who has no quiet corner in which to pursue his studies, no room but that where we all sit (to say nothing of the unwholesomeness of these low small rooms for such a number of persons). . . . We think of going into Leicestershire, Sir George B[eaumont] having offered us their house for the winter." (June 1806)

THE ODESSA STEPS (page 242)   The images of the woman with the pince-nez, the crouching mother, and the overturned baby carriage occur in a sequence from the Sergei Eisenstein film *Potemkin,* depicting an incident during the uprising of 1905, when Russian government troops advanced against unarmed civilians on the steps above the harbor at Odessa.

AN ANATOMY OF MIGRAINE (page 243)   From Thomas De Quincey, *Confessions of an English Opium-Eater* (Oxford University Press, 1985, p. 76): "The dream commenced with a music which now I often heard in dreams—a music of preparation and of awakening suspense; a music like the opening of the Coronation Anthem, and which, like *that,* gave the feeling of a vast march—of infinite cavalcades filing off—and the tread of innumerable armies."

From Simone Weil, *Gravity and Grace* (G. P. Putnam's Sons, 1952, pp. 7, 73–74): "Nothing in the world can rob us of the power to say 'I.' Nothing except extreme affliction. Nothing is worse than extreme affliction which destroys the 'I' from outside, because after that we can no longer destroy it ourselves. What happens to those whose 'I' has been destroyed from outside by affliction? It is not possible to imagine anything for them but annihilation according to the atheistic or materialistic conception.

"Though they may have lost their 'I,' it does not mean that they have no more egoism. Quite the reverse. . . . Human injustice as a general rule produces not martyrs but quasi-damned souls. Beings who have fallen into this quasi-hell are like someone stripped and wounded by robbers. They have lost the clothing of character."

From Henry James, *The Wings of the Dove,* Book First (Modern Library Edition, 1930, pp. 36, 37): ". . . all intercourse with her sister had the effect of casting down her courage and tying her hands, adding daily to her sense of the part, not always either uplifting or sweetening, that the bond of blood might play in one's life. . . . Bereaved, disappointed, demoralized, querulous, she was all the more sharply and insistently Kate's elder and Kate's own. . . . She [Kate] noticed with profundity that disappointment made people selfish. . . ."

From *The Brain: Mystery of Matter and Mind* (U.S. News Books, 1981, p. 23): "Brain surgeon Roger Sperry of the California Institute of Technology concluded that the brain's consciousness encompassed and transcended its physical workings: 'In the human head there are forces within forces within forces, as in no other cubic half-foot of the universe that we know.' "

Again, from Simone Weil in *Gravity and Grace,* p. 133: "Time bears the thinking being in spite of himself toward that which he cannot bear, and which will come all the same."

From a note by Martin Gardner to *The Annotated Alice* (Bramhall House, 1960, p. 231): "Tweedledum and Tweedledee are what geometers call 'enantiomorphs,' mirror-image forms of each other. That Carroll intended this is strongly suggested by Tweedledee's favorite word, 'contrariwise,' and by the fact that they extend right and left hands for a handshake. Tenniel's picture of the two enantiomorphs arrayed for battle, standing in identical postures, indicates that he looked upon the twins in the same way. . . ."

chī-as′ma, n.; pl. chī-as′mà·tà. [Gr. *chiasma,* two lines crossed, from *chiazein,* to mark with the Greek letter chi.]
 1. in anatomy, a crossing or intersection of the optic nerves on the ventral surface of the brain.
 2. any crosswise fusion.
chī-as′mus, n.; pl. chī-as′mi. [Mod. L.: Gr. *chiasmos,* placing crosswise.] an inversion of the second of two parallel phrases, clauses, etc.; as, do not live to eat, but eat to live.

—Webster's Unabridged Dictionary

From *The Diary of Virginia Woolf,* edited by Anne Olivier Bell (Harcourt Brace Jovanovich, 1977–84): ". . . Often down here I have entered into a sanctuary; a nunnery; had a religious retreat; of great agony once; & always some terror: so afraid one is of loneliness: of seeing to the bottom of the vessel. That is one of the experiences I have had here in some Augusts; & got then to a consciousness of what I call 'reality': a thing I see before me, something abstract; but residing in the downs or sky; beside which nothing matters; in which I shall rest & continue to exist. Reality I call it. And I fancy sometimes this is the most necessary thing to me: that which I seek. But who knows—once one takes a pen & writes? . . ." (Monday 10 September 1928; vol. 3, p. 196.)

"I've had some very curious visions in this room too, lying in bed, mad, & seeing the sunlight quivering like gold water, on the wall. I've heard the voices of the dead here. And felt, through it all, exquisitely happy." (Wednesday 9 January 1924; vol. 2, p. 283.)

MAN FEEDING PIGEONS (page 263)   From the *Paradiso* of Dante Alighieri, Canto XXX:

> E se l'infimo grado in sè raccoglie
> sì grande lume, quant' è la larghezza
> di questo rosa nell' estreme foglie?

> (And if the lowest step gathereth so large
> a light within itself, what then the amplitude
> of the rose's outmost petals?)

> —Translation by Philip H. Wicksteed

WESTWARD

DALLAS–FORT WORTH: REDBUD AND MISTLETOE (page 286)   The two quoted passages are from the *Aeneid* of Virgil, translated by Robert Fitzgerald (Random House, 1983, pp. 167 and 79).

MULCIBER AT WEST EGG (page 289)   From *The Great Gatsby* by F. Scott Fitzgerald (Scribner, 1925, p. 200):

". . . 'They picked him up when he handed the bonds over the counter. They got a circular from New York giving 'em the numbers just five minutes before. What d'you know about that, hey? You never can tell in these hick towns—'

" 'Hello!' I interrupted breathlessly. 'Look here—this isn't Mr. Gatsby. Mr. Gatsby's dead.'

"There was a long silence on the other end of the wire, followed by an exclamation . . . then a quick squawk as the connection was broken.

"I think it was on the third day that a telegram signed Henry C. Gatz arrived from a town in Minnesota. . . ."

AT A REST STOP IN OHIO (page 290)   An infant wailing in a bus terminal, T. S. Eliot's "Animula" and its sources in the work of Dante and the Emperor Hadrian: this only momentarily surprising conjunction came out of a reading by Howard Nemerov, to whose rendering of *Animula, vagula, blandula* the poem owes its concluding line.

HAVING LUNCH AT BRASENOSE (page 295) On Oxford, from *The Blue Guide to England* (Benn, 1980, pp. 274–75): "On the w. side of Radcliff Sq. is Brasenose College, founded in 1509 by Wm. Smyth, Bp. of Lincoln, and Sir Richard Sutton. The name is probably derived from the brazen knocker (a lion's head) of an older Hall, which was carried off to Stamford in 1334; this was recovered in 1890 and is kept in the college hall. Another derivation is from a supposed 'brasenhus' or brewery, on the site of the college."

WESTWARD (page 297) From *Civilization: A Personal View,* by Kenneth Clark (Harper & Row, 1969), p. 10:
"Iona was founded by St Columba, who came here from Ireland in the year 543. It seems to have been a sacred spot before he came and for four centuries it was the centre of Celtic Christianity. There are said to have been three hundred and sixty large stone crosses on the island, nearly all of which were thrown into the sea during the Reformation."

A MINOR TREMOR (page 317) From Jeremiah 32: 26, 34–35: "Then came the word of the Lord unto Jeremiah, saying: . . . But they set their abominations in the house, which is called by my name, to defile it. And they built the high places of Baal, which are in the valley of the son of Hinnom, to cause their sons and their daughters to pass through the fire unto Moloch; which I commanded them not, neither came it to my mind, that they should do this abomination, to cause Judah to sin."

AMHERST (page 319) The profile of Norwottuck, a low hill south of the town of Amherst that would have been familiar to Emily Dickinson, may be viewed from a site, new since her day, honoring graduates of Amherst College who served in the two world wars. The poet's death on May 15, 1886, has been commemorated in recent years by a gathering in the cemetery where she is buried.

Phrases lifted from the poems of Emily Dickinson will be evident. The ones represented include (using the numbers in *The Complete Poems of Emily Dickinson,* edited by Thomas H. Johnson) 526, 530, 663, 595, 658, 594, 601, 564, 593, 486. The most unlikely of these is the poet's reference (in poem 564) to "Vast Prairies of Air/Unbroken by a Settler." Her work is, however, studded with allusions to places she had never seen.

THE HURRICANE AND CHARLOTTE MEW (page 321) The devastating windstorm of October 1987, during which countless venerable trees in the south of England were uprooted, appears, according to meteorologists, to have been a strayed Caribbean hurricane. Two poems reprinted in *Charlotte Mew and Her Friends* by Penelope Fitzgerald (Addison-Wesley, 1988), entitled "The Trees Are Down" and "The Shade-Catchers," are the source of several references here.

DEJECTION: A FOOTNOTE (page 322) A letter from Samuel Taylor Coleridge to his friend Thomas Poole, dated October 16, 1797, is the source of the incident to which the poem refers.

EASEDALE TARN (page 323)   From Thomas De Quincey, *Recollections of the Lakes and the Lake Poets* (Penguin, 1985, pp. 250–51): ". . . But there is a third advantage possessed by this Easedale, above other rival valleys, in the sublimity of its mountain barriers. In one of its many rocky recesses is seen a 'force,' (such is the local name for a cataract,) white with foam, descending at all seasons with respectable strength, and, after the melting of snows, with an Alpine violence. Follow the leading of this 'force' for three quarters of a mile, and you come to a little mountain lake, locally termed a 'tarn,' the very finest and most gloomily sublime of its class."

FIREWEED (page 325)   Known to botanists as *Epilobium angustifolium,* fireweed is so called from its habit of springing up on burnt-over ground, among other unlikely places.

From "Death's Duel," the last sermon preached by John Donne at St. Paul's Cathedral in London: "Whatsoever moved Saint *Jerome* to call the journies of the *Israelites,* in the *wilderness,* Mansions, the word (the word is *Nasang*) signifies but a *journey,* but a peregrination. Even the *Israel of God* hath no mansions; but journies, pilgrimages in this life."

The effigy of John Donne that is to be seen at St. Paul's is one of the few monuments to have survived the great London fire of 1660.

MY COUSIN MURIEL (page 331)   The needlepoint lace known as *punto in aria*—literally, "a stitch in the air"—originated in Venice, according to the *Columbia Encyclopedia,* as laceworkers ventured beyond purely geometric designs on a ground of netting to freer ones with no ground at all.

Concerning Charles Wadsworth, from *The Life of Emily Dickinson* by Richard B. Sewall (Farrar, Straus & Giroux, 1980, pp. 449–50): "His popularity in Philadelphia has been compared with Henry Ward Beecher's in Brooklyn and his preaching was ranked second only to Beecher's in the country. In April 1862, he accepted a call from the Calvary Presbyterian Society in San Francisco . . . a move which was long thought . . . to account for Emily's complaint . . . of her 'terror since September . . .' In a letter to [Thomas Wentworth] Higginson a few months after Wadsworth died, he was 'my closest earthly friend.' "

THE HALLOWEEN PARADE (page 336)   From *The Portrait of a Lady,* by Henry James (New American Library, 1979, p. 271): "In the church, as she strolled over its tessellated acres, he was the first person she encountered. She had not been one of the superior tourists who are 'disappointed' in St. Peter's, and find it smaller than its fame; the first time she passed beneath the huge leathern curtain that strains and bangs at the entrance—the first time she found herself beneath the far-arching dome and saw the light drizzle down through the air thickened with incense and with the reflections of marble and gilt, of mosaic and bronze, her conception of greatness received an extension."

NOTHING STAYS PUT (page 339)   The alstroemeria, like the freesia, is a cultivated flower named presumably for the botanist who first identified or classified it.

THE PRAIRIE (page 343)   Aside from the works of Chekhov and of Emerson quoted in the text, the sources drawn upon here include the privately printed *Some Incidents in My Life: A Saga of the "Unknown" Citizen*, by Frank T. Clampitt; *Iowa: A Bicentennial History*, by Joseph F. Wall (W. W. Norton, 1978); *The Book of the Omaha*, edited by Paul A. Olson (Nebraska Curriculum Development Center, 1979); and *Pasadena: Crown of the Valley* (Windsor Publications, 1986).

The phrase quoted from George Eliot occurs in *Middlemarch*, Book II, Chapter 20.

Simone Weil wrote in her commentary entitled "The *Iliad;* or The Poem of Force": "Far from hot baths he was indeed, poor man. And not he alone. Nearly all the *Iliad* takes place far from hot baths. Nearly all of human life, then and now, takes place far from hot baths."

The descriptive phrase transliterated here as *poluphloisboio thalassēs* occurs for the first time near the beginning of the *Iliad*. It has been variously handled by translators—from "murmuring" to "loud-roaring" seas and back again. Tennyson perhaps had it in mind when he had his Ulysses say "the deep/ Moans round with many voices." Nothing in English, however, comes so close as the Greek to the hissing and tumultuous force of the breaking waves themselves.

A SILENCE OPENS

SYRINX (page 363)   "Then there gathered from out of Erebus the spirits of those that are dead, brides, and unwedded youths, and toil-worn old men, and tender maidens with hearts yet new to sorrow, and many, too, that had been wounded with bronze-tipped spears, men slain in fight, wearing their blood-stained armour. These came thronging in crowds about the pit from every side, with a wondrous cry. . . ." —*Odyssey*, XI:34–43, translated by A. T. Murray (William Heinemann Ltd., 1919), vol. 1.

DISCOVERY (page 364)   "Cape Canaveral, Fla., Jan. 22. Seven astronauts from three countries sailed flawlessly into orbit today aboard the space shuttle Discovery. . . ." —*The New York Times*, January 23, 1992.

HISPANIOLA (page 366)   "Right from the start, Columbus had a plan: to establish a sugar industry on Hispaniola much like the ones back on the Canary and Madeira islands. . . ." —Susan Miller, "Slavery: The High Price of Sugar," *Newsweek*, Special Issue, Fall/Winter 1991.

PAUMANOK (page 368)

> I too Paumanok, . . .
> I too leave little wrecks upon you, you fish-shaped island.
> —Walt Whitman, "As I Ebb'd with the Ocean of Life"

MATOAKA (page 369)   The sources drawn upon here include *Their Majesties' Royall College: William and Mary in the Seventeenth and Eighteenth Centuries,* by J. E. Morpurgo (1976); *Narratives of Early Virginia,* edited by Lyon Gardner Tyler (1907); *Pocahontas,* by Grace Steele Woodward (1969); *The Virginia Guide* (1940, 1941); and *Undreamed Shores: England's Wasted Empire in America,* by Michael Foss (1974). The lines by Sir Walter Raleigh are from "His Epitaph"; those by Michael Drayton, from "To the Virginian Voyage."

BROUGHT FROM BEYOND (page 377)   "Columbus's avidity for gold has been treated as a private obsession, but [Jacques] Attali [in *1492*] claims that all Europe was in need of gold to prevent trade 'asphyxiation.' " — Garry Wills, *The New York Review of Books,* November 21, 1991.

"There was no talke, no hope, nor worke, but dig gold, wash gold, refine gold, load gold. Such a brute of gold, as one mad fellow desired to be buried in the sandes, least they should by their art make gold of his bones. . . ." —*Narratives of Early Virginia*

"What in part distinguished Sienese painting of the 15th century from other Italian art was the liberal use of such expensive colors as gold and ultramarine. . . . Intended to reflect the wealth and generosity of the pictures' patrons, the use of such materials also had a specifically religious purpose, for by painting such opulent scenes, artists underscored the distance between the viewer's life and the realm of the divine being depicted. . . ." —Michael Kimmelman, "Sienese Gold," *New York Times Magazine,* September 11, 1988.

"**bowerbird,** common name for any of several species of birds . . . native to Australia and New Guinea, which build, for courtship display, a bower of sticks or grasses. . . . Colored stones, shells, feathers, flowers, and other bright objects . . . are used. . . . The satin bowerbird, *Ptilonorhyncus violaceus,* prefers blue decorative articles." —*The Columbia Encyclopedia*

THE UNDERWORLD OF DANTE (page 378)   This canto of the *Inferno* finds Dante with his guide, the Roman poet Virgil, halted beside the River Styx, which forms a moat about the city of Dis (the "doleful metropolis"), the stronghold of Satan and his rebel angels. The Furies or Erinyes, the Gorgon Medusa — one look at whom was said to turn the viewer to stone — the watchdog Cerberus, and the heroic figure of Theseus are all drawn from classical mythology.

SHOREBIRD-WATCHING (page 385)   The Althing is the parliament of Iceland. "Thingstead" is the name given to the meeting place of such a body.

THINKING RED (page 389)   The interview with the physicist George Wald referred to here was reported by Estelle Gilson in *Columbia Magazine,* October 1985.

THE WAR MEMORIAL (page 407)   George Fox (1624–91), the English reformer who founded the Society of Friends, reported in his *Journal* the incident referred to here.

NOTES

'EIGHTY-NINE (page 408)

> . . . Not that you could bear
> the voice of God—far from it. But hear the wind's blowing,
> the uninterrupted tidings created from silence,
> they sweep toward you now from those who died young.
>
> Every angel is terrible. And yet, alas,
> I welcome you, almost fatal birds of the soul. . . .
> —Rainer Maria Rilke, *Duino Elegies,*
> translated by C. F. MacIntyre

SED DE CORRER (page 420)   *The Complete Posthumous Poetry* of Cesar Vallejo, translated by Clayton Eshleman and José Rubía Barcia (1978), is the source of the passages quoted here. *Poet in New York,* by Federico García Lorca, translated by Greg Simon and Steven F. White (1988), has been similarly drawn upon. I am indebted to Cecilia Vicuña for particular help and inspiration.

SEED (page 425)   The characters of Mrs. Transome and her maid Denner appear in George Eliot's novel *Felix Holt.* The lines by Whitman are from his "Song of Myself." Edith Wharton's memoir, *A Backward Glance,* records the presence of Henry James at The Mount, her home in the Berkshires; an unfinished account entitled "Life and I" (in *Novellas and Other Writings,* Library of America) tells of the incident before her marriage.

MATRIX (page 428)   "The Madonna of Montserrato is one of the most revered Madonnas of Spain, before whose statue in the abbey of Montserrato St. Ignatius Loyola laid down his sword and dagger to become a warrior of the church. . . . The oil painting of the Madonna that graces the present 19th-century chapel, by style clearly of the late 16th century and hence an altar piece in the original church [built at Bellagio by Ercole Sfondrati in the year 1591], portrays a Madonna holding the Child . . . wielding a saw like those still seen in Bellagio, a small 'buck-saw,' and he is using it to cut saw teeth into the mountains in the background. Perhaps the implication is that the Child sawed off the great slab of limestone on which the Bellagio chapel stands. Have we here a kind of baroque pun? It is a fact that in the Spanish Montserrato there is a dim tradition that its saw-toothed mountains were shaped by angels wielding golden saws." —*The Castle's Keep: The Villa Serbelloni in History,* by John Marshall (1970, p. 101).

A SILENCE (page 432)   ". . . while walking one day in Boston, he saw the streets suddenly shrink and divide. His everyday preoccupations, his past, all the claims of the future fell away and he was enfolded in a great silence. . . . At the age of twenty-one [T. S.] Eliot had one of those experiences which, he said, many have had once or twice in their lives and been unable to put into words." —*Eliot's Early Years,* by Lyndall Gordon (1977, p. 15).

". . . dignity and majesty have I seen but once, as it stood in chains at midnight in a dungeon in an obscure village in Missouri." —Letter written by Parley Pratt on Joseph Smith in jail, quoted by Fawn Brodie in *No Man Knows My History: The Life of Joseph Smith* (1986, p. 243).

". . . also I saw the infinite love of God, and I had great openings."
—*The Journal of George Fox.*

INDEX OF FIRST LINES

(The use of italics denotes a first line that is also the poem's title.)

INDEX OF TITLES

PERMISSIONS
ACKNOWLEDGMENTS

Grateful acknowledgment is made to the following for permission to reprint previously published material:

Liveright Publishing Corporation: Excerpt from "Porphyro in Akron" from *Complete Poems of Hart Crane*, edited by Marc Simon. Copyright 1933, © 1958, 1966 by Liveright Publishing Corporation. Copyright © 1986 by Marc Simon. Reprinted by permission of Liveright Publishing Corporation.

University of California Press: Excerpts from "The First Elegy" and "The Second Elegy" from *Duino Elegies* by Rainer Maria Rilke, translated and edited by C. F. MacIntyre. Copyright © 1961 by C. F. MacIntyre. Reprinted by permission of the Regents of the University of California and the University of California Press.

A NOTE ABOUT THE AUTHOR

AMY CLAMPITT was born and brought up in New Providence, Iowa, graduated from Grinnell College, and from that time on lived mainly in New York City. Her first full-length collection, *The Kingfisher,* published in 1983, was followed in 1985 by *What the Light Was Like,* in 1987 by *Archaic Figure,* and in 1990 by *Westward. A Silence Opens,* her last book, appeared in 1994.

The recipient in 1982 of a Guggenheim Fellowship, and in 1984 of an Academy of American Poets fellowship, she was made a MacArthur Prize Fellow in 1992. She was a member of the American Academy of Arts and Letters and was a Writer in Residence at the College of William and Mary, Visiting Writer at Amherst College, and Grace Hazard Conkling Visiting Writer at Smith College.

She died in September 1994.

A NOTE ON THE TYPE

This book is set in a typeface called Galliard, drawn by
Matthew Carter for the Mergenthaler Linotype Company
in 1978. Carter studied and worked with historic hand-cut
punches before designing typefaces. His Galliard design
is based on sixteenth-century types of Robert Granjon, of
Paris and Lyon, a distinguished publisher, printer, type-
cutter, and founder.

Composition by North Market Street Graphics,
Lancaster, Pennsylvania
Printed and bound by Berryville Graphics
Berryville, Virginia
Designed by Harry Ford